Shakespeare
and the Idea of Western Civilization

R. V. YOUNG

Shakespeare
and the Idea of Western Civilization

The Catholic University of America Press
Washington, D.C.

Copyright © 2022
The Catholic University of America Press
All rights reserved

Names: Young, R. V., 1947– author.
Title: Shakespeare and the idea of Western civilization / R.V. Young.
Description: Washington, D.C. : The Catholic University of America Press,
[2022] | Includes bibliographical references and index. |
Identifiers: LCCN 2021062346 (print) | LCCN 2021062347 (ebook) |
ISBN 9780813235240 (paperback) | ISBN 9780813235257 (ebook)
Subjects: LCSH: Shakespeare, William, 1564–1616—Criticism and
interpretation. | Civilization, Western, in literature. | English
drama—Early modern and Elizabethan, 1500–1600—History and criticism. |
English drama—17th centur—History and criticism.
Classification: LCC PR3000 .Y68 2022 (print) | LCC PR3000 (ebook) |
DDC 822.3/3—dc23/eng/20220203
LC record available at https://lccn.loc.gov/2021062346
LC ebook record available at https://lccn.loc.gov/2021062347

For Suzanna, in gratitude for more than half a century of love and—because we are too wise to woo peacefully—patience.

Contents

Foreword	ix
Acknowledgments	xiii
Introduction: Learning from Shakespeare, Poet of Western Civilization	1
1. Shakespeare on Love (and Marriage)	25
2. Juliet's Nominalism and the Failure of Love	51
3. The Racial "Other" in *The Merchant of Venice* and *Othello*	76
4. Shakespeare's History Plays and the Erasmian Christian Prince	104
5. Freedom and Tyranny in *Julius Caesar* and *Hamlet*	133
6. "Light Thickens": Freedom and Tyranny in *Macbeth*	156
7. Hope and Despair in *King Lear*: The Gospel and the Crisis of Natural Law	173
8. *The Tempest* in the Academic Teapot	208
Afterword	234
Bibliography	239
Index	253

Foreword

It will be well from the very first to state what this book is not. It is neither a general introduction to Shakespeare's plays for beginning students nor a work of academic literary scholarship providing new information about the playwright and his dramatic output or offering a unique interpretation from a wholly novel critical perspective. While I hope that both students and their professors may find matter of interest in these pages, they are not in their narrow respective roles the intended readers. In other words, I have written neither another specialized study, like Jonathan Bate's *Shakespeare and Ovid* or Stanley Stewart's *Shakespeare and Philosophy* (admirable as both of these works are), nor a compendious account of all the plays along the lines of Stanley Wells's *Shakespeare: A Life in Drama* (1995) or Harold Bloom's *Shakespeare: The Invention of the Human* (1998). There is, however, one respect in which this book is similar to Bloom's: both have a definite polemical thesis.

Bloom's book argues an extreme, romantic view of Shakespeare: that he is, like all of Bloom's "strong poets," a moral and spiritual innovator who does not forge an exceptionally vivid and convincing representation of human experience, but rather reshapes our understanding of mankind so radically that he virtually "invents" the human. My view of Shakespeare is essentially the opposite: Shakespeare's drama achieves not a break with the Western literary and cultural tradition that has preceded him, but instead its consummate expression. Since the playwright's life coincides with a turning point in Western civilization, precipitated by the crisis of the Reformation but also by the opening of new vistas as a result of the scientific and commercial revolutions and the discovery of the New World, Shakespearean drama is favorably positioned to reaffirm the principles upon which his civilization was founded and developed, but also to witness and embody the flexibility of that civilization to retain its integrity while adapting to the inevitable changes confronting it.

By means of compelling action, sharply etched characters, and unforgettable language, Shakespeare succeeds in giving "a local habitation and a name" to the elusive and paradoxical essence of Western civilization: its solid adherence to profound and substantial tradition blended with the leaven of an inquiring, critical spirit. Shakespeare has become over the past four centuries an enduring classic of Western literature—and in the English-speaking world, at least, *the* classic—because, wherever Western culture has spread, men and women have intuitively recognized that he embodies the unique complexity of their society, which has been able to preserve its deepest commitments of its moral and spiritual vision by continually subjecting them to scrutiny.

To the best of my knowledge, no one has before now set out to consider Shakespeare precisely in this light as the poet of Western civilization. His permanent relevance (portentous word) to our reflections on love and marriage, morality, politics and social organization, and, at least obliquely, religion has, I think, been simply taken for granted—at least until the past fifty years or so. Until that time, much of what I have to say would probably have seemed obvious, and it would not have occurred to me to say it. During the past half century, however, Western civilization has been challenged as never before from within, by academics and intellectuals of an ideological bent, who are among the most favored beneficiaries of the remarkable institutions that have developed uniquely in the West and become the envy of the world as a whole. Not surprisingly, the author who has provided the most powerful dramatization of this civilization has shared in the opprobrium. While he has sometimes been expropriated as a supposed enemy of his own culture, more frequently he has been disparaged and diminished as a figure complicit in and tainted by its evils.

In attempting to demonstrate both the aesthetic and moral validity of Shakespearean drama as well as its general validation of the principles of Western civilization, I have neither discussed all of Shakespeare's plays nor offered a complete account of any of them. Rather, I have considered a number of his most powerful and enduring works insofar as they illuminate those features of our civilization that have in recent decades come under sustained and often virulent attack—namely, the West's handling of love and marriage, of race and ethnicity, of politics, of religion, of colonialism. My method has been to combine a close reading of the text with an effort to locate the work in the context of political, social, and literary history. It is my hope that my argument will not only drive my particular thesis about Shakespeare and Western civilization, but also contribute to understanding and appreciating the subtleties of his writing.

The book originated both in my undergraduate Shakespeare classes at North Carolina State University and in a number of papers that I was invited to deliver at various institutions, most commonly small colleges with what is increasingly an uncommon commitment to the liberal arts. The audiences included students and faculty members, of course, but also many members of the surrounding community with no formal connection to the institution. I have tried to retain the relaxed tone—if not the digressions and occasionally casual diction—of these oral presentations. The book is thus intended for anyone who has taken pleasure from reading or witnessing a production of Shakespeare's plays and who would value aid in understanding and appreciating them and in defending them against their strident detractors. Since Shakespeare is the principal poet of Western civilization, to defend him is to defend it at a time when such defense is much needed.

Acknowledgments

In my experience the making of a book is never the achievement of a single individual. *Shakespeare and the Idea of Western Civilization* is no exception. Although I am formally the author of this book, numerous other men and women, as well as institutions and organizations, have contributed substantially to its development and completion. Without them, it would never have been written, much less published.

The book originated in a series of papers and addresses given at various colleges, universities, and academic conferences over the course of twenty years. Chapter 1, on love and marriage in Shakespeare's plays, was given in several versions, first at Hillsdale College in Michigan in March 2003; again at Emmanuel College in Franklin Springs, Georgia, in October 2005; and finally at the International Institute for Culture in Philadelphia, in February 2007. A very short version of chapter 2 was presented as "Juliet and Shakespeare's Other Nominalists: Variations on a Theme by Richard Weaver" at a conference sponsored by the Intercollegiate Studies Institute in Snoqualmie, Washington, in August 1997. Chapter 3, on racial prejudice in *The Merchant of Venice* and *Othello*, was given in its initial form first at the University of Delaware under the sponsorship of the Delaware Association of Scholars; then at the University of the South (Sewanee); and finally at the University of Tennessee, Chattanooga, all during the first week of March 2001. A revised version was presented at Seattle Pacific University in October 2002. Chapter 4, on the history plays, went through two quite different revisions in presentations at an Intercollegiate Studies Institute conference at Ashland, Oregon, in August 1998 and at the annual convention of the Shakespeare Association of America at San Francisco, in April 1999. Chapter 5 began as "Freedom and Tyranny in Shake-

Acknowledgments

spearean Tragedy," the Edward Lee Lecture at the University of St. Thomas, Houston, in February 2003, and was presented again in an abbreviated version as a seminar paper at the Convention of the Shakespeare Association of America in Bermuda in March 2005. Chapter 6, "'Light Thickens': Freedom and Tyranny in *Macbeth*" was presented at Christendom College in Front Royal, Virginia, in April 2018.

Only several years later did I become aware that I had the makings of a book—and what that book was about. This realization was mostly a result of the give-and-take of focused discussions at academic conferences and question-and-answer periods after lectures. Listeners had challenged me by forcing me to articulate my arguments more clearly and to put them in a wider context; ultimately it occurred to me that the context was Western Civilization. Sometimes audiences were predisposed in my favor, sometimes not; but I was always received graciously, and, no matter how intense the discussions became, they were always courteous. Without the opportunity to present these lectures and talks, without the intellectual encounters thus occasioned, I could never have written *Shakespeare and the Idea of Western Civilization*.

Eventually, some of these presentations found their way into print. Some elements of chapter 2 were first published in the *Intercollegiate Review* 33, no. 1 (Fall 1997): 18–29. A shorter version of chapter 3 first appeared as "The Bard, the Black, the Jew," in *First Things*, no. 141 (March 2004): 22–28; and a much-abbreviated account of chapter 4 was published as "Shakespeare's History Plays and the Erasmian Catholic Prince," *Ben Jonson Journal* 7 (2000): 89–114. Part of chapter 5 first appeared as "Residual Catholicism in *Hamlet*: Spiritual Freedom and Political Tyranny," *Saint Austin Review* 7, no. 1 (January/February 2007): 4–8 and was reprinted in William Shakespeare, *Hamlet with Contemporary Essays*, ed. Joseph Pearce (San Francisco: Ignatius Press, 2008), 273–84. Chapter 7 was published much as it now is under the same title in *King Lear: New Critical Essays*, ed. Jeffrey Kahan (New York and London: Routledge, 2008), 253–77. Chapter 8 uses some

Acknowledgments

much-revised material from "'Fresh Piece of Excellent Witchcraft': Contemporary Theory and Shakespeare's Romances," in *Shakespeare's Last Plays*, ed. Stephen W. Smith and Travis Curtwright (Lanham, Md., Boulder, Colo., New York, and Oxford: Lexington, 2002), 217–38. I am grateful for permission to reprint this material and for the useful discussions with the editors and readers that prompted me to reconsider and reconfigure my arguments.

The comments from the two anonymous readers for the Catholic University of America Press were encouraging and insightful in suggesting revisions. I also wish to thank Aldene Fredenburg for her painstaking care in editing the text, as well as Trevor Lipscombe, the Editor of the Press, Theresa Walker, the Managing Editor, and Brian Roach, the Sales and Marketing Director, for their unfailing helpfulness and courtesy.

Brian Blackley, a North Carolina State colleague and partner in literary discussions for many years, provided indispensable insights on Shakespeare and Renaissance literature; Phoebe Spinrad was an invaluable source of information and wisdom about Renaissance drama. The only regretful acknowledgments here are to my NC State colleague and dear friend of four decades, Tom Hester; Stanley Stewart and Richard Harp, cofounders and for many years coeditors of the *Ben Jonson Journal*; and Anne Gardiner, who have all passed away. My conversations and correspondence with them about Shakespeare and so many other aspects of literature are an essential part of this book, which, to my sorrow, they have not lived to see.

Finally, I owe a debt to Joseph Pearce, editor of the *St. Austin Review* and indefatigable man of letters, that I can hardly describe, much less repay. He helped me get this project off the ground and provided indispensable aid in seeing it to fruition. It is a mystery to me how a man who achieves so much himself as a writer and an editor manages to lavish so much energy and time on the work of others, but I am very thankful that he does so.

—RVY

Shakespeare
and the Idea of Western
Civilization

Introduction

Learning from Shakespeare, Poet of Western Civilization

When John Dryden penned *An Essay of Dramatic Poesy* in 1668, it was by no means evident to everyone that Shakespeare was the foremost playwright of the Elizabethan era, much less the greatest dramatist, and possibly the greatest author, of world literature. His friendly rival Ben Jonson had the advantage in learning and in "regularity," and the team of Francis Beaumont and John Fletcher was more popular among Restoration theatre audiences. "Their plays are now the most pleasant and frequent entertainments of the stage," Dryden remarks; "two of theirs being acted through the year for one of Shakespeare's or Jonson's." Dryden, however, despite the bias of the time and his own predilection for the rules of neoclassicism, recognized in Shakespeare's drama a unique and surpassing excellence: "He was the man who of all modern, and perhaps ancient poets, had the largest and most comprehensive soul." Dryden maintained that Jonson was the more "correct" poet, but this turns out not to be the decisive feature: "I admire him, but I love Shakespeare."[1] A century later, Dr. Johnson would maintain that Shakespeare "may now begin to assume the dignity of an ancient and claim

---

1. John Dryden, *An Essay of Dramatic Poesy and Other Critical Essays*, ed. George Watson (London: J. M. Dent, 1962), 1:69, 67, 70.

the privilege of established fame and prescriptive veneration,"[2] and since then his status as a classic has only increased until our own day. His works constitute a cultural monument that continues to fascinate tourists and moviegoers as well as readers and theatre audiences.

Nevertheless, despite his continued cultural preeminence—his central place in academic literary study as well as on the stage and screen—Shakespeare's status in modern society has become somewhat equivocal. Many productions are "revisionist," making overt attempts to accommodate the plays to views typical of contemporary society; and, while in my experience Shakespeare is still quite popular among students, many colleges and universities no longer *require* a Shakespeare course, even of English majors. Academic literary scholarship during the past several decades has often treated Shakespeare with skepticism, if not downright hostility, and his work has been forced to submit to the ideological protocols of deconstruction, Lacanian psychoanalysis, new historicism, cultural materialism, and, above all, the preoccupation with race, class, and "gender" that drives so much academic activity. We may well ask, then, what qualities initially underwrote the esteem in which Shakespeare has long been held and why they no longer seem to be in favor.

Dryden has already specified Shakespeare's most remarkable distinction: it is his "large" and "comprehensive soul." Since the mere existence of such a thing as a soul is a derisory notion among many prominent members of today's cultural elite, it is no wonder that "large and comprehensive soul" has become problematic praise. It is necessary, therefore, to be more specific about the reasons both for the esteem traditionally accorded Shakespeare and for the ambivalence with which he has come to be regarded. While it is not an exhaustive explanation, Shakespeare, more than any other writer, embodies the distinc-

---

2. Samuel Johnson, "Preface" to *The Plays of William Shakespeare* (1765), in *Samuel Johnson on Shakespeare*, ed. W. K. Wimsatt Jr. (New York: Hill and Wang, 1960), 24.

tive principles of the Christian civilization of the Western world. Men and women shaped by the West's unique culture have loved Shakespeare as Dryden loved him, because his plays and poems continue to express their aspirations, to articulate their concerns, and to confront the tensions and contradictions in the Western vision.

This does not mean that Shakespeare is an uncritical encomiast of his own culture and society, but rather that he is an exemplar of the spirit, both critical and conservative, that Christianity has instilled in Western civilization by teaching that we must be in the world but not of it. It is, therefore, no surprise that literary scholars have cast doubt upon Shakespeare's exalted position at exactly the point in history when the societies of the West seem most anxious about their own integrity and probity and have, in varying degrees, become estranged from both their Christian and classical heritage.

Shakespeare may therefore be denigrated precisely for the virtue that I have proposed, howbeit in different terms: "Shakespeare," Gary Taylor complains, "discommoded reality. He dramatized the daydreams of his culture." For Taylor, one of the most acclaimed editors of Shakespeare at the turn of the twenty-first century, the ideals of Western civilization are mere "daydreams":

What I personally admire about Plautus and other writers like him is what Shakespearians so regularly deprecate: hardness, toughness, exuberant and fantastic amorality. And what I dislike about Shakespeare's comedies—and tragedies—is their softness, their central mushiness, their inevitable "love interest," their wholesomeness.

In case we miss the point, Taylor explains, "for us, 'wholesome' may be practically defined as 'suitable for schoolchildren and impressionable young adults to read.'"[3]

Although Taylor suggests that Shakespeare is in some mea-

---

3. Gary Taylor, *Reinventing Shakespeare: A Cultural History from the Restoration to the Present* (New York: Weidenfeld and Nicolson, 1989), 398, 400, 403.

sure beneath serious consideration because he is defective in the cynicism and sophistication that pass for maturity in some circles, more commonly contemporary critics complain that he is complicit in all the sins of racial, sexual, and social oppression with which they brand the Western world. Katherine McLuskie, for example, maintains that plays such as *Measure for Measure* and *King Lear* are intrinsically "sexist" and a source of frustration to feminist interpretation. The former sympathetically presents "the double bind which blames women for their own sexual oppression," and in *Lear*, "The close links between misogyny and patriarchy define the women in the play."[4] For Paul Brown, "*The Tempest* is not simply a reflection of colonialist practices but an intervention in an ambivalent and even contradictory discourse."[5]

It is not surprising, therefore, that Alan Sinfield worries about the extent to which Shakespeare's influence can be contained and exploited to suit radical political ends:

> It may be that we must see the continuous centering of Shakespeare as the cultural token which must be appropriated as itself tending to reproduce the existing order: that however the plays are presented they will exercise a relatively conservative drag, that any radical influence can hardly extend beyond the educated middle class, that in practice conservative institutions are bound to dominate the production of such a national symbol, and that for one cultural phenomenon to have so much authority must be a hindrance to radical innovation.[6]

---

4. Katherine McLuskie, "The Patriarchal Bard: Feminist Criticism and Shakespeare; *King Lear* and *Measure for Measure*," in *Political Shakespeare: New Essays in Cultural Materialism*, ed. Jonathan Dollimore and Alan Sinfield (Ithaca, N.Y., and London: Cornell University Press, 1985), 97, 99.

5. Paul Brown, "'This Thing of Darkness I Acknowledge Mine': *The Tempest* and the Discourse of Colonialism," in Dollimore and Sinfield, *Political Shakespeare*, 48. See also Thomas Cartelli, "Prospero in Africa: *The Tempest* as Colonialist Text and Pretext," in *Shakespeare Reproduced: The Text in History and Ideology*, ed. Jean E. Howard and Marion F. O'Connor (New York and London: Methuen, 1987), 112: "The text of *The Tempest* continues to allow Prospero the privilege of the grand closing gesture; continues to privilege that gesture's ambiguity at the expense of Caliban's dispossession."

6. Alan Sinfield, "Introduction: Reproductions, Interventions," in Dollimore and Sinfield, *Political Shakespeare*, 133. See also Dollimore and Sinfield, "Foreword," in

Nevertheless, Shakespeare's poetic charm and power are too pervasive in societies around the globe to be abandoned. Hence, in a later work, Sinfield remarks that, for cultural materialism, "The choice of reading modes *is strategic*: it is governed by what seems likely to disclose the political potential of the text." An "appreciative account," a "stated or implied critique of the stance (stated or implied) of the text," or "a reading against the grain"—all serve the same end: "For the ultimate allegiance of the cultural materialist is not to the text as such—not to literature—but to the political project."[7]

Of course, Shakespeare is not unique in receiving this treatment: postmodern theory generally discounts the integrity, indeed the substantial existence of all works of literature, which are all just so many "texts," essentially indistinguishable from any other "document." "Literature," Frank Lentricchia typically avers, "is inherently nothing; or it is a body of rhetorical strategies waiting to be seized";[8] and the *Norton Anthology of Theory and Criticism* pointedly omits "literary" from its title.[9] Nevertheless, Shakespeare's tremendous prestige and unrivaled stature as poet and dramatist, which many generations have—naïvely in the eyes of contemporary theorists—attributed to the greatness of his literary talent and achievement, pose a particular problem: if works of literature are not in some sense distinct entities, if they have no substantial, inherent significance, how can one set of these nullities persistently attract more favor and interest and

---

Political Shakespeare, viii: "Cultural materialism does not pretend to political neutrality.... On the contrary, it registers its commitment to the transformation of a social order which exploits people on grounds of race, gender and class."

7. Sinfield, *Shakespeare, Authority, Sexuality: Unfinished Business in Cultural Materialism* (London and New York: Routledge, 2006), 198.

8. Frank Lentricchia, *Criticism and Social Change* (Chicago: University of Chicago Press, 1988), 152. See also Stanley Fish, *Is There a Text in This Class? The Authority of Interpretive Communities* (Cambridge, Mass.: Harvard University Press, 1980), esp. 368; and the discussion of these and other similar assertions in R. V. Young, *At War with the Word: Literary Theory and Liberal Education* (Wilmington, Del.: ISI, 1999), 1–22.

9. Vincent B. Leitch, ed., *The Norton Anthology of Theory and Criticism* (New York and London: W. W. Norton, 2001). See R. V. Young, "Academic Suicide," review of *Norton Anthology*, ed. Vincent B. Leitch, *Modern Age* 44 (2002): 254–61.

exert more compelling force on successive generations and widespread societies than almost all the others?

If one ploy in the campaign to disparage Shakespeare and diminish his influence is to call into question the substantial integrity of the plays and poems as concrete works of art, another is to deny the agency of the author. The origin of this tactic, as of so much of the malaise infecting postmodern literary study, is Michel Foucault, who maintains that the *author* is a "function" of discourse and hence an "ideological product" of a particular "episteme."[10] The idea that the concept of the author is an ideological construct of printing and (eventually) copyright is absurd on its face: in the classical era Homer and Virgil, for example, were revered figures, and Horace (*Odes* III) and Ovid (*Metamorphoses* XV.871–79) claimed literary immortality. Long before Shakespeare, Chaucer's genius was acknowledged by other medieval authors such as John Gower and John Lydgate, and he was regarded as the father of English poetry by Tudor successors such as Sir Thomas Wyatt and Edmund Spenser.

New historicists and cultural materialists have countered that the case is altered with Shakespeare, because the Elizabethan plays were written collaboratively and repeatedly revised for performance by the actors and other members of the theater companies, so that the playwright's role was substantially diminished. The tawdry film *Shakespeare in Love* (1990), with Joseph Fiennes as an especially feckless Will Shakespeare, was popular among university literature professors precisely because it purported to show how little he contributed to the dramatic power of *Romeo and Juliet*. A moment's reflection, however, shows the factitiousness of these historicists' history. By 1592 Shake-

---

10. Michel Foucault, "What Is an Author?," in *The Foucault Reader*, ed. Paul Rabinowitz (New York: Random House, 1984), 118–19. See also Roland Barthes, "The Death of the Author," in *Image, Music, Text*, ed. and trans. Stephen Heath (New York: Farrar, Strauss and Giroux, 1977). For an early application of this view to Shakespeare, combined with Jacques Derrida's deconstructive attack on "logocentrism," see Harry Berger Jr., "Text Against Performance in Shakespeare: The Example of *Macbeth*," *Genre* 15 (1982): 49–79.

speare's importance as an author had already received backhanded recognition in the envious Robert Greene's *Groatsworth of Wit*: "There is an upstart crow, beautified with our feathers, that with his *tiger's heart wrapped out in a player's hide* supposes he is as well able to bombast out a blank verse as the best of you; and, being an absolute *Johannes Factotum*, is in his own conceit the only Shake-scene in a country."[11] Many Elizabethan and Jacobean plays were published with the playwright's name included, and Shakespeare led the field in this respect. Ben Jonson clearly thought of himself as the author of his plays, a point he drove home with the publication of his *Works* (1616); and the first folio publication of Shakespeare's plays seven years later (headed by Jonson's resplendent commendatory poem) by members of his theatrical company shows a clear acknowledgment of his preeminence as an author of plays.[12]

One need not romanticize Shakespeare and lapse into "bardolatry" in order to acknowledge his unique combination of imaginative intelligence, skill, and creative genius. And there is also an element of good fortune, since there was nothing inevitable about his achievement. "If John Shakespeare had remained on the land," Mark Eccles poignantly observes, "Shakespeare might, like his forefathers, have followed the ever-running year with profitable labor to his grave. But John Shakespeare came to Stratford and William had his chance to go to school."[13] The literary and dramatic treasure, acclaimed throughout the world, that we identify with the name "Shakespeare" could not have been predicted or planned; its origin is veiled in the arcana of Providence.

To an academic elite for whom "multiculturalism" is a virtual

---

11. Quoted by S. Schoenbaum, *Shakespeare: A Compact Documentary Life* (Oxford, London, and New York: Oxford University Press, 1977), 151.

12. I have benefited from the account of the "collaborationist" school of Shakespeare scholarship and its sensible refutation by Jeffrey Knapp in *Shakespeare Only* (Chicago and London: University of Chicago Press, 2009), 1–18.

13. Mark Eccles, *Shakespeare in Warwickshire* (Madison: University of Wisconsin Press, 1961), 23.

article of faith, Shakespeare is thus the most vexatious of anomalies: the chief glory of the English tongue not only continues to be cherished in the English-speaking world; he has attained the stature of the principal poet of Western civilization and has indeed transcended his origins in the West, having become not merely the subject of avid study but also of performance in India, China, Japan, and numerous other non-Western nations. His drama and poetry constitute an effective, concrete refutation of two primary premises of postmodern theory: that there are no substantial or significant differences among various cultures in their moral standing and civilizing effect, and that literature, like all other cultural "phenomena," is merely a product of social ideology rather than a uniquely and distinctively human achievement. Indeed, Shakespeare seems exemplary of a genuine cultural *diversity*, which unites a marvelous array of differing cultures in their common humanity, in contrast to a *multiculturalism*, which, at least in many contemporary formulations, uneasily separates those putatively equal in a dismaying cultural segregation.

A reductive account of Shakespeare is, then, a small but important element in the broad academic campaign to debunk Western—especially American—civilization as a whole. In a book that cheerily dismisses the "scandal" of speaking of "Shakespeare without attending to any of Shakespeare's poetry," Michael Bristol sets out to unveil "the complex links between Shakespeare as a cultural institution and the larger dispensation of bourgeois political economy." While he allows "that Shakespeare serves the interests of class domination is not, however, the whole story," nevertheless, this is only because a hegemonic ideology necessarily assimilates aspects of any dissident elements: "In the construction of Shakespeare as a complex of institutions and practices, critical and oppositional potentialities have been incorporated into various archaeological strata."[14] Bristol thus implicitly concedes that Shakespeare's work is a con-

---

14. Michael Bristol, *Shakespeare's America: America's Shakespeare* (London and New York: Routledge, 1990), 7, 61.

tribution to Western civilization, including its specifically American version, although he hardly sees this as a cause for rejoicing.

What might be seen as one of the West's virtues has been identified by its contemporary critics as a vice as well. In an influential book Tzvetan Todorov points out that, in contrast to the paganism of the Aztecs, "Christianity is, fundamentally, universalist and egalitarian.... This religion seeks to be universal and is thereby intolerant.... This fact contributes not a little to the Spaniards' victory: intransigence has always defeated tolerance."[15] Todorov remarks further, "The Europeans exhibit remarkable qualities of flexibility and improvisation which permit them all the better to impose their own way of life."[16]

Todorov never mentions Shakespeare, but many literary scholars have exploited his work to condemn the playwright as complicit in the conquest and colonization of the New World. One of the more unhinged examples is provided by Eric Cheyfitz, who seizes upon the (obvious) association between Prospero's magic and rhetorical ingenuity to denounce the imperialistic "technology" of eloquence. It has long been observed that the name "Caliban" is an anagram of "can[n]ibal"; Caliban thus becomes a victim of the West's superior verbal skills, treated as nothing more than an instrument of conquest:

It is the process of translation that places "Caliban" in *The Tempest*, dispossessing the term of its proper identity, or rather dispossessing the term of its cultural relations by translating it into the realm of property and identity.[17]

---

15. Tzvetan Todorov, *The Conquest of America*, trans. Richard Howard (New York: Harper and Row, 1984), 105–6.

16. Todorov, *Conquest of America*, 248.

17. Eric Cheyfitz, *The Poetics of Imperialism: Translation and Colonization from "The Tempest" to "Tarzan,"* rev. ed. (Philadelphia: University of Pennsylvania Press, 1997), 61. Cheyfitz bitterly denounces Todorov, a left-wing critic of colonialism, calling his book "an allegory of capitalist democracy's superiority to Communism" (xxiv), apparently because Todorov makes an effort to treat the European conquerors of the New World with a measure of impartiality. Cheyfitz's incoherent ideological screed is wholly based on the fact that *tranlatio* means *metaphor* in Latin—hence an argument based on a bilingual pun.

Introduction

Taking information from the despised Todorov, who fails to condemn the West sufficiently, Cheyfitz later fulminates against the conquistadors for informing the Indians "*in Spanish* of their place in the Catholic/Spanish imperium," a few sentences after announcing, "The burden of this book is, of course, that translation was, and still is, the central act of colonization and imperialism in the Americas."[18] Eloquence, the liberal arts in general, and the art of translation are all reduced to a "technology" of power politics, and the failure to translate and translation are both condemned as equally unjust. It is hard to see how Cheyfitz can justify the inconsistency.

The animus against Shakespeare's supposed complicity with imperialism is so relentless that even distinguished scholars who ought to know better sometimes get their facts wrong. Without saying so in so many words, Stephen Greenblatt suggests that *The Tempest* was in some fashion a part of England's colonial enterprise and hints that Miranda's reproof of Caliban's (admitted) attempt to rape her is tainted with ulterior motives in "a speech that Dryden and others have found disturbingly indelicate."[19] Greenblatt ascribes no reference for the opinion he ascribes to the Restoration poet and does not so much as mention that he collaborated with William Davenant in a revision of Shakespeare's original. The reproof of Shakespeare's Miranda is, in fact, not Dryden's at all; rather it is Dryden's biographer and editor, Sir Walter Scott, expressing his disapproval of Dryden's version of the play: "Dryden did not omit that peculiar colouring, in which his age delighted. Miranda's simplicity is converted into indelicacy, and Dorinda talks the language of prostitution before she has ever seen a man."[20]

---

18. Cheyfitz, *Poetics of Imperialism*, 104.
19. Stephen Greenblatt, *Learning to Curse: Essays in Early Modern Culture* (New York and London: Routledge, 1990), 33.
20. Sir Walter Scott, *The Life of John Dryden*, in *The Delphi Complete Works of John Dryden* (Hastings, East Sussex: Delphi Classics [Kindle Edition], 2013), loc. 105638. In a book that I highly recommend, Thomas L. Martin and Duke Pesta, *The Renaissance and Postmodernism: A Study of Comparative Critical Values* (New York and London:

Introduction

Greenblatt provides an example of another tactic in the manipulation of Shakespearean drama for ideological advantage, which is to turn him against the distinctive, subtle facets of Western civilization. In a discussion of *Othello*, Greenblatt offers a disparaging account of a theory of *empathy*, "the mobile personality of Western society," which the sociologist Daniel Lerner regards as the foundation of the West's dominant position in the modern world. "What Professor Lerner calls 'empathy,'" Greenblatt avers, "Shakespeare calls 'Iago.'"[21] Such restless discontent and frustration with Shakespeare's plays and poems are rife within the critical literature of the past several decades, and we shall consider them in more detail in conjunction with particular themes and plays in the chapters that follow. We must first briefly consider, however, what it is in Western civilization that Shakespeare represents so compellingly to the chagrin of that civilization's detractors.

We may begin by observing that the routine accusations leveled at the West by academic multiculturalism, even if they were all strictly true, provide a tenuous basis for a condemnation of the Western world as such. Patriarchy, imperialism, social hierarchy, ethno-centrism, slavery, racial prejudice, oppression of the poor by the rich—none of these are inventions of Europe and its

---

Routledge, 2016), 182, rebuke Greenblatt for his slanted view of *The Tempest*, but even they accept his misrepresentation of Dryden and further condemn Dryden for being the first to use the "racist" phrase "noble savage." It is true that Dryden did originate the phrase, but it is hardly "racist" in context: Act I, scene i, of *The Conquest of Granada*, where the Muslim hero—Dryden is at pains in his introduction to the play to stress that Almanzor is a fully heroic figure, comparing him to Homer's Achilles and Tasso's Rinaldo—is proclaiming his disdain for rulers whose only authority comes from their position, not their personal virtue. Martin and Pesta's book is excellent, and I mention this lapse only as a caution: postmodernists are not to be trusted even as sources of simple information and must always be checked.

21. Stephen Greenblatt, *Renaissance Self-Fashioning from More to Shakespeare* (Chicago: University of Chicago Press, 1980), 224–25. See also Greenblatt, *Shakespeare's Freedom* (Chicago and London: University of Chicago Press, 2010), 73, on Othello's suicide: "Othello's task was to identify and destroy an appropriate enemy, a target that the Venetian Christians had long deemed worthy of hatred." For further discussion, see R. V. Young, "Stephen Greenblatt: The Critic as Anecdotalist," *Modern Age* 51 (2009): 262–71.

extended culture. In fact, it is only in Europe and in those parts of the globe under the influence of Western cultural and moral developments that such institutions have been systematically challenged and, in some respects, repudiated. The condemnation of slavery, the liberation of women from an exclusively domestic role, and the institutions of legal equality and political democracy all emerged in the Christian West.

"Western civilization," Christopher Dawson observes, "has been the great ferment of change in the world, because the changing of the world became an integral part of its cultural ideal." Dawson attributes the revolutionary character of Western civilization to its unique historical situation: the independent development of Christian culture in the barbarous western part of Europe, which would eventually influence the politically more sophisticated East. "This marks a new departure in the history of civilization," he maintains, "since it involved a dualism between cultural leadership and political power," which was one of the main factors that produced the "freedom and dynamic activity of Western culture." The result is something genuinely new under the sun:

> It is only in Western Europe that the whole pattern of the culture is to be found in a continuous succession and alternation of free spiritual movements; so that every century of Western history shows a change in the balance of cultural elements, and the appearance of some new spiritual force which creates new ideas and institutions and produces a further movement of social change.[22]

The Western tradition is, then, a paradoxical tradition of incessant transformation in which institutions and ideals are conserved by means of modification and adaptation to the currents of history and alteration of circumstances.

Such an assessment of Western civilization will seem "Eurocentric," "triumphalist," or even racialist to many current

---

22. Christopher Dawson, *Religion and the Rise of Western Culture* (1950; repr. Garden City, N.Y.: Doubleday Image, 1958), 17, 19, 21.

Introduction

observers, but Rémi Brague shows how the accusation is quite inaccurate:

> It is now fashionable to hurl at European culture the adjective "eurocentric." To be sure, every culture, like every living being, can't help looking at the other ones from its own vantage point, and Europe is no exception. Yet, no culture was ever so little centered on itself and so interested in the other ones as Europe. China saw itself as the "Middle Kingdom." Europe never did. "Eurocentrism" is a misnomer. Worse: it is the contrary of the truth.[23]

Identifying the essence of European culture with "Romanity," Brague maintains that Western civilization has always been uniquely open to other cultures precisely because the unfolding of its history deprived it of a fully native culture of its own while provoking the aspiration to emulate the highest culture available: "In this sense," he says, "anyone is 'Roman' who knows and feels himself caught between something like a 'Hellenism' and something like a 'barbarity.'"

Like Dawson, Brague also stresses that Christianity is an indispensable factor in this composition:

> I set down therefore as a thesis that *this "Roman" structure is the very structure of the Christian reality.* The Christians are essentially "Romans" in that they have their "Greeks" to which they are tied by an invisible bond. *Our Greeks are the Jews.* To say it a little less quickly: Christianity is to the Old Covenant what the Romans were to the Greeks.[24]

Even as the literature, philosophy, art, and oratory of Rome are inconceivable apart from their relationship to the achievement of the Greeks, in an analogous fashion, Christianity, as the fulfillment of the Law and the Prophets, is inconceivable without Judaism. Notice again the distinction between a single, expansive culture with genuine diversity and a multiculturalism always threatening to disintegrate into competing tribalisms.

---

23. Rémi Brague, *Eccentric Culture: A Theory of Western Civilization*, trans. Samuel Lester (South Bend, Ind.: St. Augustine's Press, 2002), 133–34.
24. Brague, *Eccentric Culture*, 55.

A crucial consequence of the doubly derivative character of Western civilization is its unique treatment of ancient books in foreign languages. The common language of Europe during its formative centuries was Latin, which was itself not the vernacular of most Europeans, but its master texts were in Hebrew and Greek. Western civilization from the beginning is estranged from its own most intimate cultural roots. "It is then," Brague writes, "a matter of *appropriating an origin in relation to which one feels foreign, and even alienated*—and in particular, the ancient sources."[25] This sense of derivation results in an "aesthetic" grasp of books and the emergence of the idea of a classic. "The advantage of an aesthetic relationship to the texts," he continues, "is thus that it postulates that the text is inexhaustible. It is its 'inexhaustibility,' and not its value as a model, that gives the text the character of a 'classic.'" Here, without mentioning Shakespeare, Brague is drawing near to the great dramatist's core relationship to the idea of Western civilization: "A classic text is a text from which one can always extract new ideas."[26]

Western civilization is, therefore, built upon a critical perspective in regard to its own traditions and a sense of dissatisfaction with its own achievements. "One can thus describe the intellectual history of Europe," Brague writes, "as an almost uninterrupted train of renaissances."[27] But a *renaissance* is inherently paradoxical: a *rebirth* that draws inspiration and energy by reviving and reimagining the past. Hence the importance of the West's dual Roman and Christian heritage, insofar as both elements provide a traditional foundation that is ever subject to renewal. There is an established standard of perfection, but no expectation that it will ever be fully realized. Utopianism, which attempts to engineer a temporal paradise, is, therefore, a per-

---

25. Brague, *Eccentric Culture*, 122.
26. Brague, *Eccentric Culture*, 103–4. See also Dawson, *Religion and the Rise of Western Culture*, 19: "European history is the history of a series of renaissances—of spiritual and intellectual revivals that arose independently, usually under religious influences, and were transmitted by a spontaneous process of free communication."
27. Brague, *Eccentric Culture*, 114.

version of the Western tradition: "For we have not here a lasting city; but we seek one that is to come" (Hebrews 13:14). "Behind the ever-changing pattern of Western culture there was a living faith which gave Europe a certain sense of spiritual community," Dawson observes, "in spite of all the conflicts and divisions and social schisms that marked its history": but he also adds, "The Christian mystery ... was essentially the mystery of eternal life. It was not concerned with the life of nature or with culture as a part of the order of nature."[28]

Western civilization is not only an *eccentric culture*, then, but also a culture that embodies and balances apparent contradictions without ever imposing a definitive resolution. Its intertwined Christian and Roman traditions, with their Hebrew and Hellenic roots, offer instead a definitive account of human nature and the human condition; but that nature and its circumstances in the wider creation are defined by contingency. We inhabit a space of uncertainty and apprehension. We sense more than we can know; we know more than we can do. From a modern existentialist perspective our world seems absurd—an irrational chaos—human beings little more than remarkably adapted clever beasts; yet an ideal of humanity haunts our imaginations, always just beyond attainment. It is only by an act of faith that we can trust that the reality of this ideal is conserved in the divine realm of the absolute Being we call God.

William Shakespeare is the exemplary poet of Western civilization because he represents this understanding of human experience with unique and compelling vividness and power. His comedies and tragedies dramatize from opposing angles the gap between the possibilities of human flourishing and the folly and pride that vitiate even our best efforts at fulfillment. His histories offer a remarkable vision of the contradiction and conflict that beset all efforts to found a just political community, and there is no more memorable rendering of the tensions between devotion

---

28. Dawson, *Religion and the Rise of Western Culture*, 22, 42.

and desire, aspiration and disappointment, sorrow and exultation than what is provided by his sonnets.

As an individual figure Shakespeare is strikingly appropriate for the role he plays in Western civilization. His modest, middle-class origins and doubtful education along with an apparent lack of significant worldly experience have led to numerous denials that the unassuming man from Stratford could possibly have written the plays; but in fact it is just such an overachiever who properly embodies the eager striving characteristic of Western culture, which finds personal expression in the combination of ambition and insecurity that mark so many of the sonnets.[29] Further, Shakespearean drama is both derivative and strikingly original. The plots are almost never his own—derived from an array of histories, chronicles, novellas, narrative poems, and earlier plays—but Shakespeare transforms everything he touches, often turning the most leaden materials to pure gold. His literary method is thus analogous to Western culture, which conserves a traditional vision of the human situation while endlessly renewing it.

It is no wonder, then, that Western civilization and its greatest poet have together come under increasingly intense and often hostile scrutiny in recent decades and have been not infrequently subjected to opprobrium and disdain. In academic circles, liberal humanism—the conventional intellectual orientation of modern liberal democracy—has been fiercely challenged by various versions of postmodern radicalism. The secularism, relativism, and materialism (essentially different facets of the same cultural phenomenon) that are muted in liberalism are flaunted by postmodernism, which asserts that the liberal commitment to reason is "logocentric"; that is, it is a version of theology. Truth, goodness, and beauty are not intuitive realities that are beyond our complete rational grasp; they are merely constructs of an

---

29. See S. Schoenbaum, *Shakespeare's Lives*, rev. ed. (Oxford: Clarendon Press, 1991), and James Shapiro, *Contested Will: Who Wrote Shakespeare?* (New York: Simon and Schuster, 2010).

Introduction

adaptive human calculating faculty bound to the servitude of relentless, insatiable desire. To suggest otherwise is to invite the scornful label "essentialist"—the naïve belief that anything at all has an intrinsic nature.

If every conceivable aspect of human reality is totally "constructed"—by language, economic forces, society—then the only recourse for human beings is to construct a reality that suits *us*; that is, those *bien-pensants* who have seen through religion, morality, and art and who recognize that these cultural institutions and the individuals who participate in them can all be shaped by the regnant political power if it is exercised with sufficient thoroughness and ruthlessness. Hence all human activities are properly political in the sense that politics has in the modern managerial state, and the ultimate enemy of this totalizing kind of politics is religion: "What threatens our secularized profession," writes Alan Sinfield with admirable candor, "is religion."[30] In this he only affirms Christopher Dawson's insight that the independence of the religion from political power in the Western world opened up a space for free spiritual development,[31] which frustrates radically totalizing political programs.

Even as Western civilization at its best resists the reduction of every facet of human existence to politics, so Shakespeare's plays resist the political imperatives of contemporary theory and criticism; and it is in this that he has become problematic among many academics in literature departments. If Shakespearean drama does not unambiguously advance the radical political agenda, then he is complicit in all the crimes of Western civilization. Notice, for example, how Eric Cheyfitz associates *The*

---

30. Sinfield, *Shakespeare, Authority, Sexuality*, 199.

31. For a more extensive discussion of the issue raised in these two paragraphs in its specifically academic setting, see Young, *At War with the Word*, esp. 59–114. The conflict between modern relativism and traditional concepts of morality is set forth concisely and prophetically by C. S. Lewis in *The Abolition of Man* (1947; repr. New York: Collier, 1962); a treatment taking in more recent developments in more detail is William Gairdner, *The Book of Absolutes: A Critique of Relativism and a Defense of Universals* (Montreal, Kingston, London, and Ithaca, N.Y.: McGill-Queen's University Press, 2008).

Introduction

Tempest with what he treats as agents of imperialism: "From the beginning to the present, fictions of translation have rationalized this force and fraud through the figures of eloquent orators like Prospero and Tarzan and Ronald Reagan, the 'great communicator,' whose central task in these fictions is always to 'civilize' the 'savages,' to cultivate or make them proper, in whatever form they take."[32] Prescinding for the moment from the question of how we may regard the notion that Prospero, Tarzan, and Ronald Reagan—how was Margaret Thatcher overlooked?—are all wicked imperialists, what is of most significance here is the spectacle of a professor of English who is oblivious to literary distinctions among a play by Shakespeare, a novel by Edgar Rice Burroughs, and the political oratory of an American president. If Shakespeare cannot be made to serve goals of progressive politics, then he must be denounced as politically retrograde.

The situation does not want for irony. Within living memory liberals were proud to defend provocative works of art from "moralistic" censors who wished to suppress daring novels like *Lady Chatterley's Lover* or films like *The Pawn Broker*. More recently, the academic and media elites have protested indignantly efforts to remove public funding for lurid photographs of men engaged in sodomy or of a crucifix immersed in urine, or to prohibit the staging of *Vagina Monologues* on Catholic campuses. But when a Catholic bishop bans Flannery O'Connor's story "The Artificial Nigger" from the curriculum of a diocesan high school lest it give offense—never mind that the story is a devastating satire of racialism—liberal indignation was palpably silent; and Peter Erickson proposes that "we need to hold open, for black and white students alike, the possibility of a sophisticated negative assessment of a play such as *Othello*."[33] Radical censorship is, naturally, "sophisticated"; nevertheless, political utility remains the only criterion upon which literature or any other kind of art is to be judged.

32. Cheyfitz, *Poetics of Imperialism*, xii.
33. Peter Erickson, "The Moment of Race in Renaissance Studies," *Shakespeare Studies* 26 (1998): 29.

Introduction

To be sure, it is problematic to regard any work of drama as a straightforward exercise in moral or political teaching. As Horace famously observes, a poet "who mixes the useful with the sweet wins every vote, / delighting the reader and reminding him equally."[34] These words are echoed a millennium and a half later by Shakespeare's elder contemporary Sir Philip Sidney, who says that "right Poets"

> imitate both to delight and teach, and delight to moue men to take that goodnes in hande, which without delight they would flye as from a stranger; and teach, to make them know that goodnes whereunto they are mooued.[35]

The balance of the "sweet" and the "useful," of "delighting" and "teaching" (or "reminding" or "admonishing," as Horace terms it) is always in danger of being lost. Without delight the imagination will never be sufficiently engaged for any learning to take place, but if delight becomes an end in itself—if it is merely "sweet" and not at all "useful"—then the sweetness, like a diet of nothing but desserts, soon cloys and becomes nauseous. The jaded palate demands ever more pungent stimulation. The Hollywood film industry, in its preoccupation with increasingly sensational and meaningless "special effects" and brutal and lurid spectacle, provides a timely negative exemplum.

What makes the greatest works of literature great, however, is that the delight and the instruction, the sweet and the useful, the love and the learning are not only equal but, as Horace also says, emerge "at the same time."[36] That is, the knowledge and pleasure occur simultaneously and inseparably in literature because they are, finally, aspects of the same experience. Although

---

34. Horace, *Ars poetica* 343–44: "Omne tulit punctum qui miscuit utile dulci, / lectorem delectando pariterque monendo"; Horace, *Q. Horati Flacci Opera*, ed. E. C. Wickham, rev. H. W. Garrod, 2nd ed. (Oxford: Clarendon, 1912).

35. Sir Philip Sidney, *An Apology for Poetry* (1595), in *Elizabethan Critical Essays*, ed. G. Gregory Smith (London: Oxford University Press, 1904), 1:159.

36. Horace, *Ars poetica* 333–34: "Aut prodesse volunt aut delectare poetae, / aut simul et iucunda et idonea dicere vitae."

we may distinguish retrospectively and abstractly between what delights us and what we learn from, say, *Hamlet* or *As You Like It*, we cannot enjoy these components of the plays separately. In fact, the delight and learning of a literary work cannot even exist apart from one another anymore than the competitive excitement of playing a tennis match can be divided from healthy exercise. Aristotle reminds us that the essential foundation of poetry—what we usually call "imaginative literature"—is *mimesis* or representation. From our earliest years we learn by representing or imitating, and we also take a natural delight in representations, even representations of things that would repel or dismay us by their actual presence.

Now literature is primarily concerned with human beings in action displaying their virtues and vices and defining themselves according to ethical distinctions.[37] We are, therefore, delighted by a convincing representation of men and women behaving as moral beings; that is, by a dramatization of human experience that strikes us as "true" or lifelike without ceasing to be a *re-presentation* rather than an actual, historical *presence*. An actor's portrayal of Othello's murder of Desdemona and his subsequent suicide can be tremendously uplifting in the theatre, but most of us should not care to be present at such a real event. Still, the aesthetic power of the scene depends upon our sense that it is in dramatic or literary terms authentic. And because genuine morality is consonant with, indeed emerges from, human nature and our condition as mortal creatures, literature teaches by offering a compelling depiction of human experience by means of an analogical representation.

It is in this sense that we can learn from the paradoxical poetry of William Shakespeare: his complex, multilayered, and ironic verbal and dramatic structures seize our attention and grip our

---

37. Aristotle, *Poetics* 1448b, 1448a, in *Aristotle, the Poetics*, Longinus, *On the Sublime*, ed. and trans. W. Hamilton Fyfe; Demetrius, *On Style*, ed., trans. W. Rhys Roberts, rev. ed. (Cambridge, Mass.: Harvard University Press, 1932).

imagination, focusing our attention on a vision of reality embodied in an artistic image. Art of this kind, which attempts to convey an imaginative rendering of the nature of human experience rather than demonstrate a proposition about it, has emerged most forcibly in the West precisely because Western civilization has afforded such free play to our contemplation of the ambiguities and tensions in which men and women are situated in our earthly life. Even the Christian orthodoxy long dominant in the Western world rests on an acknowledgment of human fallibility and uncertainty. According to Sidney, poetry is by its very nature a constant reminder of man's divine aspiration and inevitable failure:

Neyther let it be deemed too sawcie a comparison to balance the highest point of mans wit with the efficacie of Nature: but rather giue right honor to the heauenly Maker of that maker, who, hauing made man to his owne likenes, set him beyond and ouer all the works of that second nature, which in nothing hee sheweth so much as in Poetrie, when with the force of a diuine breath he bringeth things forth far surpassing her dooings, with no small argument to the incredulous of that first accursed fall of *Adam*: sith our erected wit maketh vs know what perfection is, and yet our infected will keepeth vs from reaching vnto it.

Sidney's account of poetry's part in education similarly invests it with the task of preparing us to strive for virtue in the face of our intractably recalcitrant nature:

This purifying of wit, this enritching of memory, enabling of iudgment, and enlarging of conceyt, which commonly we call learning, vnder what name soeuer it com forth, or to what immediate end soeuever it be directed, the final end is to lead and draw vs to as high a perfection as our degenerate soules, made worse by theyr clayey lodgings, can be capable of.[38]

---

38. Sidney, *Apology*, 157, 160.

Introduction

This kind of education—a liberal education, that is, an education for moral freedom—will inevitably clash with every kind of utopian ideology, which seeks to impose earthly perfection through the exercise of human reason and technique. A liberal education essentially seeks to develop men and women with sufficient virtue and wisdom to live decently in a fallen world (this does not, of course, obviate prudently seeking economic and social improvement in specific areas); progressive ideologues, bent on changing the world and human nature rather than inducing individual men and women to change themselves through moral effort, naturally reject education of this kind. Imaginative literature, of which the works of Shakespeare are a paragon, will necessarily prove anathema to any program of social engineering, so it is not at all surprising that "Shakespeare" is no longer a required course in most university and college literature programs and that literature itself is being displaced by "culture studies," which pay minute attention to the most superficial kind of commercial entertainment. After all, "popular culture" offers little intrinsic challenge to the manipulations of the interpreter. It is no exaggeration, therefore, to maintain that the study of Shakespeare and what we learn from him will play a limited but critical part in our efforts to conserve the idea of Western civilization for future generations. *Conservatism* in this sense must be the principal work of education in our time, when the elites of our society have for several decades evinced a suicidal hostility toward the moral norms that make civilized life possible and engaged in a relentless estrangement of the populace from the sources of cultural and spiritual nurture.

An important qualification is in order: it would be a mistake to assume that Shakespeare deliberately set about to become the spokesman for Western civilization, or even that he eventually realized that he had done so. First, although he was undoubtedly aware of his literary gifts, the fact that (unlike Jonson) he seems to have made no effort to preserve his dramatic works suggests that Shakespeare was too modest even to consider such a role for himself. More important, the idea of Western civilization had not yet emerged. Europeans had long thought of themselves as participants in Christendom, but this cosmopolitan vision had come under increasing pressure from the development of aggressively independent nation-states during the late Middle Ages, and by the time of Shakespeare's death, Christendom had been rapidly disintegrating for a century in the aftermath of the Reformation. The idea of Western civilization may well be understood as a conceptual substitute for the concrete institutions of Christendom.

Some scholars, in fact, read Shakespeare's plays as an expression of withering skepticism that began to flourish in the wake of these changes. Millicent Bell, for example, emphasizes the influence of Montaigne on Shakespeare's reluctantly radical view of the human condition:

> Through the action and language of his plays he invites his audiences to question, from moment to moment, the inherited, standard truths of his time. He also allows his audiences to view fearfully the results of abandoning the prop of such beliefs.... One of the secrets of his high poetry is the way its complex verbal effects both enrich and contradict one another.[39]

---

39. Millicent Bell, *Shakespeare's Tragic Skepticism* (New Haven, Conn., and London: Yale University Press, 2002), 5. For a more balanced and insightful account of the relation between Montaigne and Shakespeare and the limits of their skepticism, see Robert Ellrodt, *Montaigne and Shakespeare: The Emergence of Modern Self-Consciousness* (Manchester, UK: Manchester University Press, 2015), esp. 163: "The present tendency among literary critics is to reject any presence of essentialism in the thought of Montaigne and Shakespeare. It is only justified if one has in mind a Platonic type of essentialism." This book is the author's English rendering of his work in French, *Montaigne et Shakespeare: L'émergence de la conscience moderne* (Paris: José Corti, 2011). Stanley Cavell, *Disowning Knowledge in Six Plays of Shakespeare* (Cambridge: Cambridge University Press, 1987), says, "My intuition is that the advent of skepticism as manifested in Descartes's *Meditations* is already in full existence in Shakespeare, from the time of the great tragedies in the first years of the seventeenth century, in the generation preceding that of Descartes" (3); and "It is in taking tragedy as the display of skepticism, and skepticism with respect to other minds as allegorical of skepticism with respect to material objects, that in my experience the treatment of the object forces its attention upon us" (8). So far as I can discover no evidence is offered for these remarkable assertions besides Cavell's "intuition."

Introduction

As an examination of the plays in the succeeding chapters will seek to show, however, Bell is mistaking for radical skepticism Shakespeare's embodiment of precisely that critical spirit that is not a negation of what we know as Western civilization, but rather its essence.

I

Shakespeare On Love (and Marriage)

Nowhere is the alienation of contemporary men and women from the Christian traditions of the past—and hence from the moral vision embodied in Shakespeare's plays—more manifest than in the realm of sexual morality. The uneasiness of our society with the world that Shakespeare represents is blatantly displayed in the reduction of the greatest poet of the English language to the level of the feckless "leading man" of the 1995 film *Shakespeare in Love*, which is more than anything else an adolescent fantasy of adultery. While we have no means of knowing whether William Shakespeare was involved with a real "dark lady" as is his persona "Will" in Sonnets 127 through 150, there is certainly no portrayal of the spiritual devastation wrought by lust more unnerving than what emerges from these poems. The plays from first to last likewise reveal a horror at uncontrolled sexual desire that leads to promiscuity and infidelity. Premarital chastity and the depth and permanence of the conjugal bond are correspondingly portrayed as the beneficent norm.

Some contemporary scholars are sufficiently forthright to condemn Shakespeare for what they regard as his outdated morality. As one clause in a lengthy repudiation of Shakespeare's superior standing in world literature, Gary Taylor asks, "Do we really believe anymore, do students believe, do we want them to believe, in the overwhelming moral importance of premarital female virginity?"[1] By far the more common ploy, however, is to recruit Shakespeare to the interpreter's own favorite ideological project. Catherine Belsey writes a book about love and marriage in Shakespeare's plays with the explicit goal of showing "that family values as we understand them have nothing to do with nature." Worse still, "the close-knit, supportive nuclear family can also appear as a form of heterosexist oppression, and ... the location not only of affection and support, but also of domestic violence and child abuse."[2] Belsey proceeds to show how families formed by presumably loving marriages become the sites of irrational jealousy in *Othello, The Winter's Tale,* and *Cymbeline* and murderous sibling rivalry in *As You Like It* and *Hamlet.* Without even taking up the relevance of these observations to Shakespeare's plays, we may observe that to eliminate jealousy by eliminating romantic love or to eliminate fratricide by eliminating brothers is analogous to solving the problem of tooth decay by abolishing teeth: it may work, but eating would be greatly inconvenienced.

Dr. Johnson rightly observes that a distinctive feature of Shakespearean drama is its comparatively restrained attention to love: "Upon every other stage the universal agent is love, by whose power all good and evil is distributed and every action quickened or retarded." Johnson continues in a vein that suggests the extent to which our current preoccupation with what we coarsely call "sex" would dismay him:

For this, probability is violated, life is misrepresented, and language is depraved. But love is only one of many passions; and as it has no great influence upon the sum of life, it has little operation in the dramas of a poet who caught his ideas from the living world and exhibited only what he saw before him. He knew that any other passion, as it was regular or exorbitant, was a cause of happiness or calamity.[3]

---

1. Taylor, *Reinventing Shakespeare*, 403.
2. Catherine Belsey, *Shakespeare and the Loss of Eden: The Construction of Family Values in Early Modern Culture* (New Brunswick, N.J.: Rutgers University Press, 1999), 19.
3. Johnson, *Johnson on Shakespeare*, 26–27.

Shakespeare on Love (and Marriage)

Those who think first of *Romeo and Juliet* when they think of Shakespeare may find this judgment surprising, but it is one of only three tragedies—the others are *Othello* and *Antony and Cleopatra*—in which passionate sexual love is a principal concern.[4] In the histories, love is noticed only incidentally and in passing, so Shakespeare's depictions of love are largely the business of the comedies and romances.

In the most substantial and moving of these plays Johnson's observation is still vindicated, if somewhat obliquely. The fulfillment of amorous desires and emotional longing is never sufficient unto itself, because erotic gratification is constrained and qualified by competing personal needs and interests and by the imperatives of social convention and political order. *The Taming of the Shrew* is, for example, about love and marriage; but it introduces myriad other factors besides the urge for sexual consummation and emotional union. Both the attraction and the conflict between lovers must be resolved within a communal context. As Wolfgang Riehl points out, even this rowdiest of Shakespeare's comedies embodies a social vision:

> Contrary to a widespread view, Shakespeare's *Taming* is not a mere farce. Instead, it proves to reflect a humanist corrective purpose. What seems so genuinely farcical, namely the process of taming itself, is motivated by Petruchio's intention of showing Kate, as in a mirror, the social misconduct that produces her shrewishness.[5]

What distinguishes Shakespeare's treatment of romantic sexual love is not just its diminished importance in his plays, as Dr. Johnson urges, but also an insistent questioning of the relationship between love and social and religious institutions—above all, marriage.

About the time Shakespeare was a young man, the relationship between love and marriage was becoming a social issue as

---

4. *Troilus and Cressida* is thus classified not as a tragedy, but as a "problem" comedy.
5. Wolfgang Riehl, *Shakespeare, Plautus and the Humanist Tradition* (Cambridge: D. S. Brewer, 1990), 213.

well as a literary topic. At the beginning of the twenty-first century in the Western world, the relationship between ardent romantic love and marriage seems self-evident, even if lifelong, faithful marriage has become an increasingly doubtful proposition over the past half-century or so. But before "falling in love" could become the basis for marriage, the rather idealized, not to say rarified notion of love thus implied had to be conceived and become a cultural reality. Obviously, men and women have always desired one another, and as long as there has been some form of human society, what we call "love" has involved not merely sensual gratification, but also attractions of appearance and personality. But for a man to find himself willy-nilly preoccupied intensely with a single woman whom he regards with quasi-religious adoration and views as the cynosure of beauty, virtue, and delight—this is a new development that C. S. Lewis, among others, traces to eleventh-century Provence. "There can be no mistake about the novelty of romantic love," he writes; "our only difficulty is to imagine in all its bareness the mental world that existed before its coming—to wipe out of our minds, for a moment, nearly all that makes the food of both modern sentimentality and modern cynicism."[6]

The emergence of this transfiguration of sexual desire and affection did not easily become associated with marriage. The expectation that a man and woman would marry because they had met and "fallen in love" does not reflect the realities of most societies throughout most of the world during most of history, and even in the Western world such passion only gradually and grudgingly became routinely linked to marriage. The common

---

6. C. S. Lewis, *The Allegory of Love: A Study in Medieval Tradition* (London, Oxford, and New York: Oxford University Press, 1936), 4. Much of the discussion of the development of love and its relation to marriage between eleventh-century Provence and sixteenth-century England in this chapter depends upon Lewis's book, which remains the classic discussion of its topic. Although critics have succeeded in calling into question various details of Lewis's argument, his fundamental thesis, that romantic love, its eventual amalgamation with marriage, and the poetry thus inspired constitute a unique historical development of the West, is unassailable.

cultural norm has been—and is—for parents or dominant members of extended families to arrange the marriages of young men and women according to criteria that considered first the social and economic advancement of the family as a whole. Insofar as the individual spouses were considered, in addition to the hope of fertility, the qualities that would be looked for in a bride were dutifulness and faithfulness toward her husband as well as frugality, industriousness, and strength of character in order to rear sound children and manage a household. The groom ought to be a man with prudence to conserve the family's prosperity, prestige, and interests and the initiative to advance them. If the couple also enjoyed one another's company—so much the better. But no sensible adult would have regarded the passionate desires and emotional infatuation of a pair of adolescents as a sound basis for establishing a lifelong conjugal union with the purpose of procreation and participation in the important business of the community.

This was undoubtedly the dominant, conventional view of Shakespeare's day, but there was already a cultural trend in the direction of what is now called "companionate marriage," usually associated with the Puritan wing of Protestantism.[7] This cultural movement was embodied in the work of the greatest nondramatic poet of the sixteenth century, Edmund Spenser, a man of moderate Puritan inclinations. C. S. Lewis observes that Spenser provides the literary climax of the transformation of passionate desire and emotional attachment into a suitable motive for marriage: "The last phase of the story—the final defeat of courtly love by the romantic conception of marriage—occupies the third book of *The Faerie Queene* and much of the fourth."[8]

He might have included, in addition, Spenser's love sonnet sequence *Amoretti* along with the *Epithalamion* placed at its end. The typical English imitator of the love sonnet sequence estab-

---

7. William Haller and Malleville Haller, "The Puritan Art of Love," *Huntington Library Quarterly* 5 (1942): 235–72, remains the definitive treatment.
8. Lewis, *Allegory of Love*, 298.

lished in the fourteenth century by Francesco Petrarcha followed the Italian master in depicting a frustrating passion for an enchantingly perfect but hopelessly unattainable woman. To be sure, the English sonneteers were often less content than Petrarch's lover to admire the object of their desire with melancholy resignation from afar. Sir Philip Sidney's Astrophil is typical in closing out a sonnet detailing all the perfections of body, mind, and soul of Stella—which ought to inspire purely spiritual devotion—with a burst of defiant anguish: "But ah, desire still cries: 'Give me some food!'"[9]

Spenser's *Amoretti*, in contrast, provides an account of a courtship that eventually results in the marriage celebrated in the *Epithalamion*, or marriage hymn, appended to the end of the sonnet sequence. The lady is beautiful, chaste, and a paragon of all virtue; at times she treats her lover with the disdainful mockery of the proud Petrarchan mistress. Nevertheless, she is not inaccessible or forbidden, and eventually the poetic persona succeeds by winning her consent. Although the passionate desire and emotional attachment of the lovers are emphasized, their love is assimilated to Christian charity: "Loue is the lesson which the Lord vs taught."[10]

This idealized view of marriage both as a religious and social institution and as the fulfillment of the personal longings and aspirations of the spouses informs the view of marriage dramatized in many of Shakespeare's plays, but he makes us aware as well of the complex tensions involved with such a conception of marriage. In this complexity of outlook, Shakespeare embodies in dramatic form a characteristic feature of Western civilization: its paradoxical maintenance of conflicting principles and predi-

---

9. Sir Philip Sidney, *Astrophil and Stella* (1591), sonnet 71, in *Sir Philip Sidney: The Oxford Authors* (Oxford and New York: Oxford University Press, 1989).

10. Edmund Spenser, *Amoretti* (1595), sonnet 68. See also, especially, sonnets 65 and 67 for the theme of the lady's consent. The *Epithalamion* culminates in the bridegroom's prayer that the long-desired wedding night consummation will lead to offspring, who will ultimately reach heaven, "Of blessed Saints for to increase the count" (Spenser, *Epithalamion* 423).

lections in a dynamic cultural matrix. For example, Christianity, a fundamental element in the Western synthesis, is a revealed religion requiring faithful adherence to dogmas that transcend reason, but ecclesiastical institutions have nonetheless permitted, nay, encouraged the development and elaboration of an extensive and probing body of theological speculation with the purpose of explaining rationally and justifying what is by definition inexplicable and accessible only by the submission of reason to faith. Similarly, since the democratic experiment began in Athens more than 2,500 years ago, the politics of the Western world has—at its best—been a struggle to maintain social order and the common good while providing the space for individual liberty. And so with marriage: while it has been a social and religious institution in every society, since the revaluation of personal affection and desire began to emerge in the second millennium of the Christian era, Western civilization has offered an often uneasy accommodation between intimate longings of individual men and women and public norms of matrimony.

Shakespeare concludes his most memorable and powerful comedies with conventional happy marriages, which are presumed to furnish enduring pleasure, prosperity, and contentment; but these endings are never altogether unambiguous. This provocatively equivocal treatment of love and marriage can be no more effectively illustrated by two of his most unsettling comedies, *The Merchant of Venice* and *Much Ado About Nothing*. For some commentators, the questions that trouble thoughtful audiences at the end of these plays constitute a dramatic flaw. Maurice Charney, for instance, contrasts "certain structural problems" in the latter unfavorably with "most of Shakespeare's earlier comedies":

The danger of the comic villainy in *Much Ado* is that it heats the plot up so torridly that it is difficult to get rid of Don John and his paid conspirators, revive Hero, reanimate Claudio, and produce the happy ending of comedy without some sense of needless effort and overly hasty regeneration. Probably worst of all, Claudio and Hero remain an undeveloped pair of lovers alongside some of Shakespeare's most successful, witty players in love-game comedy: Beatrice and Benedick.[11]

Charney likewise calls attention to "the imperfect love actions" of *The Merchant of Venice* and complains that it "ends more with 'this muddy vesture of decay' than with the immortal harmony that only angelic creatures can hear."[12] But this acknowledgment of imperfection, this undertone of disharmony and anxiety, is the source of the compelling vividness of Shakespeare's representation of human love and its consummation in marriage.

The Merchant of Venice entangles its marriage plot with a fairy-tale motif of winning a wife through choosing correctly among three metal chests, and the overt statements about love and marriage in *Much Ado About Nothing* are largely nervous jokes about marriage as a "yoke" and the "horns" in the forehead of the cuckolded husband. These two romantic comedies, nevertheless, embody a specifically Christian wisdom about the perennial issues of human conjugal relations. Moreover, discomfort with the moral orientation exemplified by these plays is an important source of the revisionist interpretations of Shakespeare, often shading into overt hostility, that are so prominent a feature of the current academic scene. Informing with moral substance the sometimes farcical misadventures of both comedies is an idea about marriage and the love it requires, as well as its relation to friendship, that can only be suggested in the actions of the characters and the style of their speech, not stated as a prudential maxim. Like so much of the world's greatest literature, Shakespearean drama stages the paradoxical nature of human existence.

---

11. Maurice Charney, *Shakespeare on Love and Lust* (New York: Columbia University Press, 2000), 46–47.

12. Charney, *Shakespeare on Love and Lust*, 48. Charney is referring to Lorenzo's speech on the music of the spheres in *Merchant of Venice* V.i.54–65, but he seems to miss the point of the reference: we cannot in our mortal condition hear the celestial music, but only intimations of it. This is the reason for including the equivocal invocation at the play's conclusion.

Shakespeare on Love (and Marriage)

The Merchant of Venice begins with Antonio, the merchant of the title, in a mood of inexplicable melancholy: "And such a want-wit sadness makes of me, / That I have much ado to know myself"(I.i.6–7).[13] The other characters speculate in the scene that he is worried about the success of his numerous commercial adventures or else is in love. It soon becomes apparent, however, that what is gnawing unconsciously at his peace of mind is his friend Bassanio's hope of making a good marriage, which will inevitably alter the relationship of the two men. Shakespeare thus shapes our sense of the nature of marriage by contrasting it with, and in some measure opposing it to, masculine friendship, a familiar sixteenth-century theme,[14] which appears as early as *Two Gentlemen of Verona*, resurfaces in his late collaboration with John Fletcher, *The Two Noble Kinsmen*, and plays a prominent role in his mature comedies, *Twelfth Night* and, as we shall see, *Much Ado About Nothing*. The merchant, Antonio, is willing to do anything—"if it stand ... / Within the eye of honor" (I.i.136–37)—to advance his friend's prospects, even if it means helping Bassanio to a wife who will come between them.

Indeed, when Shylock claims the forfeit pound of flesh that Antonio has offered as security to fund Bassanio's courtship journey, Antonio triumphantly asserts the superiority of his friendship over the love of a wife:

> Commend me to your honorable wife,
> Tell her the process of Antonio's end,
> Say how I lov'd you, speak me fair in death;
> And when the tale is told, bid her be judge
> Whether Bassanio had not once a love.
>
> (IV.i.273–77)

---

13. Unless otherwise specified, Shakespeare's works are quoted throughout from William Shakespeare, *The Riverside Shakespeare*, ed. G. B. Evans et al., 2nd ed. (Boston and New York: Houghton Mifflin, 1997).

14. See, e.g., Edmund Tilney, *The Flower of Friendship: A Renaissance Dialogue Contesting Marriage* (1568), ed. Valerie Wayne (Ithaca, N.Y., and London: Cornell University Press, 1992).

Bassanio, at this terrible moment with Shylock brandishing a knife over his friend, is all too willing to assent to this invidious comparison between friend and spouse:

> Antonio, I am married to a wife
> Which is as dear to me as life itself,
> But life itself, my wife, and all the world,
> Are not with me esteem'd above thy life.
> I would lose all, ay, sacrifice them all
> Here to this devil, to deliver you. (IV.i.282–87)

Of course the tragic terror of the scene is mitigated by comic irony, as Portia, present in disguise as the youthful jurist, Balthazar, who will save Antonio and discomfit Shylock, quips: "Your wife would give you little thanks for that / If she were by to hear you make the offer" (IV.i.288–89).

When Portia and Nerissa, in their disguises as Balthazar and his clerk, inveigle their husbands into rewarding judicial success with the rings that they have promised their brides to keep forever as a sign of their fidelity, they take humorous revenge upon their husband's willingness to sacrifice them for Antonio, while furnishing Act V with a bit of highly amusing confusion. But they establish the point that marriage takes precedence over friendship, or, put differently, that a man's wife ought to be his best friend. Bassanio and Gratiano are nonplussed at the demand of their new wives for the rings entrusted to them, momentarily horrified at the women's threat to take the doctor and his clerk for their bedfellows, and simultaneously abashed and relieved when the deception is revealed. Portia does not prolong their anxiety for more than a few moments, because the offense involving the rings has been slight. Nevertheless, although rings for men were not formally part of an Elizabethan wedding ceremony, the rings given by Portia and Nerissa remind their husbands that the same obligations of fidelity are laid upon them as upon the bride, whose ring is a necessary part of the wedding. Even the bawdiness implicit in Gratiano's speech that closes the play only adds a comic edge to the moral symbolism of a permanent bond: "Well, while I live I'll fear no other thing / So sore as keeping safe Nerissa's ring" (V.i.306–7).

Bassanio has already demonstrated that he understands the true significance of marriage as the ultimate earthly commitment, albeit he has briefly forgotten during the terrible strain of the trial scene. As so often happens in Shakespearean drama, the casket test is a bit of folk mythology that the playwright adapts to the purposes of moral realism. Bassanio's correct choice of lead casket in Act III is a figurative means of showing that his hero has more character and maturity than his spendthrift ways and dependency on Antonio would suggest.

The Prince of Morocco chooses the gold casket, which bears the inscription, "Who chooseth me shall gain what many men desire" (II.vii.5). It is as if he were choosing a wife on the basis of her popular appeal—a "trophy wife," who would enhance his status among other men. When he opens the casket, he is confronted by a skull and the message, "All that glisters is not gold" (II.vii.65).[15] The Prince of Aragon, whose name suggests "arrogance" to Anglophone ears and who would be especially opprobrious in the wake of the Spanish Armada, even more thoughtlessly chooses the silver casket with its inscription, "Who chooseth me shall get as much as he deserves" (II.vii.7).

In the wedding ceremony of the *Book of Common Prayer*, the minister asks the bride if she is willing to yield herself completely to her husband: "Wilt thou obey him and serve him, love, honor, and keep him, in sickness and in health? And forsaking all other, keep thee only unto him, so long as you both shall live?"[16] What

---

15. Geraldo U. de Sousa, *Shakespeare's Cross-Cultural Encounters* (Houndmills, Basingstoke, Hampshire: Palgrave, 1999), 80, maintains that the Prince of Morocco does not understand the "trite, well-known proverb" because he is "an outsider," lacking the appropriate cultural knowledge. This explanation is, however, improbable, because the proverb appears earliest in the fables of Aesop, an essentially mythical figure, first mentioned by Hesiod. By Shakespeare's day, the stories and proverbial "moral" were the common property of the Mediterranean world.

16. *The Book of Common Prayer: The Elizabethan Prayer Book* (1559), ed. John E. Booty (Charlottesville: University Press of Virginia, 1976), 292.

man can possibly *deserve* that? Or what woman can *deserve* a similar reciprocal promise from her husband? The gift of self in holy matrimony is as close as most of us ordinary mortals will ever come to bestowing something like *grace*—the divine favor that no one can possibly merit—upon another person. It is doubtless, for this reason, that St. Paul compares Christ's relation to the church to matrimony and adjures husbands to "love your wives, as Christ also loved the Church and delivered himself up for it" (Ephesians 5:25).

Bassanio, who has only been able to come wooing on borrowed money and at great risk to his friend Antonio, cannot call for such a sacrifice just because of a woman's beauty and wealth, which "many men desire"; and he cannot fail to realize that he does not deserve Portia. While Morocco and Aragon have scornfully rejected the lead casket with its threatening inscription, "Who chooseth me must give and hazard all he hath" (II.vii.9), Bassanio recognizes in the pallor of this metal his own humble claim to such a blessing as the hand of Portia:

> ... but thou, thou meager lead,
> Which rather threaten'st than dost promise aught,
> Thy paleness moves me more than eloquence,
> And here choose I. (III.ii.104–7)

To "give and hazard all he hath" is exactly what marriage demands of both spouses, who promise fidelity "from this day forward, for better, for worse, for richer, for poorer, in sickness, and in health."[17] In the contingent world of fragile humanity, who can know which of these alternatives will obtain? In recognizing what marriage truly demands, Bassanio shows that he is ready to be a good husband, that he recognizes that it may entail sacrifice. Even so, the trial scene with its terrible threat to Antonio, ultimately caused by Bassanio's wooing of Portia, subjects him sooner than he would have expected to the kind of sorrow that can arise in marriage; and Portia's ruse involving the rings em-

---

17. *Book of Common Prayer*.

phatically displays how forgiveness is a necessary element of any conjugal relationship.

Portia, likewise, acknowledges that marriage is a gift of self and, insofar as we can never know the future, a "hazard." She further willingly submits to the subordinate position that was a woman's lot in Elizabethan England, but not without bestowing upon Bassanio, along with herself and all her worldly goods, the ring that reminds him of his equal obligations:

> But now I was the lord
> Of this fair mansion, master of my servants,
> Queen o'er myself; and even now, but now,
> This house, these servants, and this same myself
> Are yours—my lord's!—I give them with this ring,
> Which when you part from, lose, or give away,
> Let it presage the ruin of your love,
> And be my vantage to exclaim on you. (III.ii.167–74)

Shakespeare's romantic comedies are often quite amusing, and they end in typical comic fashion with the principal characters happily married. They are also "comic," however, in the sense that Dante's *Commedia* is comic; that is, they point beyond the realm of merely earthly happiness to the blessedness of heaven. Marriage is not merely celebrated as a fulfillment of earthly desire and aspiration but is also seen as a grave responsibility that can raise men and women to a higher good than they had imagined or plunge them into the depths of despair. Like *The Merchant of Venice*, *Much Ado About Nothing* is a comic play that draws nigh unto tragedy and modulates its humor and sparkling wit with ominous overtones.

Scholars have long noted that in this comedy Shakespeare combines the Beatrice and Benedick "sub-plot" with a version of the tale of the slandered woman, which was very familiar in Renaissance literature and had roots in ancient Hellenic romance. Readers since Charles I have preferred the "sub-plot," and Hector Berlioz made it stand alone as the opera *Béatrice et Bénédict* in 1861. As Anne Barton remarks, however, the all-important sub-plot is diminished when it is turned into a self-sufficient main plot: "A Beatrice who has no need to ask Benedick to 'Kill Claudio' (IV.i.289), forcing him to choose abruptly between his old world of male friendships and the new world of love, cannot fully reveal either her own nature or the depth of her lover's commitment."[18] Barton's observation raises two important points. First, in *Much Ado About Nothing* as in most of his plays, Shakespeare's apparent violation of the Aristotelian canon of unity of action by the deployment of multiple plots eventually discloses a deeper thematic, even spiritual, unity. Second, Shakespeare highlights the nature of marital love by juxtaposing it to masculine friendship. In other words, we learn about love and marriage from Shakespeare not from what he tells us—he *tells* us nothing—but from the contrasts between two approaches to marriage and between the love of a man and a woman and the nonsexual love between friends.

Meaning is not, then, something that the playwright adds on to the plot; it is generated by the plot as the strength and durability and beauty of a building are aspects of its structure. In *Much Ado About Nothing* we see two sets of lovers moving toward marriage with very different attitudes and expectations; the import of the comedy emerges, in large measure, from the contrast between these couples. Claudio and Hero are, ostensibly, the traditional romantic lovers. Their betrothal seems to be the culmination of mutual attraction, and it has the approval of the appropriate third parties, the bride's father, Leonato, and Claudio's patron, Don Pedro. So free of obstacles seems their pathway to wedded bliss that they can while away the time before the ceremony in an elaborately devious matchmaking scheme

---

18. Introduction to *Much Ado About Nothing*, in Evans et al., *The Riverside Shakespeare*, 361. John Traugott, "Creating a Rational Rinaldo: A Study of the Mixture of the Genres of Comedy and Romance in *Much Ado About Nothing*," Genre 15, nos. 1–2 (1982): 157–81, points out that Shakespeare strengthens the impact of the tale by making the comic "joker" play the role of Rinaldo, from Ariosto's *Orlando Furioso*, who comes to the aid of a similarly slandered woman.

aimed at those recalcitrant enemies of Cupid Beatrice and Benedick. These latter appear unlikely to make a happy pair, since they are both set in their ways, suspicious, and endowed with an acerbic wit that would give pause to any potential spouse who reflected upon how it might wear after twenty years of marriage. It is a characteristically ironic twist of Shakespeare that the crisis involving Claudio and Hero becomes equally crucial in the developing love of Beatrice and Benedick. By the time Claudio repudiates his bride at the door of the church on their wedding day, Beatrice and Benedick have been maneuvered by their friends into acknowledging their love for one another, but they must confront the prospect of tragedy in order to know what that love means and what it demands. Most important, they learn truly to know one another by uniting in response to Claudio's ill treatment of Hero.

It is the lack of such knowledge—of the requirements of love and of the character of one's prospective spouse—that nearly brings about the ruin of Hero and the irredeemable descent of Claudio into shameful villainy. It would be easy enough to blame the deceit of Don John and his henchmen, but it is probably safe to assert that at some point every marriage has to face the moral equivalent of a Don John. Claudio and Don Pedro are deceived by Don John even as they are complicit in the deception of Benedick, but Benedick still must make a decision—and so must Claudio. Shakespeare is careful to dramatize the character flaws that make the latter such an easy mark for Don John's deceptions early in the play. We should not, perhaps, condemn Claudio excessively for his interest in Hero's status as the sole heiress of Leonato's wealth, but it is disappointing that the very *first* question that he asks Don Pedro about her is not about her at all: "Hath Leonato any son, my lord?" (I.i.294). In addition to the indication of ambition and avarice, this question suggests that Claudio knows very little about the object of his erotic ardor, and his willingness to allow Don Pedro to woo on his behalf indicates a disinclination to make any effort to know better the woman he would make his wife. Finally, he instantly doubts the integrity of his longtime patron, Don Pedro, on the word of Don John and reveals an unpleasant strain of cynicism blended with callow naïveté. In his approach to marriage, Claudio displays a good deal of immaturity.

Hero is even more passive and disengaged from her marital future than her betrothed. The text of the play affords no evidence that Hero has an inclination toward any man when the play opens, though it is not unreasonable to infer that she has had her eye on Claudio, or at least noticed his eye on her. In any case, when her father instructs her to accept Don Pedro's suit, should he make an offer, she does not demur; and when, as it turns out, Pedro woos instead for his young protégé, she is instantly won. It is not incumbent upon her to be so absolutely submissive. Although fathers in Shakespeare's time exercised a good deal more authority over daughters than we can easily imagine in twenty-first-century America, no one could be lawfully forced to marry without giving consent.[19] When Hero's uncle Antonio says, "Well, niece, I trust you will be rul'd by your father," Beatrice answers for her cousin:

> Yes, faith, it is my cousin's duty to make cur'sy and say,
> "Father, as it please you." But yet for all that, cousin, let him
> be a handsome fellow, or else make another cur'sy and say,
> "Father, as it please me." (II.i.50–56)

Beneath the banter of her tone, Beatrice is seriously admonishing her cousin that she ought not to give herself for life to a man who in no way appeals to her; but Hero, as so often in the course

---

19. This is ancient Catholic teaching, succinctly stated by St. Thomas Aquinas quoting St. John Chrysostum, *Summa Theologiae* Supplementum 45.2: "*Matrimonium non facit coitus, sed voluntas.* . . . Ergo consensus facit matrimonium." It did not vanish in Reformation England. In Edmund Tilney's *The Flower of Friendship*, 127–28, women are warned to be as careful in choosing husbands for virtue as men are in choosing wives. See also T. E., *The Law's Resolutions of Women's Rights: Or, the Law's Provision for Women* (1632), 2.18, 2.21, 2.22, in *Sexuality and Gender in the English Renaissance: An Annotated Edition of Contemporary Documents*, ed. Lloyd Davis (New York and London: Garland, 1998), 382–83, where it is made clear that mutual consent is essential to marriage.

of the play, says nothing and allows herself to be wholly guided by others. It seems clear that Claudio and Hero have agreed to marry, having little mutual knowledge or understanding; each of them is merely a fitting spouse—a "good catch," we should say now—on superficial grounds.

If it is not surprising, given these circumstances, that Claudio is quick to condemn Hero once Don John has deceived him, Claudio is certainly less forgivable than Robert G. Hunter maintains, in saying the "error ... cannot deserve, in itself, our very strong censure."[20] After all, Don John has already deceived Claudio once about Don Pedro's intentions. Surely a man less self-absorbed, less preoccupied with his own privileges and position, would be a little more wary of such an insinuating tale-bearer. But there is worse, and the bill of indictment cannot be better articulated than by the victim's cousin:

> O that I were a man! What, bear her in hand until they come to take hands, and then with public accusation, uncover'd slander, unmitigated rancor—O God, that I were a man! I would eat his heart in the market-place. (IV.i.303-7)

Even if the accusation against Hero had been true, Claudio's behavior is unconscionable. He ought to have known better, and Shakespeare's audience would have known how a man is to conduct himself in such a situation from the gospel reading for the Sunday after Christmas in the *Book of Common Prayer*, taken from St. Matthew:

> The birth of Jesus was on this wise: When his mother Mary was married to Joseph (before they came to dwell together) she was found with child by the Holy Ghost. Then Joseph her husband (because he was a righteous man, and would not put her to shame) was minded privily to depart from her.[21]

---

20. Robert G. Hunter, *Shakespeare and the Comedy of Forgiveness* (New York: Columbia University Press, 1965), 95.
21. *Book of Common Prayer*, 90.

Even prescinding from the duty of Christian charity, mere secular decency would require more: "It is almost a definition of a gentleman," Cardinal Newman remarks, "to say he is one who never inflicts pain."[22]

While the dominant voices of contemporary society would generally agree in condemning Claudio's accusation as wicked, it is questionable whether they would agree that the deed of which he accused Hero was also quite as wicked. But it is precisely because the slander is so dire that it is so monstrous; it robs Hero of her sense of personal identity and casts her into oblivion. Faced with the accusation, she cries, "Is it not Hero? Who can blot that name / With any just reproach?" (IV.i.80–81). Unchastity is a virtual denial of her being, because it *blots her name*; that is, it deprives her of her purpose and her place in family and community. There is a horror of fornication and adultery and of the lust that provokes them throughout Shakespearean drama, and it emerges in explicit terms in the "Dark Lady" series among the *Sonnets*:

> Th'expense of spirit in a waste of shame
> Is lust in action, and till action, lust
> Is perjur'd murd'rous, bloody, full of blame,
> Savage, extreme, rude, cruel, not to trust,
> Enjoy'd no sooner but despised straight,
> Past reason hunted, and no sooner had,
> Past reason hated as a swallow'd bait
> On purpose laid to make the taker mad:
> [Mad] in pursuit and in possession so,
> Had, having, and in quest to have, extreme,
> A bliss in proof, and prov'd, [a] very woe,
> Before, a joy propos'd, behind, a dream.
> All this the world well knows, yet none knows well
> To shun the heaven that leads men to this hell.
> (129.1–14)

---

22. John Henry Newman, Discourse VIII.10, in *The Idea of a University*, ed. Martin J. Svaglic (Notre Dame, Ind.: University of Notre Dame Press, 1982), 159.

The relentless stringing together of phrases and clauses, never allowing for a pause, embodies the relentless—indeed the ruthless—obsession that is lust; and the crumbling syntax provides a verbal image of the disintegration of character that results. Such is the charge that Claudio brings against Hero: "But you are more intemperate in your blood / Than Venus, or those pamp'red animals / That rage in savage sensuality" (IV.i.59–61).

Beatrice defends her cousin not with an alibi, but with an assured knowledge of her character: "O, on my soul, my cousin is belied!" (IV.i.146). The friar, the only man present whose ego is not in some measure bound up with Hero's virginity, is likewise certain that she is innocent *because she is too virtuous for such vile conduct*:

> Call me a fool,
> Trust not my reading, nor my observations,
> Which with experimental seal doth warrant
> The tenure of my book; trust not my age,
> My reverence, calling, nor divinity,
> If this sweet lady lie not guiltless here
> Under some biting error. (IV.i.164–70)

The woman who truly knows Hero, the man who looks at her as she is rather than through the eyes of outraged vanity—they see that she must be pure because the sin laid against her is so ugly that it must needs be visible in her conduct and countenance.

Shakespeare is not, for this view of lust, a prude, much less a puritanical despiser of the flesh and blood nature of human beings. *Much Ado About Nothing* is, after all, a comedy that begins with a bawdy pun in its title, features prominently the erotically charged skirmishes of wit between Beatrice and Benedick, and closes with a double marriage. As Mary Beth Rose points out, plays like *Much Ado About Nothing* affirm the benefit of human sexuality, but with a critical qualification:

> Shakespeare's romantic comedies … reveal an increasing sense of confidence that sexuality as individual assertion can be organized

for society's good. At the same time—and the difference from modern conceptions of romantic love is crucial—sexual desire is never idealized for its own sake, never seen as by itself leading to personal happiness, never conceived as a positive value—as love—apart from marriage or procreation.[23]

Such an affirmation of the importance of chastity both before and after marriage comes into conflict with the glorification of sexual "liberation" that is pervasive not only among the elites of the mass media and the entertainment industry, but also in the universities of our time. "Hero, having died for the imagined crime of the independent use of her sexuality," complains Jean Howard of Columbia University, "is reborn when rewritten as the chaste servant of male desire."[24] Jonathan Dollimore similarly sneers at "critics ... liking their women chaste."[25]

Shakespeare's celebration of chastity is not, however, as Howard, Dollimore, and countless others imply, merely the imposition of patriarchal rule on unfettered, innocent sexuality. The playwright creates an imaginative vision that dramatizes the necessity of chastity, loyalty, and integrity to the flourishing of individual and society. The lust that is so horrifying in Sonnet 129 and countless other passages throughout Shakespeare's works is evil because it fragments both the individual personality and the community as a whole. Men and women find themselves and prosper only within a stable network of human relationships, which in turn constitute the larger community. A man or woman in the grip of lust is not a whole human being, and "pamp'red animals / That rage in savage sensuality" cannot form a human society.

The reluctance of Beatrice and Benedick to wed is a manifes-

---

23. Mary Beth Rose, *The Expense of Spirit: Love and Sexuality in English Renaissance Drama* (Ithaca, N.Y., and London: Cornell University Press, 1988), 37.
24. Jonathan Dollimore, "Renaissance Antitheatricality and the Politics of Gender and Rank in *Much Ado About Nothing*," in Howard and O'Connor, *Shakespeare Reproduced*, 181.
25. Howard, "Transgression and Surveillance in *Measure for Measure*," in Dollimore and Sinfield, *Political Shakespeare*, 82.

tation of their intuitive awareness of the perils of crossing the sexual divide in marriage and of the responsibilities that such commitment entails. Their incessant mock warfare of wit is undoubtedly an expression of their unconscious mutual attraction, which they are both wise enough to fear. If Claudio and Hero do not know each other well enough when they are first betrothed, what Beatrice and Benedick both lack is knowledge of their own hearts. Their friends play a trick on them—a trick ironically parallel to the deception that Don John practices on Claudio and Pedro—that leads them to confess their love. They soon discover, however, that love—the mutual sexual attraction and delight in one another's company—is not sufficient. "Come, bid me do any thing for thee," Benedick offers as so many infatuated men have done before and since. "Kill Claudio," comes the reply (IV.i.289-90). What Beatrice demands of Benedick is not, fundamentally, a gallant display of martial boldness, but his trust in her judgment. If he is going to marry her, it is not enough that he desire her; he must also believe in her. Despite what she claims in her outburst of righteous indignation, Beatrice does not really wish to be a man. What she wants is exactly what she gets: that Benedick be a man, instead of merely one of the boys.

The clash between sexual love and friendship is a common theme in Renaissance literature, and in Shakespeare love—leading to marriage—always prevails, except in tragedies like *Othello*. This choice represents a significant change from the classical era, when Aristotle, for example, regards marriage as a kind of friendship, but certainly not a friendship of equals.[26] Or consider Catullus. Casting about to find a way of expressing the depth of his devotion to a woman who has proven wholly unworthy, he plaintively cries, "I have loved you, then, not only so much as the common crowd loves a mistress, but as a father loves the sons he has begotten and his sons-in-law."[27] Not as a husband loves

---

26. Aristotle, *The Nicomachean Ethics* VIII.xi.4, ed. H. Rackham (Cambridge, Mass.: Harvard University Press, 1945).

27. Catullus, *C. Valerii Catulli Carmina* lxxii.3–4, ed. R. A. B. Mynors (Oxford:

his true and faithful wife, but as a father loves his sons and sons-in-law. The shock value in Catullus's simile is his suggestion that a man might hold a woman, any woman, in the same reverence and esteem as a cherished man.

But Benedick, in order to be a fit husband for Beatrice in the Christian world of the sixteenth century, must regard her as at least equal in moral stature to the men who are his friends. This does not mean that he will always necessarily defer to her judgment, but on the issue of Hero's guilt or innocence the mere fact that he remains at the church, rather than leaving with Claudio and Don Pedro, suggests that his own inclination is already for the slandered bride.[28] Benedick's decision is certainly Shakespeare's. There is no more distinctive feature of his mature drama than his creation of women characters who are witty and admirably independent and yet enchantingly feminine. Beatrice, with her gay intelligence, strength of character, and sober acceptance of reality, is typical. Antonio says of her, "In faith, she's too curst" (II.i.20), meaning "shrewish"; but Shakespeare makes an ironic joke of this in her name, which suggests that she is not "cursed" but "blessed." And of course, as "Beatrice" suggests "beatified," so "Benedick" suggests "benediction"; and we may infer that this couple will be blessed in their union because they have entered it with cautious hesitation, but also humor: "Thou and I are too wise to woo peaceably," Benedick tells her (V.ii.72).[29]

Portia and Beatrice prepare the way for Shakespeare's two most luminous heroines, Rosalind of *As You Like It* and Viola of *Twelfth Night*, which mark the culmination of the playwright's foray into the composition of high romantic comedy. Both

---

Clarendon Press, 1958), 89: "Dilexi tum te non tantum ut uulgus amicam, / sed pater ut gnatos diligit et generos."

28. On this point see Anne Barton, Introduction to Evans et al., *Riverside Shakespeare*, 363.

29. For a critical and historical disquisition on the Shakespeare's comic heroines, see Ellrodt, "Et Shakespeare créa la jeune fille," in *Montaigne et Shakespeare*, 249–66. I have cited the French version of the book, because Ellrodt did not include this appendix ("Annexe") in the later English version.

of these characters, disguised as young men in order to avoid the perils of an isolated, unprotected woman, carry out what amounts to an education in love for men who will claim them as brides at the end of the drama. Rosalind, disguised as the youth Ganymed, teaches her callow lover Orlando to woo by suggesting that he pretend that she is the beloved Rosalind and practice on "him." The process is, naturally, amusing; but the ploy also allows her to discover whether there is more to Orlando's love than mere desire and to test his constancy by injecting a dose of stern realism into their mock courtship. When Orlando claims that he would die were the "real" Rosalind to reject his proposal, for example, she replies, "Men have died from time to time, and worms have eaten them, but not for love" (IV.i.106–8). Viola, disguised as Cesario, whom Orsino, Duke of Illyria, takes under his wing and makes his confidant, falls in love with her new master. The comic business here arises from the Duke's employing his new young friend to press his suit for the hand of the disdainful Olivia. The Duke, although older, is even less mature than Orlando; a great deal of comic confusion will be required before he realizes that the virtues of the "youth" who has recently come into his life are more appropriate to a marriage partner than the affectations of the self-centered Olivia.

Both comedies have elicited a good deal of tendentious commentary arising from the postmodernist preoccupation with "gender." The masculine disguises of the Rosalind and Viola are routinely referred to as "cross-dressing," and the fact that Elizabethan theatrical convention mandated that women's roles be taken by boys further inflames the imaginations of many current critics. Finally, both Rosalind and Viola, in their disguises as male youths, provoke the desire of other female characters: Rosalind the shepherdess, Phebe, and Viola the very same Olivia, whom "he" has been sent to woo on behalf of the Duke. Hence Jean Howard makes a great deal of the epilogue to *As You Like It*, in which the boy actor playing Rosalind jokingly identifies himself as really male and therefor qualified to speak the final words:

"Dressed like a woman but declaring she is not, this unpredictable figure, this he/she, continues to the end to defy the fixed identities and exclusionary choices of the everyday world, offering instead a world of multiple possibilities and transformable identities, a world as perhaps we might come to like it." Similarly, Stephen Greenblatt maintains, "Though by divine and human decree the consummation of desire could be licitly figured only in the love of a man and a woman, it did not follow that desire was inherently heterosexual. The delicious confusions of *Twelfth Night* depend upon the mobility of desire."[30]

But this will not do. A disguise assumed for prudential reasons is not the same as cross-dressing; the absence of women from the Elizabethan stage reflected longstanding English ideas about appropriately modest deportment for women in public (contemporary Italians were not so straitlaced), and there is no indication at all that either Phebe or Olivia *really knew* that "Ganymed" and "Cesario" were actually women. Although much of the point is simply the extremely funny possibilities inherent in sexual confusion of this kind—Shakespeare was a shareholder in the company and interested in selling tickets—the confusion also has moral significance. Phebe and Olivia, who are so completely deluded, are vain, frivolous, and rather haughty women who have treated perfectly plausible suitors with scorn. Their blindness to the sex of the persons on whom they arbitrarily fix their ardor is not a sign of underlying homoerotic inclinations, but rather of their obliviousness to other persons and their ignorance of the true nature of love. In any event, both Rosalind (V.ii.87–121) and Viola (III.i.162) tell their aspiring female lovers that they are simply incapable of loving them as they wish. The assertions are made equivocally in order to preserve the disguises of Rosalind and Viola and thus drive the plot; but, in both

30. Jean Howard, "Introduction" to *As You Like It*, in *The Norton Shakespeare*, ed. Stephen Greenblatt et al., 3rd ed. (New York and London: W. W. Norton, 2016), 1621; Greenblatt, *Shakespearean Negotiations: The Circulation of Social Energy in Renaissance England* (Berkeley and Los Angeles: University of California Press, 1988), 92. On the latter, compare R. V. Young, *At War with the Word*, 111.

instances, Shakespeare's heroines imply that love between two women can never be the equivalent of love between a man and a woman. Similarly, the Duke is not so much in love with Olivia as with his own romantic melancholy in face of rejection by an unattainable Petrarchan mistress. Only when "Cesario" is revealed to be the lovely young woman Viola does he become aware that his affection for this "youth" was stronger than his ersatz love for Olivia. In this respect, all three are reminiscent of Claudio and Hero in *Much Ado* and of the unsuccessful suitors in *Merchant of Venice*.

The vision of love and marriage offered by *The Merchant of Venice* and *Much Ado About Nothing* is still compelling, and its promulgation could not be more urgent. Just as Europe and North America seem to have largely repudiated their Christian moral heritage, a resurgent Islam regards the democratic nations of the Western world as hopelessly degenerate and, in its more extreme forms, imposes on its own peoples an arbitrary and draconian moral code, while relegating women to the status of children. Sadly, the laws, the popular culture, and all too frequently the behavior of the citizens of the Western world in the present age provide a great deal of evidence of our depravity. Moreover, it is hard to see in the hostility toward Shakespeare emanating from certain quarters of the academy as anything but an expression of discomfort with the poet's luminous presentation of the sane and balanced moral vision of traditional Western civilization.

Shakespeare's comedies provide a demonstration, however, that our only choice is not between Al-Qaeda or ISIS and the morals of cable television. Shakespeare does not preach to us in *The Merchant of Venice* and *Much Ado About Nothing* or in any of his other dramas, but he does provide an analogue, a model if you will, by which we may vicariously experience the dismay of Claudio's arrogant self-righteousness and the joy of forgiveness, reconciliation, and the restoration of harmony. Above all, he reminds us that the happy, wholesome, and fruitful enjoyment of human sexuality requires a delicate balance between desire and duty, between self-fulfillment and social obligation, between our rights as individuals and our responsibilities as members of a community. If we are to preserve our way of life, it will not be enough to defeat "terrorism"; we must recover the habit of self-control that is essential to the ordered liberty, which is a distinctive feature of Western civilization. Shakespearean drama is an especially valuable resource in this quest, because the experience of his plays not only strengthens our intellectual convictions; it also nurtures our moral imagination by providing us a sense of the joy that comes with practicing justice and charity.

Joy in the prospect of faithful, fruitful, enduring marriage is not in itself a guarantee against the ills that trouble spouses and families; the sources and effects of sexual sin and marital sorrow must be confronted and grasped. This Shakespeare does in a few tragedies and in his "problem comedies," which complicate and confound even more than usual an audience's conventional expectations of comic drama. While the romantic comedies that are most characteristic of his work from the mid-1590s until the turn of the seventeenth century are largely celebrations of the emergent blending of marriage as a social and religious institution with marriage as the fulfillment of the passionate longings of a particular man and woman, Shakespeare's tragedies of marriage and problem comedies are dramatizations of the clash of individual ego and desire with communal norms and needs. What is more, the playwright offers us awareness that the most severe intellectual and moral perils that threaten the West arise within the civilization itself. Implicitly, the playwright links personal rebellion with the development of nominalism, a philosophical perspective from the late Middle Ages. The spread of the nominalist perspective from the Scholastic theologians and philosophers of the universities to the thoughtful part of the larger populace both contributes to the growth of the characteristically modern world and undermines some of its most cherished and distinctive features—marriage among them—as we shall see in chapter 2.

2

Juliet's Nominalism and the Failure of Love

"It was William of Occam," writes Richard Weaver, "who propounded the fateful idea of nominalism, which denies that universals have a real existence." Weaver compares this development in the intellectual history of Western man to Macbeth's ominous meeting with the Weird Sisters: "Have we forgotten our encounter with the witches on the heath? It occurred late in the fourteenth century...." The eventual result of the "evil decision" made on this "blasted heath" of the mind was an alteration in the moral and spiritual orientation of Western culture:

> The issue ultimately involved is whether there is a source of truth higher than, and independent of, man; and the answer to the question is decisive for one's view of the nature and destiny of humankind. The practical result of nominalist philosophy is to banish the reality which is perceived by the intellect and to posit as reality that which is perceived by the senses.[1]

It is appropriate that Weaver should choose a scene from *Macbeth* to dramatize his understanding of Western man's philo-

---

1. Richard Weaver, *Ideas Have Consequences* (1948; repr. Chicago and London: University of Chicago Press, 1984), 2–3. Since Ockham's death is now usually set in 1347, it is hard to see why Weaver specifies the "late" fourteenth century.

sophical crisis. Shakespeare lived at the time when the metaphysical or, better, anti-metaphysical implications of nominalism were beginning to exert a practical, if obscure, influence over the actual life of European society. One of the defining features of great poetry is an extraordinary sensitivity to the spiritual currents of the age—to disturbances in the fabric of a culture's moral consciousness. It is, therefore, not surprising that the greatest poet of the English language should manifest an awareness of the nominalist assumptions that had begun to permeate the web of daily life by the end of the sixteenth century. The poet, of course, provides no disquisition on this issue any more than he does on other philosophical topics; nominalist attitudes and utterances are attached to particular characters involved in a variety of dramatic situations and actions. The extent of our sympathy for these characters is also various, as is the extent to which the deeds and declarations of such characters is validated or rejected by the overall course of the play. A consideration of a number of Shakespearean characters who seem associated with nominalism, however, suggests that the playwright recognized the corrosive effect of this philosophical outlook as it suffused the traditional culture of Christendom. In regarding Shakespeare as the preeminent poet of Western civilization, we must acknowledge that his awareness of the problematic developments in our culture is as acute as his attachment to its richest traditions. In this he embodies, again, its spirit both conservative and critical.

The power of dramatic poetry, along with other literary genres, to provide a concrete, imaginative vision of the consequences of ideas is especially significant and ironic in this context; for it is precisely the capacity of literature to embody truth that is denied by Occam's contemporary successors, the postmodern literary theorists who have most persistently called the poet's worth into question. Shakespeare furnishes a double refutation of the current crop of his nominalist critics: the fictional substance of his plays dramatizes the moral consequences of nominalism, and the very existence of plays as transcendent structures of meaning open to interpretation by readers and audiences undermines the reductive nominalist premise about the nature of reality.

To be sure, the exact status and nature of universals are not a simple matter: the moderate realism represented by St. Thomas Aquinas, for example, does not attribute substantial being to abstract concepts in the same way as Plato regarded the ideas or forms as the essential realities of the universe. Universals only attain actual, concrete existence in particular entities, just as color is only realized in this or that colored object. "Similarly," St. Thomas writes, "humanity, as it is understood, does not exist except in this or that human being: but in order that humanity may be grasped without individual peculiarities, the concept of humanity itself must be abstracted and so it follows that under the aspect of universality, humanity as it is perceived by the understanding attains the likeness of a nature, and not of individual principles."[2] The important point here is that, although the universal does not exist separately, it does actually exist in particulars, and the mental abstraction "humanity" or "human nature" has a substantial basis in the individuals that it unites as a class. For Occam, universals are mere constructs of the mind with only a conventional relationship to individual entities.[3]

The work of William of Occam (ca. 1258–ca. 1347) would hardly seem to be the stuff either of drama or of far-reaching changes in mankind's moral consciousness. Occam's principal contribution to Western philosophy is a proposition about the

---

2. St. Thomas Aquinas, *Summa theologiae* (hereafter *ST*), Cura Fratrum Eiusdem Ordinis, 3rd ed. (Madrid: Biblioteca de autores Cristianos, 1961), *ST* I, q. 85, a. 2, ad 2: "Similiter humanitas quae intelligitur, non est nisi in hoc vel in illo homine: sed quod humanitas apprehendatur sine individualibus conditionibus, quod est ipsum abstrahi, ad quod sequitur intentio universalitatis, accidit humanitatis secundum quod percipitur ab intellectu, in quo est similitudo naturae specie, et non individualium principiorum."

3. Some scholars have asserted that Occam was not in fact such a radical nominalist as to deny universals any reality or correspondence to extra-mental reality, but the precise orientation of his thought is less significant for present purposes than its effect on subsequent generations. For the distinction between Occam and St. Thomas, see Frederick Copleston, SJ, *A History of Philosophy* (New York: Doubleday, 1963), 3:58.

Juliet's Nominalism and the Failure of Love

relationship between extra-mental realities and the way in which they are known by human beings. The entire range of the former, of things existing independently of the mind, comprises exclusively singular or particular things. Universals or general concepts are nothing but a species of intellectual fiction: the mind's way of organizing knowledge of particular things derived from sensory experience. According to Occam, these conceptual abstractions fall into two classes:

> Nonetheless, one should know that there are two kinds of universal. One kind is naturally universal, in that it is evidently a sign naturally predicable of many things, in a fashion analogous to the way smoke naturally signifies fire, a moan the pain of the sick, and laughter an inner gladness. Such a universal is nothing except a notion of the mind, and so no substance outside the mind nor any accident outside the mind is such a universal.... The other kind of universal is so by established convention. In this way a word that is produced, which is really one quality, is a universal, because clearly it is a sign established by convention for the signifying of many things. Hence just as a word is said to be common, even so it can be said to be universal; but this does not obtain from the nature of the thing, but only by agreement of those who have coined the term.[4]

The effect of this view is to deprive the external world of any inherent meaning apart from human convention—that is, apart from what is *convenient* for men and women to attribute to it. Similarly, language ceases to be an organic element of the gener-

---

4. William of Occam, *Summa totius logicae* I. 14: "Verumtamen sciendum, quod universale duplex est: Quoddam est universale naturaliter, quod scilicet naturaliter est signum praedicabile de pluribus ad modum proportionaliter, quo fumus naturaliter significat ignem et gemitus infirmi dolorem et risus interiorem laetitiam: et tale universale non est nisi intentio animae, ita quod nulla substantia extra animam nec aliquod accidens extra animam est tale universal.... Aliud est universale per voluntariam institutionem. Et sic vox prolata, quae est vere una qualitas, est universalis, quia scilicet est signum voluntarie institutum ad significandum plura. Unde sicut vox dicitur communis, ita potest dici universalis; sed hoc non habet ex natura rei, sed ex placito instituentium tantum." The Latin text is taken from Ockham, *Philosophical Writings*, ed. and trans. Philotheus Boehner, OFM, rev. Stephen F. Brown (Indianapolis and Cambridge, Mass.: Hackett, 1990), 34. The introduction maintains, unconvincingly in my view, that "Ockham is ... a realist in his epistemology" (xxv).

al human patrimony and becomes a collection of blank counters, with only such meaning as it pleases individual human beings arbitrarily to grant it ("non ... ex natura rei, sed ex placito instituentium tantum").

"The question of what the world was made for now becomes meaningless," Weaver observes, "because the asking of it presupposes something prior to nature in the order of existents."[5] "Meaning" can only *mean* in a general sense: isolated particulars have no meaning by themselves because they have no universal referent. But if universals, or general concepts, are only a function or intention of the individual mind (and minds, like every entity, are by nominalist definition also individual or singular), then all meaning can only be conventional, agreed upon, arbitrary. Nothing has intrinsic meaning.

To be sure, one can hardly surmise that Shakespeare, even with his wide-ranging interests, spent much time poring over the crabbed Scholastic Latin of Occam's treatises. By the end of the sixteenth century, however, nominalism had seeped into the popular mind as a result of its role in the Reformation. Luther's early theological studies were largely based on the nominalism of late Scholasticism. Although he rebelled against Scholastic theology, nominalism nonetheless shaped the way he thought about religious questions. When Occam confined universals to the thought processes of the individual mind, he effectively severed reason and faith and laid the groundwork for a purely empirical view of the natural world. Although Luther and most of the Protestant Reformers shared the humanists' scorn for Scholastic theology in all its forms, nominalist skepticism of the capacity of the mind to grasp substantial reality seems to anticipate Luther's debunking of the "whore," reason, and his insistence on faith alone—*sola fide*—as the only means of salvation.

In his most important theological treatise, *On the Bondage of the Will* (*De Servo Arbitrio*, 1525), Luther excoriates Erasmus (an

---

5. Weaver, *Ideas Have Consequences*, 5.

inveterate enemy of Scholastic nominalism) for the failure of his *Discussion or Collation Concerning Free Will* (*Diatribe seu collatio de libero arbitrio*, 1524) to recognize the futility of any rational speculation about the transcendent nature of divine ideas:

> The Diatribe makes itself ridiculous through its own ignorance, so long as it makes no distinction between God preached and God hidden; that is, between the Word of God and God Himself. God does a great deal that He does not reveal to us in His Word. He wills a great deal that He does not reveal Himself as willing in His Word. Thus He does not will the death of a sinner, namely, in His Word; He does, however, will it in His inscrutable will.[6]

Similarly, the draining of the physical world of all innate significance may be regarded as an anticipation of the abyss opened up by Calvinism, in a parallel development, between nature and grace. The Protestant Reformation was, among other things, a rebellion against the perceived corruption of a church too entangled with worldly material concerns; nevertheless, one effect of the zealous effort to purify religion was eventually to diminish the influence of divinity on daily life by depriving the material realm of intrinsic spiritual meaning. In other words, the Reformation contributed, howbeit inadvertently, to the gradual secularization of Western culture.

There is an obvious connection here to Max Weber's thesis of a "disenchanted world" resulting from the desacralization set in motion by Protestantism. Although Weber's argument has been refuted from a number of angles and in numerous details since its

---

6. Martin Luther, *De Servo Arbitrio* (Nuremberg, 1526), 151 [accessed online at books.google.com]: "Illudit autem sese Diatribe ignorantia sua, dum nihil distinguit inter deum praedicatum & absconditum, hoc est, inter uerbum dei et deum ipsum. Multa facit deus, quae uerbo suo non ostendit nobis, multa quoque uult, quae uerbo suo non ostendit sese uelle. Sic non uult mortem peccatoris, uerbo scilicet, uult autem illa uoluntate illa imperscrutabile." For various viewpoints on the role of nominalism in the Reformation, see, e.g., A. G. Dickens, *The English Reformation* (New York: Schocken, 1964), 64, 85; Erik H. Erikson, *Young Man Luther: A Study in Psychoanalysis and History* (New York: W. W. Norton, 1958), 187–91; Philip Hughes, *The Reformation in England* (London: Hollis and Carter, 1958), 1:101n2; and Lewis W. Spitz, *The Protestant Reformation, 1517–1559* (New York: Harper and Row, 1985), 79–81.

first proposal in *Die Protestantische Ethik und der Geist des Kapitalismus* (1905), it nonetheless continues to influence discussions of the Reformation period and its relationship to the secularization of the modern world.[7] Charles Taylor offers a good recent example of a scholar who both deploys Weber's argument and substantially modifies it. In Taylor's view, the cataclysm of the Protestant Reformation was preceded by a reforming spirit, which became pervasive in Latin Christendom a few centuries before Luther, and which sought to purify the worship and belief of the faithful by making them less superstitious, more inward, personal, and sincere. The eventual result is the emergence of the "buffered self" of modern individualism in tension with more traditional ways of experiencing the world and one's place in it.[8] Taylor acknowledges the relationship of nominalism to the secularizing tendencies of the Reformation, and, more recently, Brad Gregory's *The Unintended Reformation* and Carlos M. N. Eire's *Reformations*, with its significantly plural title, have further confirmed this view.[9] For our purposes, the point is the continuing awareness among scholars that Western civilization, with its sometimes uneasy balance of intellectual restlessness and deference to traditional norms, bears within itself the basis for conflict.

The conflict in Shakespearean drama is not infrequently a testimony to the growing sense that familial and communal institutions are losing their sacred character or religious sanction. "God in His Majesty and sacred nature, therefore, is to be left alone," Luther writes, "for in this respect we have nothing to do with Him, nor does He will that we make Him our concern

---

7. See Max Weber, *The Protestant Ethic and the Spirit of Capitalism*, trans. Talcott Parsons (1934; repr. New York: Scribner and Sons, 1958).

8. Charles Taylor, *A Secular Age* (Cambridge, Mass., and London: Harvard University Press, 2007), 37.

9. Taylor, *Secular Age*, 94, 97, 284, 295, 773; Brad Gregory, *The Unintended Reformation: How a Religious Revolution Secularized Society* (Cambridge, Mass., and London: Harvard University Press, 2012), Kindle ed., loc. 1127, 1186; Carlos M. N. Eire, *Reformations: The Early Modern World, 1450–1650* (London and New Haven, Conn.: Yale University Press, 2016), 144. See also R. V. Young, "How Drie a Cinder This World Is: Dissociation of Sensibility Redux," *Ben Jonson Journal* 24, no. 2 (2017): 163–86.

in this way; but only insofar as He is adorned and displayed in His word, in which He offers himself to us."[10] In this doctrinal formulation, the *only* sacred or Godly manifestation available to man on earth is the Bible, the word of God—a word that tells us nothing about God's true nature, but rather leaves Him hidden (*Deum absconditum*) in inscrutability, and mankind subject to His apparently arbitrary will. Not surprisingly, the Protestant Reformation reduced the number of sacraments from seven to two, and many of the ceremonies of everyday life began to lose their "religious" or quasi-sacramental character.

It is particularly significant that holy matrimony, deemed a sacrament of Christ by the Medieval church (and still by the Roman Catholic and Orthodox churches), was denied sacramental status in Protestant doctrine. When marriage ceases to be a sacrament—that is, a channel of grace mediated by ecclesiastical ritual—either it becomes vulnerable to reabsorption into a rigidly patriarchal system modeled on Greco-Roman customs, or, conversely, its communal nature may dissolve into a wholly new individualistic model characteristic of the modern world. The powerful interests of wealth and property in sixteenth-century England favored and attempted to institute the former in the wake of the church's loss of social and political authority, but the pressures of an expansive bourgeois culture, with its focus on the individual aggrandizement reinforced by nominalist thinking, served to reshape the social institution of marriage in the interests of particular personal goals and aspirations.

It is unsurprising that the call for person-centered devotional inwardness, which Charles Taylor identifies as a significant feature of the reforming spirit spreading through Latin Christendom in the late Middle Ages, would spill over into erotic experience as well. Hence it is also unsurprising that the most explicitly

---

10. Martin Luther, *De Servo Arbitrio*, 151: "Reliquendus est igitur Deus in maiestate & natura sua, sic nihil nos cum illo habemus agere, nec sic uoluit à nobis agi cum eo. Sed quatenus indutus & proditus est uerbo suo, quo nobis sese obtulit, cum eo agimus, quod est decor et gloria eius, quo Psalmista eum. caelebrat indutum."

nominalist speech in all of Shakespeare's plays is made by Juliet Capulet and that it is a direct challenge to the traditional conception of marriage and family. In the famous balcony scene, after she has first met Romeo, who has come in disguise to the ball in her father's house, Juliet cries out her sudden passion for this scion of the enemy Montague clan, while he overhears her in the garden:

> O Romeo, Romeo, wherefore art thou Romeo?
> Deny thy father and refuse thy name:
> Or, if thou wilt not, be but sworn my love,
> And I'll no longer be a Capulet....
> 'Tis but thy name that is my enemy;
> Thou art thyself, though not a Montague.
> What's Montague? It is nor hand nor foot,
> Nor arm nor face, nor any other part
> Belonging to a man. O, be some other name!
> What's in a name? That which we call a rose
> By any other name would smell as sweet;
> So Romeo would, were he not Romeo call'd,
> Retain that dear perfection which he owes
> Without that title. Romeo, doff thy name,
> And for thy name, which is no part of thee,
> Take all myself. (II. ii. 33–49)

As an evidently approving Harry Levin observes, "She calls into question not merely Romeo's name but—by implication—all names, forms, conventions, sophistications, and arbitrary dictates of society, as opposed to the appeal of instinct directly conveyed in the odor of a rose."[11] An epistemological doctrine about the nature of universals thus turns out to have momentous social and moral implications.

The nominalist significance of Juliet's famous speech is exploited in the title of Umberto Eco's novel *The Name of the Rose*, set in 1327 and having as its hero a certain William of Baskerville,

---

11. Harry Levin, "Form and Formality in *Romeo and Juliet*," *Shakespeare Quarterly* 11 (1960): 4.

a Franciscan friar who has a "friend from Occam" and who follows Occam and Michael of Cesena in resisting the new constitution mandated for the Franciscans by Pope John XXII.[12] For Eco, nominalist epistemology seems to be a step in the direction of postmodern liberation from the constraints of political and religious hierarchies. In taking the title of his work from Shakespeare's otherwise irrelevant tragedy, Eco implies that, like Levin, he thinks that the instinctive appreciation of a rose's fragrance necessarily supersedes "arbitrary dictates of society."

What interests Shakespeare is not, of course, an epistemological theory in itself, but its effect in the moral lives of his characters. The idealized erotic transport of the two young lovers comes in direct conflict with the conception of family ties that prevailed not only in Verona, the dramatic setting, but also in Shakespeare's England. When Juliet yearns for Romeo to "Deny thy father and refuse thy name," she is effectively asking him to abandon his identity. In traditional communal societies, a man *is* the son of his father, the kinsman of his other relatives, the subject of his prince. To assert that *Romeo Montague* would suffer no substantial alteration if he were to become *John Doe* implies a radically new, individualistic understanding of personal identity. Shakespeare thus shows that attitudes toward sexual love and marriage emerging during the Renaissance parallel developments in the religious sphere, where the Reformation doctrine stresses the dependence of salvation upon an individual's encounter with Christ rather than his participation in the sacramental life of the church. Marriage conceived as a private agreement between two persons rather than as a sacrament, a religious and social institution involving the wider community, similarly opens the way for a modern, individualistic conception of sexual relations. The relevance of nominalism is manifest: if the only substantial realities are particular things, and universals are *mere names*—labels attached to heterogeneous items grouped

---

12. See Umberto Eco, *The Name of the Rose*, trans. William Weaver (San Diego, New York, and London: Harcourt Brace Jovanovich, 1983), 17–18, 498–99.

together for mental convenience—then the immediate, pressing desires of individuals are obviously more important than abstract notions like family honor and obligation.

Shakespeare's greatness as a dramatist is perhaps most marked in his ability to define moral issues in the words and actions of characters and thus to affect audiences in complex and paradoxical ways. Romeo and Juliet are quite obviously sympathetic, and their love is, in many respects a powerful, affirmative experience. No audience has ever doubted that Romeo's feeling for Juliet is the "real thing," in contrast to the melancholy infatuation that he has affected for "Rosaline," who is literally no more than a *name* in the play. In the same way, it is clear that the moral force of Juliet's personality grows along with her love for Romeo. What is more, this ardent love stands in sharp contrast to the gnawing, irrational hatred of the prolonged feud between the Capulets and Montagues, which has plagued Verona for generations. Shakespeare's "star-cross'd lovers" (*prol.* 6) are the most attractive characters in the drama, and they command our good will and sympathy.

But it is an index to the triumph of the Romantic revolution over the past two and a half centuries that the sympathies of most audiences and readers lie so completely with the young lovers. The tragedy probably seems more sentimental to modern men and women than it did to Shakespeare's contemporaries, because we are not shocked by the impiety of Juliet's call to abandon family name and honor, because we are not truly horrified at the prospect of a secret marriage carried out against the will of parents and extended family. Almost everyone in modern Western society—whatever his considered judgment about a specific situation—makes an unreflecting assumption in favor of the individual as opposed to society or family and takes it for granted that the purpose of marriage is the gratification and fulfillment of a particular man and woman, rather than the achievement of social and religious goals of paramount concern to the family and the wider community of the spouses.

There is no better illustration, then, of the tension between competing goods that is always at play in Western civilization. A distinctive achievement of our culture, the insistence upon consent as a necessary element in marriage and the elevation of the role of personal love in its success, can become an assertion of the exclusive demand of individual will and desire, which threatens the institution of marriage as a fundamental part of the common good of society. Marriage in an imperfect world among fallen men and women will not infrequently fail to achieve or maintain the ideal blend of intense personal love and deference to the reasonable claims of family and society dramatized in Shakespeare's romantic comedies.

Engaging as Romeo and Juliet are, there is a striking parallel between the heedless abandon of their erotic passion and the ferocity of the hatred between their families embodied in Juliet's cousin, Tybalt. Love can be as irrational and destructive as hate. Friar Lawrence, who vainly hopes to end the feud between the Capulets and Montagues by means of the love of Romeo and Juliet, recognizes the explosive potential of sexual desire as he admonishes Romeo:

> These violent delights have violent ends,
> And in their triumph die, like fire and powder
> Which as they kiss consume. (II. v. 9–11)

The tragic conclusion of the play is in part the result of chance—of sheer bad luck—but, as in all true tragedy, it is essentially an expression of the character of the protagonists: the impetuous ardor of Romeo and Juliet, which makes their story so gripping, also deprives them of the virtues of patience and humility and leads them inexorably to destruction.

After Juliet has first met Romeo, she sends her nurse to discover his name and adds this fateful comment: "If he be married, / My grave is like to be my wedding-bed" (I.v.134–35). When Romeo learns that he has been banished from Verona for slaying Tybalt, he refuses to accept Friar Lawrence's argument that Prince Escalus has treated him with mercy, and that all is not lost:

> 'Tis torture and not mercy. Heaven is here
> Where Juliet lives, and every cat and dog
> And little mouse, every unworthy thing,
> Live here in heaven and may look on her,
> But Romeo may not. (III.iii.29–33)

Responding to the frenzy of these words, Friar Lawrence reproves in the suicidal Romeo "The unreasonable fury of a beast" (III.iii.131). When Romeo says that Juliet's presence is heaven, he is substituting her for God: this attitude is not only blasphemous and idolatrous; it also suggests that his love cannot be contained within the limits of mortal life. Hence Shakespeare turns the indecent Elizabethan pun on "die" as slang for attaining orgasm into the central meaning of the plot: the language of these lovers is haunted by death throughout the drama, and the final consummation of their love is suicide within a sepulcher. Moreover, when Friar Lawrence attempts to reason with Romeo on the basis of proverbial wisdom, the frantic lover asserts the imperious ethics of nominalist individualism: "Thou canst not speak of what thou dost not feel" (III.iii.64). Universal moral principles are of no force in the face of immediate, particular emotion.

The pattern established in *Romeo and Juliet* is a familiar one in Shakespearean drama: the guardians of traditional order—princes, priests, parents—have neglected or betrayed their trust and allowed the institutions they rule to become oppressive and vulnerable to rebellion. Ideal standards of conduct and belief are never perfectly realized in this world; but when the gap between principle and practice becomes excessive, then the nominalist assertion that universals are insubstantial abstractions—mere empty "names"—seems more plausible. In *Romeo and Juliet* parents have produced a world inhospitable to love by making the institution of the family a vehicle of unruly pride and hatred. We sympathize with the lovers, although their love is finally antisocial and destructive, because their society is itself in some measure unnaturally constraining and corrupt.

Juliet's Nominalism and the Failure of Love

The tension generated by the clash between sclerotic traditional idealism, nominalist skepticism, and individualism is not confined to disruptions of the family; in the second tetralogy of history plays, comprising *Richard II*, the two parts of *Henry IV*, and *Henry V*, we observe the corruption of traditional authority on a national scale. A subsequent chapter will treat the political aspects of the history plays in more detail, but it is worth pausing for a moment here over what we might call the nominalist subtext. The eponymous tragic hero of *Richard II*, a king even more inept than malicious, assumes that the institution of royalty maintains itself. The opposite of a nominalist, he believes—or wishes to believe—that a name is a talisman possessing not just meaning, but also power. When he learns that his own indecisiveness and delays have caused the desertion of twelve thousand of his troops, he recovers confidence by remembering who he is:

> I had forgot myself, am I not a king?
> Awake, thou coward majesty! thou sleepest.
> Is not the king's name twenty thousand names?
> Arm, arm, my name! a puny subject strikes
> At thy great glory. (III.ii.83–87)

Richard's extravagant reification of his name would tempt anyone to nominalism. His successful rival, Henry Bullingbroke, who usurps his throne and becomes Henry IV, is by contrast, a man of few words. When Richard is finally brought to abdicate, he delays handing over his crown in a lyrical speech of nearly thirty lines: Bullingbroke's reply is a single curt line: "I thought you had been willing to resign" (IV.i.190).

In *I Henry IV* Sir John Falstaff offers, after Juliet, the most explicitly nominalist speech in the Shakespeare canon. As the decisive battle approaches, the braggart knight lets Prince Hal see how fearful he is of real danger, eliciting this curt reply: "Why thou owest God a death." With the Prince offstage, Falstaff delivers this famous soliloquy:

Juliet's Nominalism and the Failure of Love

> 'Tis not due yet, I would be loath to pay him before his day. What need I be so forward with him that calls not on me? Yea, but how if honor prick me on? Yea, but how if honor pricks me off when I come on? how then? Can honor set to a leg? No. Or an arm? No. Or take away the grief of a wound? No. Honor hath no skill in surgery then? No. What is honor? A word. What is in that word honor? What is that honor? Air. A trim reckoning! Who hath it? He that died a' Wednesday. Doth he feel it? No. Doth he hear it? No. 'Tis insensible then? Yea, to the dead. But will't not live with the living? No. Why? Detraction will not suffer it. Therefore I'll none of it, honor is a mere scutcheon. And so ends my catechism. (V.i.126–41)

What Juliet says about the name "Romeo Montague" Falstaff says about the abstract term "honor." It is only a name, only a word, mere air. It has no substantial existence. What this means in practical terms, as we shall see in a subsequent chapter, is manifest in Falstaff's conduct: not only that of a coward but also a scoundrel.

Shakespeare's most profound treatment of the everyday effects of nominalist philosophy, both in the family and the commonwealth, comes in *King Lear*, which will require a chapter of its own. But before abandoning the theme of nominalism and the failure of love, it is necessary to reflect briefly on the treatment of love in those plays usually designated "problem comedies." These works, even when concluding with a marriage, leave many audiences uneasy, even dissatisfied, and numerous issues they raise are left manifestly unresolved.

Troilus and Cressida undoubtedly poses the greatest problems among these problem plays. The (probably pirated) 1609 quarto edition of the play identifies it as *The History of Troilus and Cressida* on its title page, but the quarto also adds a preface extolling it as "passing full of the palme comicall; for it is the birth of your braine, that neuer vnder-tooke any thing commicall vainely...."¹³ The folio of 1623, however, omits the play from the table of contents while placing it ambiguously between the history and tragedy sections and giving it the title *The Tragedie of Troylus and Cressida*. Modern commentary has pointed out its resemblances in tone and style to the satires so popular in London at the end of the Tudor period. Whatever generic designation the work receives, it is surely Shakespeare's most bitterly cynical vision of the human condition, offering not only an especially jaundiced view of sexual love, but also a witheringly sardonic characterization of the noble and tragic heroes of the *fons et origo* of Western literature, Homer's *Iliad*.

This statement requires, however, immediate qualification: when Shakespeare was writing *Troilus and Cressida*, the *Iliad* did not occupy the same place in Western culture as it has over the past three centuries. Julius Caesar Scaliger, probably the most influential classical scholar of the late sixteenth century, ranked the *Aeneid* over the *Iliad*; and the former was certainly more widely read and more influential, if for no other reason than because very few men read Greek well enough to appreciate Homer's poetry. Moreover, a number of European royal houses traced their lineage to Aeneas. The British, for example, accepted their founder as Brute (or Brut or Brutus), the mythical grandson of Aeneas, who led a band of Trojans to the Island of Albion—renamed Britain—even as Rome was named after Romulus, another of Aeneas's descendants.¹⁴ Most of the literary accounts of the story of Troy written during the Middle Ages take a Trojan perspective. Hence an account of noble but flawed and foolish Trojans overcome by the wiles of deceitful Greeks would not seem to undermine the foundation of Western culture for Shakespeare's audience as it does for many modern scholars.

When Shakespeare was writing *Troilus and Cressida* the only English versions of the *Iliad* available to him would have been

13. Shakespeare, *Riverside Shakespeare*, 526, textual notes.
14. A number of literary accounts exist; the most convenient source is the first book of Geoffrey of Monmouth's twelfth-century *British History*.

Juliet's Nominalism and the Failure of Love

Arthur Hall's translation of the first ten books of Hugues Salel's French translation of the Greek (1581) and George Chapman's English version of the first seven books of the *Iliad* (1598), although some have suggested that Shakespeare may have gone directly to Salel's French rendering (1580, first complete version) or Jehan Samxon's version in French prose (1530) or one of the several translations into Italian or Latin prose. Geoffrey Bullough says, "I have no doubt that Shakespeare read the *Seaven Bookes*, and suspect that his satiric treatment of the Greeks and his use of high-sounding language was partly to mock at the hero-worship shown by Chapman in the prefatory material to his versions."[15]

Troilus and Cressida offers one of Shakespeare's most impressive purple passages of blank verse. Ulysses attributes the Greeks' failure to conquer the Trojans to a failure to observe proper hierarchy of command (of which Achilles's withdrawal from battle as a result of his dispute with Agamemnon over a slave girl is the most egregious instance):

> Take but degree away, untune that string,
> And hark what discord follows. Each thing meets
> In mere oppugnancy: the bounded waters
> Should lift their bosoms higher than the shores,
> And make a sop of all this solid globe;
> Strength should be lord of imbecility,
> And the rude son should strike his father dead;
> Force should be right, or rather, right and wrong
> (Between whose endless jar justice resides)
> Should lose their names, and so should justice too!
> Then everything include itself in power,
> Power into will, will into appetite,
> And appetite, an universal wolf
> (So doubly seconded with will and power),
> Must make perforce an universal prey,
> And last eat up himself. (I.iii.109–24)

---

15. Geoffrey Bullough, ed., *Narrative and Dramatic Sources of Shakespeare* (New York: Columbia University Press, 1966), 6:87.

Juliet's Nominalism and the Failure of Love

There is undoubtedly an element of incongruousness in the placement of this speech in the midst of a play whose action turns on sexual jealousy, injured male pride, and incessant deceit and betrayal, and in its attribution to Ulysses, who is portrayed as a Machiavellian schemer. It is not, however, so obvious which way the irony cuts.

In the introduction to the play in the *Riverside Shakespeare*, Anne Barton maintains that the playwright's "most elaborate presentation of the medieval great chain of being, finishes by portraying a chaos which can no longer be remedied by traditional means. Accepted ideas of degree and rule, of personal honor, reputation, and love, do not, in this society, require reaffirmation so much as radical redefinition." Walter Cohen, who provides the introduction to the play in the *Norton Shakespeare*, similarly asserts, "The dramatic context undermines this judgment [that the speech represents "Shakespeare's own orthodox credo"]. The play, he continues, "dramatizes a cynical world antithetical to the norms of trust that are necessary, early modern political theorists argued, in any reasonably functioning society."[16]

But this is to assume that the flouting of political or moral standards proves them false, or that Shakespeare's contemporaries and the poet himself expected that men would ordinarily live up to their professed principles and were shocked when they did not. Shakespeare lived, after all, in a Christian society, which took very seriously the wisdom of St. Paul, who admits, "For the good that I would, I do not: but the evil which I would not, that I do" (Romans 7:19). How surprised would they be that the pagan Ulysses fails to embody the high-minded ideals of his "degree" speech; or that Hector, after making a sound, moral argument for ending the war by returning Helen to her lawful husband, immediately reverses course and agrees to continue the conflict on behalf of a flawed notion of honor; or that Achilles turns out to be a vain braggart who murders a helpless, unarmed Hector

---

16. Shakespeare, *Riverside Shakespeare*, 481; Greenblatt et al., ed., *The Norton Shakespeare*, 3rd ed. (New York and London: W. W. Norton and Company, 2016), 1986.

Juliet's Nominalism and the Failure of Love

who had expected fair play from the greatest of the Greek heroes. Ulysses has warned that *right*, *wrong*, and *justice* would "lose their names"; that is, in nominalist fashion, they will be regarded as mere names. The result is what we see in *Troilus and Cressida*: an anarchic world of violence and betrayal.

The depiction of sexual love in this play is by no means incompatible with what we see in the romantic comedies. In his infatuation with Cressida, Troilus reminds us of Claudio at the beginning of *Much Ado* or the Duke Orsino at the beginning of *Twelfth Night*. Like these men, Troilus does not really know the object of his desire, and he is more in love with his idea of love than with an actual woman. He also manifests the relativism that follows from nominalism's insistence that only individual particulars are real. Attempting to convince his brothers that Helen ought to be restored to Menelaus, Hector says that "she is not worth what she doth cost / The Keeping," to which Troilus replies, "What's aught but as 'tis valued?" Hector's rejoinder is an assertion of intrinsic value, which implies that universal terms ("good," "true," "beautiful," etc.) are not without substantial meaning:

> But value dwells not in particular will,
> It holds its estimate and dignity
> As well wherein 'tis precious of itself
> As in the prizer. (II.ii.51–56)

Neglect of this principle, by Hector himself as well as by his brothers, eventually will cost the Trojans everything, so the action of the play, rather than repudiating, affirms traditional wisdom.

Unfortunately for Troilus there is in Troy no Beatrice or Viola, no Rosalind or Portia to educate him in the nature of mutual love between a man and a woman. Cressida is weak, vulnerable, and feckless—lacking the resources of character and intellect that characterize the heroines of the romantic comedies. When Ulysses has led Troilus secretly into the Greek camp where Cressida has been forced to follow her father and the young Trojan witnesses his beloved making an assignation with the Greek Diomedes, he is unable to reconcile the mistress of his passionate fantasy with the sordid reality he beholds. "This she? No, this is Diomed's Cressida." "This is, and is not, Cressid! / Within my soul there doth conduce a fight ... " (V.ii.137, 146–47). Troilus has no universal rational categories to guide him in processing the experience of his senses, which are peculiar to each individual. When Agamemnon asks Ulysses what excuse Achilles offers for refusing to fight against the Trojans with his comrades, Ulysses replies, "He doth rely on none, / But carries on the stream of his dispose / Without observance or respect of any, / In will peculiar and in self-admission" (II.iii.163–66). The observation is equally true of Troilus and, indeed, of most of the play's major characters.

The affirmative vision of love and marriage in Shakespeare's romantic comedies is, then, a genuine ideal, but this is not to say that it is often or easily realized. The light-hearted joyousness of these plays is a testament to danger and difficulty overcome. In Shakespeare's two other "problem plays," *All's Well That Ends Well* and *Measure for Measure*, seemingly intractable obstacles are in fact surmounted: the plays end with marriages. But in both of them there are ambiguous, even dubious, elements at work even in the traditional comic close.

In *All's Well That Ends Well*, the heroine, Helena, daughter of a court physician who has died leaving her orphaned and impoverished, has long been hopelessly smitten with Bertram, the son of the Count whom her father had served. Helena is beautiful, intelligent, resourceful, and virtuous; Bertram is, however, vain, deceitful, self-indulgent, and arrogant. When Helena succeeds in curing the King of France of a wasting disease, he willingly accedes to her sole request, Bertram's hand in marriage. The groom goes through with the ceremony, but he is mortified at being wed to a poor commoner and flees before the wedding night, leaving Helena a disconsolate, virgin bride. Eventually, by means of a combination of perseverance, shrewdness, and luck, Helena succeeds in tracking Bertram down and getting into his bed, acquiring thus both his ring and his child (this is the notorious "bed trick"—Bertram thinks that he is enjoying an adulterous affair with a certain Diana). When Helena confronts him with indisputable evidence of the consummation of their marriage at the court of the King, Bertram promises, "I'll love her dearly, ever, ever dearly" (V.iii.316).

For our present purpose, two points are worth noting. First, in contrast to the typical way of comedy, it is the authoritative elders—the King, his chief courtier, Lord Lafew, and even Bertram's widowed mother, the Countess of Rosillion—who acknowledge that Helena's good qualities make her a fit bride for Bertram, despite her poverty and lowly birth. It is Bertram and his companion Parolles, a despicable poltroon, who has fabricated a fantastic tale of his own martial valor, who scorn her. Second, the audience or reader is left with a feeling of uneasiness: Bertram's change of heart and promise of love and fidelity are abrupt, even perfunctory. In the romantic comedies Bassanio, Orlando, Benedick, even Claudio and the Duke Orsino all give evidence that they will prove worthy as husbands to their brides. With Bertram, it is far more a matter of hope than assurance.

Parolles, whose name suggests that he is a creature merely of words (*paroles* in French and *parole* in Italian mean *words*), seems included in the cast mainly as a way of characterizing Bertram: his adherence to a character who is merely talk without substance suggests that he embodies on a practical level the implications of nominalist philosophy. The King recognizes this distorted view when he attempts to persuade Bertram of Helena's value:

> If she be
> All that is virtuous—save what thou dislik'st,
> A poor physician's daughter—thou dislik'st
> Of virtue for the name. But do not so.
> From lowest place when virtuous things proceed,

> The place is dignified by th' doer's deed.
> Where great additions swell's, and virtue none,
> It is a dropsied honor. Good alone
> Is good, without a name; vileness is so:
> The property by what it is should go,
> Not by the title. (II.iii.121–31)

A superficial reading may equate this passage with Juliet's "A rose by any other name" speech, but while the impassioned girl is making her own imagination and desire the measure of reality, the King is insisting upon the intrinsic nature and worth of things apart from immediate individual feeling. Human folly may abuse language and misattribute words, but that does not mean that authentic rational judgments of good and vileness, as the King puts it, are merely arbitrary.

For all Helena's virtue, we are left with the realization that her heart has clouded her judgment: men and women of admirable character and good sense about most matters can fall in love with altogether unsuitable partners. Sometimes such matches work out well enough; sometimes they do not. We are again reminded that the great good fortune and blessed happiness depicted at the close of plays such as *Much Ado About Nothing* cannot be counted on or taken for granted. A happy ending is a blessing and a wonder, which must surmount many perils. Shakespeare's dramatizations of marriage reflect with remarkable moral realism both the ideal vision of marriage that has emerged in Western civilization and the difficulties besetting it.

Perhaps his most uncomfortable treatment of the comic happy ending with multiple marriages comes in *Measure for Measure*. Much of the ambivalence about these marriages results from their entanglement with an equivocal effort to restore the rigorous administration of justice in Vienna, which is undertaken by the Duke in a disturbingly peculiar fashion. Having allowed the city's severe laws regarding sexual conduct to be disregarded and thus to fall into contempt, the Duke tells his lieutenants, Angelo and Escalus, that he is going on a journey of unspecified destination and duration. Angelo is left in charge with full power to enforce the laws with unbending exactitude. The Duke claims that if he were to attempt such a rigorous restoration, his inconsistency would seem unfair and earn him deserved opprobrium from the people. In fact, the Duke remains in Vienna, disguised as a friar in order to determine whether Angelo's reputation for stern morality and integrity can survive the test of unchecked power.

When a young gentleman, Claudio, is discovered to have impregnated his betrothed, Juliet, before they have been formally married, Angelo sentences him to death on the basis of a long-neglected law against fornication. One of Claudio's rather dubious acquaintances, Lucio, persuades Claudio's sister, a novice at a Viennese convent who is on the brink of taking her final vows, to go to Angelo and plead for her brother's life. The result is predictable because the plot device has been used so often across a wide variety of literary genres. The "prenzie Angelo"—*prenzie* is a hapax legomenon, but its meaning is obvious—is smitten with Isabella and promises to spare her brother if she will yield herself to him sexually.

It turns out that the Duke's apprehensiveness regarding Angelo's character has been aroused by his knowledge that Angelo has, some years before, abandoned his betrothed, Mariana, when her dowry is lost through no fault of her own. Duke convinces Isabella to agree to Angelo's repugnant terms with the stipulation that Mariana will substitute for Isabella in the dark room where the assignation is to be carried out. As in *All's Well That Ends Well*, a worthy woman wins a husband of—at best—doubtful character by means of the "bed trick." Our expectation that this couple will live "happily ever after" is at least as diminished as in the case of Helena and Bertram. Not only has Angelo jilted Mariana for coldly mercenary considerations, but he has also attempted to coerce Isabella into sexual submission by promising to spare her brother and then ordered Claudio's immediate execution as soon as he thinks he has gained his sexual prey.

Angelo, in addition to his ruthlessness toward Claudio

and his criminally corrupt treatment of Isabella, has also been tricked into committing exactly the same crime for which he has condemned Claudio. The Duke proposes to formalize the marriage of Angelo and Mariana in order to secure her honor and then have Angelo put to death. Like Helena, however, Mariana still wants the husband that most of us would think her well rid of. She begs Isabella to join her in pleading with the Duke for Angelo's life. Only after the initially reluctant Isabella falls to her knees beside Mariana in supplication before the Duke does he reveal that he had intervened and saved Claudio's life. Isabella, who has been in her own way as sternly moralistic as Angelo, is thus given the opportunity to show the mercy associated with Christ rather than stern judgment, thereby recalling the gospel source of the play's title.

Anyone who finds it improbable that women such as Helena and Mariana would choose men such as Bertram and Angelo and refuse to relinquish them in the face of painful demonstrations of their unworthiness has clearly not been reading the newspapers—especially the "agony columns." But there are even more problematic nuptials in *Measure for Measure*. Although we may be reasonably hopeful about the future of the chastened Claudio and Juliet, what is an audience to make of the Duke's ordering Claudio's louche companion Lucio to marry Kate Keepdown, a prostitute whom he has impregnated? "Marrying a punk, my lord, is pressing to death, whipping, and hanging" (V.i.537), Lucio protests, but in vain; for the Duke is as unbending as his erstwhile lieutenant, Angelo: "Slandering a prince deserves it" (V.i.538). And then there is the Duke's sudden proposal to Isabella, which comes only fifty lines before the end of the play with no advance warning at all. To this sudden proposal Isabella makes no reply at all, indeed, never speaks after she has pled with the Duke for the life of Angelo. Does she accept the proposal? Is possible for her to decline it? What becomes of her vocation to the religious life on the threshold of her taking her permanent vows? The play provides no answer.

It is a critical commonplace to maintain that Isabella's decision to enter a convent resulted more from a puritanical rejection of the world than from a genuine, single-minded love of God. From this assumption one may infer that she would willingly, even eagerly accept the Duke's offer, having learned true charity for her neighbor and hence an appreciation of the world from her bridegroom's stratagem that led her to forgive the man she thought guilty of her brother's death. The evidence for this conjectural dénouement in the text nonetheless remains tenuous. We are on firmer ground in seeing in *Measure for Measure* and the other "problem" comedies of the 1600s Shakespeare's acknowledgment that the glorious triumph of conjugal love in the comedies of the 1590s is rare. The men and women depicted in the problem plays, like the eponymous hero and heroine of *Romeo and Juliet*, tend all too easily toward the self-absorbed individualism fostered by a nominalist worldview. The result is, if not tragedy, "comic" endings that leave the audience, as well as many of the characters, with a sense of uneasy perplexity.

3

The Racial "Other" in *The Merchant of Venice* and *Othello*

Although the status of sexual morality in the modern world is exceedingly problematic, still, no issue has proven more vexatious than race in the assessment of the moral stature of Western civilization. The drive toward multiculturalism, which is especially vigorous in the academic world, rests on the proposition that the culture of the West, in virtually all its manifestations, is an elite hegemony of white European males, which routinely marginalizes, represses, and generally victimizes women, the poor, adherents to non-Christian religions, and—above all—the dark-skinned races indigenous to other continents. The chief playwright of the Western world is, according to this view, fully implicated in the crimes of his culture. Exhibit "A" for the prosecution—this may seem surprising to the uninitiate—is *The Tempest*. This proposition is absurd on its face, and we shall defer considering it until chapter 8, our final chapter. We shall instead consider here *The Merchant of Venice* and *Othello*, plays in which Shakespeare offers characters and incidents with a plausible relation to contemporary concerns and that also complicate his understanding of love and marriage by introducing elements of racial and ethnic tension.

The Racial "Other" in *The Merchant of Venice* and *Othello*

Shakespeare is undoubtedly a man of his own era, and it is mistaken and mischievous to force his dramatic creations into the political categories of our time; nevertheless, his insight into the perennial quandaries of human experience is sufficient to afford his dramas a resonance with the preoccupations of any particular society. Shakespeare's persistence both as a popular favorite and as a topic of learned speculation and intellectual contention suggests that he challenges while he pleases, that he disturbs even as he exhilarates. *The Merchant of Venice* and *Othello* are hardly mere ideological products, affirming the prejudices of the subjects of Queen Elizabeth and King James; but then they are equally deadly to the complacent pieties of postmodernity. To unsettle assumptions and disturb the conscience—these are effects of great works of art and features of the essential genius of Western civilization.

The Merchant of Venice, for instance, can be an extremely troubling play for contemporary audiences. Barbara Lewalski takes note of the "acrimonious critical debates ... concerning whether Shakespeare's attitude in the play is humanitarian or anti-Semitic, whether Shylock is presented as the persecuted hero or as a crude monster and comic butt, whether Antonio and Bassanio are portrayed as worthy Christians or as crass hypocrites."[1] Peter Berek asserts, "Quite independently of Elizabethan ideas, the figure of Shylock shapes stereotypes of Jews and provides ammunition for the racial antisemitism of the nineteenth and twentieth centuries. And in retaliation or recompense, a humanized reading—or misreading—of *The Merchant of Venice* becomes a resource for both Christians and Jews who argue for such modern concepts as religious toleration and human equality."[2] While Lewalski wishes to save Shakespeare and the Christian characters from the charge of intolerance and anti-Semitism by turning

---

1. Barbara Lewalski, "Biblical Allegory and Allusion in *The Merchant of Venice*," in *Twentieth Century Interpretations of the Merchant of Venice*, ed. Sylvan Barnet (Englewood Cliffs, N.J.: Prentice-Hall, 1970), 33.
2. Peter Berek, "The Jew as Renaissance Man," *Renaissance Quarterly* 51 (1998): 159.

the play into an allegory, Berek maintains, to the contrary, that Shakespeare—with help from Christopher Marlowe's Barabas in *The Jew of Malta*—lays the groundwork for the anti-Semitism of a later era in the character of Shylock. It seems especially reprehensible to Berek that, in his view, Shylock may provoke attitudes not reflective of the realities of Elizabethan society.

Now, *The Merchant of Venice*, although it involves significant symbolic elements, is not an allegory; and, although it has certainly had an impact on European culture, the play has not—among reasonable persons—contributed to the rise of anti-Semitism. Such "ammunition for racial antisemitism" as it provides has been there in the culture all along, and the principal effect of *The Merchant of Venice* is to disrupt any ideological complacency deriving from the apparent Jewish stereotype presented by Shylock. This disruption does not entail Shylock's romantic transmogrification into a tragic hero; in fact, it is his stubborn villainy that generates the uneasy tension that runs through the drama. Shylock is certainly a more malicious individual than Antonio, Bassanio, or Portia, yet there can be no question that the Jew suffers ill use at the hands of the Christians. Shakespeare's critical spirit is nowhere more manifest: in literature as in life, the individual whom we find pleasant or engaging is not always good, not always fair; and justice is not always served by just *any* action taken against a malefactor. It is precisely because Shylock is so cruel and repellent that his appeal to our common humanity is so poignant.

Regarded as a depiction of a Jew, what stands out about *The Merchant of Venice* is that there is nothing else like it. Villainous Jews are not unusual in medieval literature, although they are not commonplace in the Renaissance;[3] Jews who compel our attention as suffering human beings are virtually unheard of in Renaissance literature before Shakespeare. It is generally agreed

---

3. See Robert Ornstein, *Shakespeare's Comedies: From Roman Farce to Romantic Mystery* (Newark: University of Delaware Press, 1986), 91.

that Shakespeare takes most of the plot from the tale of Giannetto, which appears in a fourteenth-century Italian collection, *Il Pecorone* (the "blockhead" or "dolt"). As John Gross remarks, "The most striking thing about Shakespeare's use of *Il Pecorone* is how much he made out of how little."[4] As Gross proceeds to show, and as anyone who has read the Italian model can see, Shakespeare adds depth of meaning and richness of texture to every element of plot and character that he has imitated, but especially in his creation of Shylock, who is a nameless, dimensionless figure in *Il Pecorone*. Shakespeare not only provides the Jewish usurer with a name, but also with a daughter who elopes with a Christian, as well as a history of hostility and abuse from Antonio. Above all, Shakespeare gives Shylock an intense bitterness and sense of humiliation that certainly explain—although they do not excuse—his murderous intentions toward Antonio.

But Shakespeare had in Christopher Marlowe a more formidable competitor in the dramatization of a villainous Jew than the anonymous compiler of *Il Pecorone*. "*The Jew of Malta*," Gross points out, "offered Shakespeare the precedent of a Jew who was articulate, who dominated the action, who had his own point of view and his own grievances."[5] But as Gross adds, Marlowe's Jew, Barabas, is a caricature out of medieval mystery and miracle plays.[6] As he recruits the Turkish slave Ithamore to his nefarious services, he gives an account of himself in close accord with the superstitious folk image of the Jew as ritual murderer, poisoner, and ruthless enemy of humanity—but especially of Christians:

> Hast thou no trade? Then listen to my words,
> And I will teach that that shall stick by thee.
> First, be thou void of these affections:
> Compassion, love, vain hope, and heartless fear;

---

4. John Gross, *Shylock: A Legend and Its Legacy* (New York: Simon and Schuster, 1992), 16.
5. Gross, *Shylock*, 20.
6. Gross, *Shylock*, 22–25.

> Be mov'd at nothing, see thou pity none,
> But to thyself smile when the Christians moan.
>
> As for myself, I walk abroad a-nights,
> And kill sick people groaning under walls;
> Sometimes I go about and poison wells;
> And now and then, to cherish Christian thieves,
> I am content to lose some of my crowns,
> That I may, walking in my gallery,
> See 'em go pinion'd along by my door.[7]
> (II.iii.169-74, 176-82)

To this image of mythical terror out of the Middle Ages Marlowe adds a very "modern" Elizabethan fear of the amoral Machiavellian schemer—"Machavill" speaks the prologue to the play and claims Barabas as his follower. The title character of *The Jew of Malta* is thus an epitome of archetypal villainy for Shakespeare's age.

When *The Merchant of Venice* was first performed, probably in 1596 or 1597, *The Jew of Malta* had enjoyed an extraordinarily successful revival, having been staged at least thirty-six times between February 26, 1592, and June 21, 1596. What may have kept interest in the subject alive and even provided an occasion for the composition of Shakespeare's play was the notorious affair of Roderigo Lopez, a Portuguese Jew who had served as physician to Queen Elizabeth. Jews had been officially banished from England in 1290 by King Edward I, and Lopez, like the rest of the handful of Jews living in London in the sixteenth century, was at least nominally a Christian convert. Such conversions were, however, always suspect among Christians throughout Europe, and when Lopez became implicated in an alleged Spanish plot to poison the Queen in 1594, old fears of Jewish duplicity and cruelty were seemingly confirmed.[8]

---

7. Christopher Marlowe, *Complete Plays and Poems*, ed. E. D. Pendry and J. C. Maxwell (London: J. M. Dent, 1976), 355.

8. For contemporaneous accounts of the affair, see G. B. Harrison, ed., *An Elizabethan Journal: Being a Record of Those Things Most Talked About During the Years 1591-1594* (New York: Cosmopolitan, 1929), 295, 297-99, 301, 304-5, 306-12, 316, 323, 344, 372.

The trial and execution for treason of Roderigo Lopez thus furnished a sensational backdrop for *The Merchant of Venice*; but, in sharp contrast to the model he had in *The Jew of Malta*, Shakespeare mutes the sensational possibilities in the material. Both Barabas and Shylock have only daughters who, the fathers feel, betray them by becoming Christians. Abigail, the daughter of Barabas, having counterfeited a religious vocation in order to help her father recover his money, turns nun in earnest after he conspires in the death of her Christian lover—a man whose advances Barabas has, for his own purposes, required her to encourage. Barabas responds by poisoning her along with all the nuns in the convent. Jessica, the daughter of Shylock, is unhappy at home and elopes with a rather prodigal Christian, Lorenzo, stealing large sums of money and jewels—including an important keepsake—when she goes. Shylock is enraged over the loss of his ducats, but he is also heartbroken over his daughter's heartless betrayal of him. He cries out in his rage and frustration, "I would my daughter were dead at my foot, and the jewels in her ear! Would she were hears'd at my foot, and the ducats in her coffin!" (III.i.87–90). The discrepancy between Barabas's atrocity and Shylock's malevolent but perfectly understandable human exclamation could hardly be more pronounced. The one is monster, the other a man.

From the outset Shakespeare sets about providing Shylock with powerful motivation for his hatred of Antonio. When Antonio offers Shylock surety for a loan of 3,000 ducats to the improvident Bassanio, the aggrieved money lender reminds the merchant of the affronts he has offered:

But see Berek, "Jew as Renaissance Man," 151–52: "In the few documents where Lopez's Jewishness figures as more than identifying ascription, Jewishness becomes assimilated to Roman Catholicism as a figure of otherness and enmity. In none of the accounts of the Lopez case is there the explicit Jew-baiting we find in the plays of Marlowe and of Shakespeare." But in fact, in the Calendar of State Papers, as excerpted by Harrison, Lopez is called "a perjured murdering traitor and Jewish Doctor, worse than Judas himself" (307) and "a vile Jew" (309). See also de Sousa, *Shakespeare's Cross-Cultural Encounters*, 88.

> You call me misbeliever, cut-throat dog,
> And spet upon my Jewish gaberdine,
> And all for use of that which is mine own.
> Well then, it now appears you need my help.
> Go to then, you come to me, and you say,
> "Shylock, we would have moneys," you say so—
> You that did void your rheum upon my beard,
> And foot me as you spurn a stranger cur
> Over your threshold; moneys is your suit.
> What should I say to you? Should I not say,
> "Hath a dog money? Is it possible
> A cur can lend three thousand ducats?"
> (I.iii.111–22)

Antonio is unmoved by Shylock's indignant response to such humiliations:

> I am as like to call thee so again,
> To spet on thee again, to spurn thee too.
> If thou wilt lend this money, lend it not
> As to thy friends, for when did friendship take
> A breed for barren metal of his friend?
> But lend it rather to thine enemy,
> Who if he break, thou mayst with better face
> Exact the penalty. (I.iii.130–37)

Antonio is, in modern parlance, "asking for it"; and we may suspect that a modern playwright with this plot on his hands would make the long-suffering Jew first conceive his hatred here, when his genuine longing for reconciliation is rebuffed one time too many. Shakespeare, however, has already let us know, in an aside earlier in the scene, that Shylock hates Antonio because "he is a Christian," and because

> He lends out money gratis, and brings down
> The rate of usance here with us in Venice.
> If I can catch him once upon the hip,

> I will feed fat the ancient grudge I bear him.
> ... Cursed be my tribe
> If I forgive him! (I.iii.42, 44–48, 51–52)

But Shylock's studied malice no more justifies Antonio's self-righteous complacency than Antonio's insults justify Shylock's premeditation of murder. In fact, the Christian merchant is more of a "Pharisee," in his self-assured moral and spiritual superiority, than the Jewish usurer; and the sharp edge of ironic tension adds a bite to the gaiety of this romantic comedy. Antonio's acceptance of the "merry bond" (I.iii.171) of a pound of his flesh to be granted Shylock in the unlikely event of forfeiture allows Antonio to avoid entering an agreement involving interest, to which he was willing to agree "only to supply the ripe wants of my friend" (I.iii.63). As Robert Ornstein points out, "His selflessness declared, he feels justified in continuing to revile Shylock. Indeed, precisely because his moral situation is slippery, he must be unbending in his scorn."[9] It is important to note that Antonio's complete condemnation of any taking of interest is an extreme view for Elizabethan England during Shakespeare's time. Although usury was theoretically forbidden, in practice it was allowed at rates of no more than 10 percent. Francis Bacon probably spoke for the common attitude when he maintained,

> That it is a Vanitie to conceiue, that there would be Ordinary Borrowing without Profit; And it is impossible to conceiue, the Number of Inconueniences, that will ensue, if Borrowing be Cramped. Therefore, to speake of the Abolishing of *Vsury* is Idle. All States haue euer had it, in one Kinde or Rate, or other. So as that Opinion must be sent to *Vtopia*.[10]

There is, in fact, evidence that Shakespeare's father took interest on loans.[11]

---

9. Ornstein, *Shakespeare's Comedies*, 99.
10. Francis Bacon, "Of Usury" (1625), in *A Harmony of the Essays, etc. of Francis Bacon*, ed. Edward Arber (1871; repr. New York: AMS, 1966), 543–44.
11. Eric Sams, *The Real Shakespeare: Retrieving the Early Years, 1564–1594* (New Haven,

Although Shylock holds within him a settled hatred for Antonio, based on religious and moral antipathy and inflamed by the Christian's open hostility and public insults, there is no indication that he is actively plotting revenge. Even when he proposes the pound-of-flesh bond, he has no more cause than Antonio to suppose that it will ever come due. He immediately concedes to Bassanio that his friend is "a good man" insofar as he is "sufficient" to pay back the loan. Although Shylock calculates the extent to which Antonio's "means are in supposition," he never imagines that *all* his enemy's ventures will fail—or appear to fail, as the event proves (I.iii.15–26). The fairy-tale bond is not a probable means to catch Antonio "upon the hip," and we must surmise that Shylock's offer to lend the money gratis, with a pound of Antonio's flesh as surety, is a spontaneous rejoinder to the Christian's inveterate and insufferable disdain. Shylock admits that he has "borne it with a patient shrug" (I.iii.109), but now he wants to talk back to his tormentor, to assume a superiority both by making Antonio and Bassanio beholden to him and by holding over Antonio's head a grotesque, but apparently altogether fanciful threat.

What turns Shylock from a petty, circumspect miser into a bloodthirsty ogre is his daughter's elopement with another spendthrift Christian, Lorenzo, and her theft of his money and jewels. It is this betrayal by his own flesh and blood and the jeering of the Christians Solanio and Salerio that render Shylock implacable. The contrast with *The Jew of Malta*, again, could not be more striking. Marlowe's Barabas is a scheming mass murderer who ruthlessly destroys his daughter Abigail when she sincerely becomes a Christian nun after her father has betrayed her. Shylock is a man who sets out to do evil, but unlike the mythical Jew of medieval fantasy, he is not a remorseless cannibal. When James Shapiro assimilates Shylock's metaphors to this tradition, he fails to appreciate the moderation of Shakespeare's portray-

---

Conn., and London: Yale University Press, 1995), 8–10; and Park Honan, *Shakespeare: A Life* (Oxford and New York: Oxford University Press, 1998), 36–37.

al.¹² Salerio asks what purpose would be served if Shylock actually took a pound of Antonio's flesh, and the Jew responds in rage, "To bait fish withal—if it will feed nothing else, it will feed my revenge" (III.i.53–54). The important point here is that Salerio and Solanio do not, at first, take Shylock seriously; they cannot believe that he will go through with his threat. Shylock, for his part, has indeed become remorseless in his murderous intention toward Antonio, but it is strictly a matter of personal hatred growing out of a sense of wounded pride. Despite Shapiro's literalizing of a metaphor, Shylock's vendetta has nothing to do with ritual murder or Judaism per se. If the Christian Venetians would only look at him with unbiased eyes, they would see that he acts with a human, perfectly understandable motive.

In a masterstroke of irony, Shakespeare has Shylock claim his common humanity most poignantly in the course of justifying his most inhuman act. In one of the play's two most famous speeches, he berates the Christians for failing to acknowledge his equally human status even as he is bent upon shedding his humanity:

> Hath not a Jew eyes? Hath not a Jew hands, organs, dimensions, senses, affections, passions; fed with the same food, hurt with the same weapons, subject to the same diseases, heal'd by the same means, warm'd and cool'd by the same winter and summer, as a Christian is? If you prick us, do we not bleed? If you tickle us, do we not laugh? If you poison us, do we not die? And if you wrong us, shall we not revenge? If we are like you in the rest, we will resemble you in that. If a Jew wrong a Christian, what is his humility? Revenge. If a Christian wrong a Jew, what should his sufferance be by Christian example? Why, revenge. The villainy you teach me, I will execute, and it shall go hard but I will better the instruction. (III.i.59–73)

Nothing I can say will enhance the power of this speech. Allan Bloom complains that "Shylock bases his claim to equality

---

12. See James Shapiro, *Shakespeare and the Jews* (New York: Columbia University Press, 1996), 110.

with his Christian tormentors" only on "things which belong to the body; what he finds in common between Christian and Jew is essentially what all animals have in common."[13] It is of crucial importance, however, that Shylock make his plea on a very basic level, even as it is important that he not be a very good man himself. A man ought not to be required to appeal to others on an exalted spiritual plane in order to have his fundamental humanity acknowledged. The decisive test of a society's tolerance and compassion is not its response to a distinguished, cultivated Nobel laureate, who happens to be of a different race and religion; the test comes with the foreigner who dresses peculiarly, has an odd accent and an abrasive manner, and rejects the manners and customs of the host country. It is important, in other words, that neither the Christian characters in *The Merchant of Venice* nor the audience *like* Shylock. Essential human dignity should not be contingent upon a winsome personality.

Hence the trial scene in Act IV, which has proven so unsettling to modern audiences, manifests not the failure of Shakespeare's art, but rather its triumph; and the success is a direct result of the tremendous tension it is likely to generate in readers and theatregoers of almost any persuasion. While it is a mistake to attempt to save the play's gaiety and romance by turning its turbid religious conflict into an abstract allegory in which the feelings and experiences of the individual characters do not count for much, critics who diminish or dismiss the importance of their religion to the Christian characters are equally in error. The trial scene is constructed from a Christian perspective, which highlights the Pauline dichotomy of Old Testament legalism opposed to the New Testament gospel of grace. Before Portia, disguised as Balthasar, ever enters the scene the issue is framed in an exchange between the Duke and Shylock. "How shalt thou hope for mercy," asks the former, "rend'ring none?" To which the Jew replies, "What judgment shall I dread, doing

---

13. Allan Bloom, with Henry Jaffa, *Shakespeare's Politics* (1964; repr. Chicago: University of Chicago Press, 1981), 23.

no wrong?" (IV.i.88–89). Shylock is persistent in his demand that the legal contract be carried out exactly as it is written, confident in the justice of his cause: "My deeds upon my head! I crave the law, / The penalty and forfeit of my bond" (IV.i.206–7). Having uttered one of the most moving speeches in all of Shakespeare's plays, he is deaf to another, uttered by Portia:

> The quality of mercy is not strain'd
> It droppeth as the gentle rain from heaven
> Upon the place beneath. It is twice blest:
> It blesseth him that gives and him that takes.
> 'Tis mightiest in the mightiest, it becomes
> The throned monarch better than his crown.
> His sceptre shows the force of temporal power,
> The attribute to awe and majesty,
> Wherein doth sit the dread and fear of kings;
> But mercy is above this sceptred sway,
> It is enthroned in the hearts of kings,
> It is an attribute of God himself;
> And earthly power doth then show likest God's
> When mercy seasons justice. Therefore, Jew,
> Though justice be thy plea, consider this,
> That in the course of justice, none of us
> Should see salvation. We do pray for mercy,
> And that same prayer doth teach us all to render
> The deeds of mercy. (IV.i.184–202)

Ornstein is skeptical of the sincerity—or at least of the depth—of Portia's Christianity and says, "She knows she cannot ask the Jew to follow the example of Christ; she can only remind him that mercy is an attribute of God and becomes kings of this world better than their crowns."[14] But in fact the prayer that "doth teach us all to render / The deeds of mercy" is the "Our Father," and the notion that we cannot be saved by our own justice is the heart of the gospel, especially as preached by St. Paul. The opposition

---

14. *Shakespeare's Comedies*, 110. See also Bloom and Jaffa, *Shakespeare's Politics*, 24.

between the covenants of law and grace, which comes to the fore in the trial scene, is central to the play as whole; and there is no reason to assume that this understanding of moral and spiritual reality is not integral to the minds of the Venetian Christians.

They are not, even so, especially fervent or exemplary Christians. Fervent, exemplary Christians are called *saints*, and their number is regrettably small. As is so often the case in Shakespeare, the irony is doubled: Shylock gives utterance to an impassioned plea for the common humanity in all men even as he is hardening his heart to exact a terrible vengeance; Portia eloquently extols the virtue of mercy in the hearts of kings and seems promptly to forget her own speech when she comes to exercise power herself. The Duke, Bassanio, and Antonio—once the threat is past—are all willing to allow a chagrined Shylock to walk away with his money; it is the iron-willed Portia who demands that he be held to the strict letter of the law, just as he has insisted. The end of the play would be much more comfortable for us if we could treat the Portia of the trial scene as an allegory of the Divine Judge, who forces Shylock (the allegorical sinner) to relinquish all his wealth with the conditional restoration of a part of it upon his baptism—that is, he must throw down everything he has and follow Christ. But this will not work because we already know Portia as the high-spirited, self-possessed mistress of Belmont and as a tender, longing young bride. She has no business playing God.[15]

Here again is Shakespeare's critical spirit at work: Portia provides a fine account of mankind's universal need for the grace of forgiveness, but then fails to be gracious and forgiving herself. Even she, "A Daniel come to judgment" (IV.i.223), is fallible and in need of forgiveness. If we miss the point, Shakespeare under-

---

15. Craig Bernthal, *The Trial of Man: Christianity and Judgment in the World of Shakespeare* (Wilmington, Del.: ISI, 2003), 85–87, maintains that the characters in *The Merchant of Venice* present both allegorical and realistic components. He also points out, 89, that "Shakespeare's first move is to blur the distinction between Venetian Christians and stereotypical Jews."

scores it with a further irony. The character who immediately begins jeering at Shylock when Portia turns the tables on him, the character who offers Shylock only "A halter *gratis*—nothing else *for God's sake*" (IV.i.379; italic added), is named *Gratiano*, which of course suggests *grazia*, the Italian word for "grace." The character contradicts the name. After Gratiano has upbraided Antonio in the first scene of the play for his melancholy, grave demeanor, Bassanio thus describes Gratiano:

> Gratiano speaks an infinite deal of nothing, more than any man in all Venice. His reasons are as two grains of wheat hid in two bushels of chaff; you shall seek all day ere you find them, and when you have them, they are not worth the search.
> (I.i.113–17)

Such is the man who most avidly seconds Portia in her complete humiliation of Shylock, though the others join in readily enough. The Christian principle of gracious forgiveness is, then, a good one, but it is extremely difficult for Christians themselves to observe. Shylock is prevented from cutting away a pound of Antonio's flesh from very near his heart, but in a sense the Christians cut Shylock's heart out of his body without shedding a drop of his blood. And they do so with satisfied—if blinded—consciences. In thus dramatizing the doctrine of grace by showing how necessary it is to those who profess it because they fail to fulfill it, Shakespeare highlights a distinctive and specifically Christian element of Western civilization: its inability to live up to its own finest insights, which are always too exalted to be grasped by mortal men and women.

The devastated Shylock slinking off the stage casts a shadow over the comedy and romance of *The Merchant of Venice*, but we cannot suppose it is mere inadvertence on Shakespeare's part, because he does the same thing in other plays. Falstaff certainly ought to be banished from the royal court at the end of *II Henry IV*, but his dismissal still disrupts the solemnity of the coronation. Even more striking is the storming off the stage of the "much abus'd" Malvolio at the end of *Twelfth Night*.¹⁶ As his name indicates, Malvolio is a man of ill will—a *malevolent* character. His genuine grievance against Olivia's other servants, however, dampens the gaiety of the play's conclusion. What is more, the parallel with Malvolio assimilates Shylock to another category: in *Twelfth Night* Maria calls Malvolio "a kind of puritan" (II.iii.140). Shakespeare's audience, which would have had little chance to associate with Jews, would have found Shylock's disapproval of masques, plays, and revelry familiar enough:

> What, are there masques? Hear you me, Jessica:
> Lock up my doors, and when you hear the drum
> And the vile squealing of the wry-neck'd fife,
> Clamber not you up to the casements then,
> Nor thrust your head into the public street
> To gaze on Christian fools with varnish'd faces;
> But stop my house's ears, I mean my casements;
> Let not the sound of shallow fopp'ry enter
> My sober house. (II.v.28–36)

Everything in Shakespeare's plays—not to mention his profession as playwright—suggests that he was not fond of puritans. Yet as a man who was surely reared a Catholic, and who may have died a Catholic, in the ferociously anti-Catholic England of Elizabeth and James, he may well have sympathized with anyone under the pressure of religious conformity. This fact may well explain the poignancy of Shylock's forced conversion, troubling the penultimate act of this comedy. Shylock is thwarted, but we cannot forget him and his demand to be recognized as a man, not a monster.

Portia, who is for the most part a thoroughly engaging heroine, provides another moment that brings a modern reader up short and anticipates the concerns of *Othello*. Among the unsuccessful suitors for her hand who precede Bassanio is the Prince of Morocco. When she first hears of his arrival, Portia remarks

---

16. See Ornstein, *Shakespeare's Comedies*, 117, who notes the same parallels.

to her maid Nerissa, "If he have the condition of a saint, and the complexion of a devil, I had rather he should shrive me than wive me" (I.ii.130–31); and when he fails the test by picking the gold casket, she sighs in relief: "A gentle riddance. Draw the curtains, go. / Let all of his complexion choose me so" (II.vii.78–79). This is certainly color prejudice, but it does not seem to be racialism in the modern sense. There is no indication that the Prince's suit is any more objectionable than that of the other failed aspirants, and it certainly does not seem to be regarded as outrageous. Portia is far more belittling in her comments about the suitors from France, Scotland, and Naples; and the Prince of Morocco departs with far more dignity than the Prince of Arragon, who fails by choosing the silver casket. Portia seems typical of her time in her bias for fair features, but nothing in her conduct suggests that dark skin is a badge of innate inferiority. She seems to have distaste for the Moor and may possibly fear him, but she does not despise him. Finally, it is worth observing that the Prince of Morocco speaks eloquently in defense of his virtue and noble dignity, fully aware that Europeans, including Portia, are likely to look askance upon his "complexion, / The shadowed livery of the burnish'd sun" (II.i.1–2).[17]

In *Othello* Shakespeare develops the ambiguous status of the dark-skinned African in European society of the Renaissance. As in *The Merchant of Venice*, religious issues complicate considerations of race or ethnicity, but Shakespeare's drama again leaves an attentive audience or reader with a powerful realization of the essential humanity of the racial "other." And yet, although he does not depict a society that is racialist, as Europe and North America would become in the following centuries, the play reveals the seeds of racialism, which is confirmed in subsequent

---

17. While the earliest meaning of "complexion" in English derives from the notion of the temperament or mixture of bodily humors and the consequent physical and moral effects, including skin color, by Shakespeare's day it could mean simply skin color, without reference to physiology. The OED uses this passage as an illustration of this meaning, and the Prince clearly introduces the term with his own dark color in mind.

responses to it by some commentators. *Othello* is not, then, a manifestation of an established racialism, but it does highlight the danger of racial categorization at a point in European history when it was soon to become a problem.

Ironically, it is Shakespeare himself, rather than Marlowe, who furnishes a sensational counterpart to Othello in the character of Aaron the Moor from *Titus Andronicus*, the poet's first and worst tragedy. Bassianus, brother to the new Emperor Saturninus and bridegroom to Titus's daughter Lavinia, expresses the standard view of Aaron when he finds him alone during a hunt in the forest with the Emperor's new bride, the Gothic Queen Tamora:

> Believe me, Queen, your swart Cimmerian
> Doth make your honor of his body's hue,
> Spotted, detested, and abominable.
> Why are you sequester'd from all your train,
> Dismounted from your snow-white goodly steed,
> And wand'red hither to an obscure plot,
> Accompanied but with a barbarous Moor,
> If foul desire had not conducted you? (II.iii.72–79)

In *Titus Andronicus* the assumption that a Moor's dark skin is a reliable indicator of his "dark" wickedness proves correct: Aaron not only fathers a bastard child on the Empress; he also engineers the rape and mutilation of Lavinia, the murder of her husband, Bassianus, the framing and execution of two of Titus's sons for this murder, Titus's severing of his own hand in a vain effort to save these sons, and the banishment of a third son. When this last son, Lucius, returns at the head of a Gothic army and captures Aaron, the Moor is defiantly impenitent for his "heinous deeds" in lines reminiscent of Barabas's speech to Ithamore:

> Even now I curse the day—and yet I think
> Few come within the compass of my curse—
> Wherein I did not some notorious ill:
> As kill a man, or else devise his death,

> Ravish a maid, or plot the way to do it,
> Accuse some innocent, and forswear myself,
> Set deadly enmity between two friends,
> Make poor men's cattle break their necks,
> Set fire on barns and haystalks in the night,
> And bid the owners quench them with their tears.
> (V.i.125–34)

This rant goes on for another ten lines and serves to remind us that even Shakespeare had not only to learn his craft but also to grow in wisdom and moral vision in order to create characters of compelling humanity and depth.

Othello is a play of considerably increased sophistication and complexity. Although the ominous portent of race-baiting is evident in the opening scene, it emerges in a situation of subtle ambiguity. Iago, Othello's discontented "ancient" or ensign, is desperately seeking to persuade Roderigo, an idle young gentleman with too much money as well as time on his hands, not to give up his hope of possessing Desdemona, the beautiful daughter of the wealthy merchant Brabantio, despite the news that she has eloped with Othello. Iago must sustain Roderigo's resolution in order to maintain access to Roderigo's purse with promises of help in attaining his amorous quest. And, of course, there is Iago's obscure but virulent malice toward his Moorish master. A striking aspect of this scene lies in the two men's several disdainful references to Othello's black skin, African features, and general foreignness mingled with brutish sexual images. "What a full fortune does the thick-lips owe," exclaims Roderigo, "If he can carry't thus!" (I.i.66–67). Iago rouses Brabantio by shouting under his window, "Even now, now, very now, an old black ram / Is tupping your white ewe" (I.i.88–89), and soon adds, "I am one, sir, that comes to tell you your daughter and the Moor are now making the beast with two backs" (I.i.115–17). The less imaginative Roderigo horrifies the old man by describing his daughter in "the gross clasps of a lascivious Moor," who is also "an extravagant and wheeling stranger" (I.i.126, 136). When Brabantio first confronts Othello, he denies that his daughter without magical compulsion "Would ever have, t' incur a general mock, / Run from her guardage to the sooty bosom / Of such a thing as thou" (I.ii.69–71).

In the face of such scurrility, the dignity and calm of Othello emerge with great force when he takes the stage in the second scene. More than any other Shakespearean tragic hero, he commands respect and radiates authority as the drama begins and embodies the values of aristocratic chivalry. Iago attempts to ruffle the Moor's magnificent self-possession to no avail. "You were best go in," Iago warns, when he thinks that Brabantio and his retainers approach. "Not I; I must be found," Othello tranquilly replies. "My parts, my title, and my perfect soul / Shall manifest me rightly" (I.ii.30–32). He is supremely confident in his virtues, in his standing in the city, and above all in his clear conscience. When the outraged father's party does finally confront Othello and the officers who have come to summon him to the Duke's council chamber "Upon some present business of the state" (I.ii.90) and the blades of drawn weapons are gleaming in the torchlight, the Moorish general quells the threatened tumult with a relaxed yet magisterial authority: "Keep up your bright swords, for the dew will rust them" (I.ii.59). Only a man accustomed to command and to be obeyed could utter these words with such self-assurance. After the vile slanders of Iago and Roderigo, who would paint Othello as a lecherous savage in the first scene, Shakespeare is at pains to present the Moor as a gentleman of fully heroic stature.

Othello's stature is confirmed when the marriage is considered before the Duke and his Council. Assembled to deal with a new Turkish threat to the Venetian possession Cyprus, the senators must first hear Brabantio's accusation that his daughter "is abus'd, stol'n from me, and corrupted / By spells and medicines bought of mountebanks" (I.iii.60–61). Belying his claim to be "Rude... in ... speech" (I.iii.81), Othello gives an account of wooing Desdemona—at first inadvertently—by means of the stories he told, invited by Brabantio himself, of perilous adventure and suffering in exotic lands:

> She lov'd me for the dangers I had pass'd,
> And I lov'd her that she did pity them.
> This only is the witchcraft I have us'd.
> (I.iii.167–69)

The Duke himself affirms Othello's conclusion: "I think this tale would win my daughter too" (I.iii.171). For her part, Desdemona dispels the aspersions cast upon her bridegroom's appearance and supposed barbarism with an exemplary assertion of the spiritual transcendence of human dignity:

> I saw Othello's visage in his mind,
> And to his honors and his valiant parts
> Did I my soul and fortunes consecrate.
> (I.iii.252–54)

When we consider the racial or ethnic dynamics of the play, two points stand out: first, racial difference is a source of animosity, suspicion, and disdain; second, the animosity, suspicion, and disdain are nowhere near sufficiently dominant for us to call Venice, as Shakespeare depicts it, a *racialist* society in the modern sense of the term. Brabantio's denigrations are the response of a man who has lost a daughter on whom he doted to a foreigner who was welcome as a guest, but not as a son-in-law. Roderigo, who refers to Othello as "the thick-lips," is apparently a wastrel whom both Desdemona and Brabantio have scorned as a suitor.[18] And then there is Iago. Surely, he is the most wicked of Shakespeare's villains, a man who seems to delight in evil for its own sake to such an extent as to inspire Coleridge to his

---

18. See Brabantio's initial dismissal of Roderigo when the latter comes to break the news about Desdemona's elopement: "I have charg'd thee not to haunt about my doors. / In honest plainness thou has heard me say / My daughter is not for thee ..." (I.i.96–98).

famous phrase, "the motive-hunting of motiveless malignity."[19] Over against the malicious slanders of these men is the nearly universal admiration for Othello. Plainly, the Duke and Venetian senators regard him as their best general and only hope against a Turkish invasion of Cyprus. Even Iago is constrained to admit to Roderigo "that, for their souls, / Another of his fadom they have none / To lead their business" (I.i.151–53).[20] Finally, and most importantly, there is the generic evidence: Othello is a tragic hero, and although a tragic hero necessarily has a flaw, he cannot be despicable or inferior. Tragedy, Aristotle observes, is "a representation of men better than ourselves."[21]

The significance of Othello's status as a tragic hero may be easily gauged from the response it calls forth from Thomas Rymer at the end of the seventeenth century. *Othello* was one of the more popular tragedies on the English stage throughout the century, and in 1693, Rymer complains that it "is said to bear the Bell away."[22] He is quite evidently incensed at the changes Shakespeare has made in the source, a novella by Giraldo Cinthio, all of which serve to ennoble the characters and elevate the action:

Shakespear alters it from the Original in several particulars, but always, unfortunately, for the worse. He bestows a name on his *Moor*, and styles him the Moor of *Venice*,—a Note of pre-eminence which neither History nor Heraldry can allow him. *Cinthio*, who knew him best, and whose creature he was, calls him simply a *Moor*. We say the Piper of *Strasburgh*, the Jew of *Florence*: and if you please, the Pindar of *Wakefield*;—all upon Record, and memorable in their Places. But we

19. Samuel Taylor Coleridge, *Coleridge's Writings on Shakespeare*, ed. Terence Hawkes, introduction Alfred Harbage (New York: G. P. Putnam's Sons, 1959), 171.
20. The suggestion by Bloom and Jaffa, *Shakespeare's Politics*, 49, that "he [Othello] is not so much the best general as reputed to be the best general," is frivolous. Iago, who again has no reason to extol Othello's virtues, tells Roderigo about his own campaigns with the Moor in various locales (I.i.28–30), and the minor character Montano, whom the audience has no reason to doubt, likewise says, "For I have serv'd him, and the man commands / Like a full soldier" (II.i.35–36).
21. Aristotle, *Poetics* xv.11 (1454d): Επει δε μιμησις εστιν η τραγωδια βελτιονων.
22. Thomas Rymer, *A Short View of Tragedy* (1693), in *Critical Essays of the Seventeenth Century*, ed. J. E. Spingarn (Oxford: Clarendon, 1908), 2:219.

see no such Cause for the *Moors* preferment to that dignity. And it is an affront to all Chroniclers and Antiquaries to top upon 'um a *Moor*, with that mark of renown, who yet had never faln within the Sphere of their Cognizance.[23]

Rymer will grant to a black African not even the "dignity" of a name, much less the nobility of a soldier or the grandeur of a heroic figure. He scornfully quotes a few lines of Othello's account of the "magical" wooing and remarks, "This was sufficient to make the Black-amoor White, and reconcile all, tho' there had been a Cloven-foot into the bargain"; and he is outraged that a white Venetian like Iago should be depicted as a conniving liar: "He is no Black-amoor Souldier, so we may be sure he should be like other Souldiers of our acquaintance."[24]

Clearly something has happened that enables or impels white Englishmen (and other Europeans) to regard black Africans as naturally inferior. Basil Davidson suggests that 1592 is crucial. In that year the king of Spain greatly increased the slaving assiento or license between Africa and the New World because of the enormous profits that were beginning to be made in the sugar trade, which required slave labor. In the course of the seventeenth century the other European nations would get into the trade in a large way. Once slaving became the chief point of contact between Europe and Africa, Davidson observes, profit became more important than humanity: "Race contempt crept in when free men could justify their material interests by the scorn they had for slaves."[25] When *Othello* first appears on the stage in 1603 or 1604, slavery is not yet seen as an institution exclusively imposed by Europeans and Arabs upon black Africans, but there are straws in the wind. Less than ninety years later, Thomas Rymer finds the notion of a noble black man winning the love of a

---

23. Rymer, *Short View of Tragedy*, 2:220.
24. Rymer, *Short View of Tragedy*, 2:222, 223.
25. Basil Davidson, *The African Slave Trade: Precolonial History 1450–1850* (Boston: Atlantic–Little Brown, 1961), 5. On the 1592 expansion of the "assiento" and the rapid growth of the Atlantic slave trade, see 49–53. See also Hugh Thomas, *The Slave Trade: The Story of the Atlantic Slave Trade, 1440–1870* (New York: Simon and Schuster, 1997), 134–35ff.

noble white woman and marrying her intolerable. The power of this viewpoint is displayed in the less than edifying spectacle of various critics in the course of the next two and half centuries attempting to make Othello merely swarthy or "tawny," and not a sub-Saharan African. Samuel Taylor Coleridge, who ought to have known better, will serve as an example: "It would be something monstrous to conceive this beautiful Venetian girl falling in love with a veritable negro."[26] In his effort to save the tragedy from Rymer's strictures, Coleridge is blithely unaware of how much he sounds like Brabantio.

Postmodern efforts to "save" the play—to make it "relevant"—to contemporary audiences are often equally unsatisfactory and substitute patronizing pity of Othello for Rymer's unvarnished contempt. Stephen Greenblatt, for instance, reads *Othello* as a virtual allegory of the European conquest of the New World. Greenblatt takes up the theory of Daniel Lerner that the dominance of the "mobile society" of the modern West is characterized by "empathy" and comments thus:

> Professor Lerner is right to insist that his ability is a characteristically (though not exclusively) Western mode, present to varying degrees in the classical and medieval world and greatly strengthened from the Renaissance onward; he misleads only in insisting further that it is an act of imaginative generosity, a sympathetic appreciation of the situation of the other fellow. For when he speaks confidently of the "spread of empathy around the world" we must understand that he is speaking of the exercise of Western power, power that is creative as well as destructive, but that is scarcely ever wholly disinterested and benign.[27]

---

26. Coleridge, *Coleridge's Writings on Shakespeare*, 169. See Maynard Mack, *Everybody's Shakespeare: Reflections Chiefly on the Tragedies* (Lincoln and London: University of Nebraska Press, 1993), 129–30. In the introduction to his Arden edition of *Othello* (Walton on Thames, Surrey: Thomas Nelson and Sons, 1997), E. A. J. Honigmann makes a reasonably convincing case that Shakespeare was specifically thinking of a "tawny" north African, the Moorish ambassador to Queen Elizabeth, who made quite a stir from 1600 to 1601, but he also concedes that it makes little difference to our reading of the play: "Be he a black or a north African Moor, Othello's otherness remains" (27).

27. Greenblatt, *Renaissance Self-Fashioning from More to Shakespeare*, 227–28; see "Introduction," n. 21.

Iago, Greenblatt presumes, is a master of this sinister "empathy" that enables a man to enter into the situation of another and beguile him; that is, Iago is the embodiment of Western civilization in its aggressive essence.

Now there are two major problems here only if we consider the play and not the implications of the schema as a definition of Western civilization. First, there is the problem that Iago is the villain of the play and not its hero: far from looking like the complete Renaissance man, he resembles nothing so much as the unstable, decentered postmodern subject. "I am not what I am," he confides to Roderigo (I.i.65). Like so many of Shakespeare's tragic antagonists—think of Edmund in *King Lear*—Iago is best regarded as a threat to traditional Western civilization, not as its exemplar. Second, the "empathetic" relationship that Greenblatt proposes between Iago and Othello reduces the latter to little more than a "noble savage"—precisely the "erring barbarian" out of his depth in a marriage to a "super-subtle Venetian." Now everything in the text of the play tells us that Othello is certainly noble, but not in the least savage. Greenblatt would make Othello's vulnerability to deception by Iago no different from Roderigo's, but Iago plays on the passions of the latter. It is just his nobility that makes Othello vulnerable, and in this he is very much like Hamlet. When Claudius is planning to murder Hamlet by means of a poisoned foil in what is ostensibly a friendly fencing match, he tells Laertes that Hamlet, "Most generous, and free from all contriving, / Will not peruse the foils" (IV.vii.135–36). Similarly, in a soliloquy at the end of Act I of *Othello*, Iago informs the audience that his general bears the same character: "The Moor is of a free and open nature, / That thinks men honest that but seem to be so" (I.iii.399–400).

But Greenblatt sees Othello as the victim of an even darker aspect of Western civilization, the tension between "erotic intensity" and "Christian orthodoxy." Othello's blackness becomes a symbol of the sexual guilt that torments a man who must be ever proving his place in society: "This tension is less a manifestation of some atavistic 'blackness' specific to Othello than a manifestation of the colonial power of Christian doctrine over sexuality, a power visible at this point precisely in its inherent limitation."[28] The basis for Greenblatt's alarm about the "colonial power of Christian doctrine over sexuality" comes in Othello's response to Desdemona's request to accompany her new bridegroom on the campaign in Cyprus; otherwise, "The rites for why I love him are bereft me" (I.iii.257). Othello certainly wants the company of his bride, but he is anxious lest the senators take the wrong impression from her impassioned plea:

> Vouch with me, heaven, I therefore beg it not
> To please the palate of my appetite,
> Nor to comply with heat (the young affects
> In me defunct) and proper satisfaction;
> But to be free and bounteous to her mind.
> And heaven defend your good souls, that you think
> I will your serious and great business scant
> For she is with me. No, when light-wing'd toys
> Of feather'd Cupid seel with wanton dullness
> My speculative and offic'd instruments,
> That my disports corrupt and taint my business,
> Let housewives make a skillet of my helm,
> And all indign and base adversities
> Make head against my estimation! (I.iii.261–74)

Now the obvious interpretation of this passage would stress both Othello's interest in reassuring his employers that he will in no way "scant" their "great business" and his becoming modesty in wishing to deflect any general speculation about the sexual ardor of the newlyweds.

For Stephen Greenblatt and other postmodern critics, however, this passage suggests that Othello is a sexual cripple captured by "a still darker aspect of Christian orthodoxy," which the scholar illustrates by quoting St. Jerome out of context from a

---

28. Greenblatt, *Renaissance Self-Fashioning*, 242.

secondary source: "An adulterer is he who is too ardent a lover of his wife."[29] Likewise, Karen Newman maintains, "As the object of Desdemona's illegitimate passion, Othello figures both monstrosity *and* at the same time represents the white male norms the play encodes through Iago, Roderigo, Brabantio."[30] Now Greenblatt could have found the passage from Jerome quoted and interpreted by a contemporary of Shakespeare's in a wedding sermon by John Donne: "*Nihil foedius, quam uxorem amare tanquam adulteram*, There is not a more uncomely, a poorer thing, then to love a Wife like a Mistresse."[31] Certainly the sexual standards of both Shakespeare's era and Jerome's were generally sterner than what we encounter at the beginning of the twenty-first century, but it is another question whether husbands ought to treat their wives as they would an adulteress. In any event, Newman makes explicit what Greenblatt only implies: the postmodernist interpretation of Othello as a helpless, psychologically crippled victim of Christian sexual morality depends upon making Iago the exemplar of Western civilization. The man who is simply identified as a *"Villaine"* in the list of characters in the first folio edition of the play, in this view, "encodes the white male norms" that govern it. After Roderigo has witnessed the expressions of love that pass between Othello and Desdemona in the presence of the Duke and the senators, he is ready to give up his hopes of ever possessing her; but Iago rekindles his ardor by assuring him that "love" is a mere illusion of carnal passion: "It is merely a lust of the blood and a permission of the will" (I.iii.334–35). Postmodernist interpreters join Iago in scorning the protestations of Othello and Desdemona that their love is, truly, something more than mere sensual attraction, and only by this great negation can they deny that Othello, like all Shakespeare's tragic he-

---

29. Greenblatt, *Renaissance Self-Fashioning*, 247–48.
30. Karen Newman, "'And Wash the Ethiop White': Femininity and the Monstrous in *Othello*," in Howard and Connor, *Shakespeare Reproduced*, 153.
31. John Donne, *The Sermons of John Donne*, ed. George R. Potter and Evelyn M. Simpson (Berkeley, Los Angeles, and London: University of California Press, 1955), 2:345.

roes, is the embodiment of an ideal virtue of Western civilization who fails and suffers catastrophe. As Maynard Mack points out, "There would be nothing tragic, in the senses of tragic that apply to drama, in the commission of a murder by one who in fact was a barbarian—that is melodrama."[32]

Othello, like *The Merchant of Venice*, is both an affirmation of the principles of the Western world and a daring challenge to that civilization to embody its principles with more constancy. *The Merchant of Venice* sets a concept of justice tempered with mercy over against unbending legalism and self-righteousness, but it reminds us in the troubling figure of Shylock and the failure of the Christian characters to integrate him into the comic close that even expressions of mercy can be tainted with self-righteousness. The challenge is all the greater—and Shylock's eloquent denunciation of the way he has been dehumanized all the more poignant—because he is in many ways such an unattractive individual. It is, after all, sinners who require grace. In a still more daring fashion, *Othello* exemplifies the highest virtues of Western Christendom—fortitude, courtesy, devotion to duty, and sexual delicacy—in a character who seems, to some observers, their antithesis: a black African could routinely be associated with Islam or with barbarism. Shakespeare thus reminds us that the essence of Western civilization is a matter of the mind and the heart, not outward appearance or blood inheritance. In his tragic fall—a tragedy deepened by the loftiness of his nobility at the play's outset—we see the fragility of virtue and honor, especially their vulnerability to betrayal by those, like Iago, who

---

32. Mack, *Everybody's Shakespeare*, 139. Cavell, *Disowning Knowledge*, 133, maintains, "However far he [Othello] believes Iago's tidings, he cannot just believe them; somewhere he also *knows* them to be false.... We must understand Othello ... to want to believe Iago, to be trying, against his knowledge, to believe him." I can find no substantial evidence or argument that Cavell presents for these assertions, and they are thoroughly refuted (without being mentioned) by Brian Vickers, *Appropriating Shakespeare: Contemporary Critical Quarrels* (New Haven, Conn., and London: Yale University Press, 1993), 74–93, who provides a detailed exposition of how Iago gradually undermines Othello's trust of Desdemona and self-confidence by manipulating his expectations that speech is intended to communicate.

seem to be their champions. Anti-Semitism and racial prejudice against black Africans are two of the uglier maladies in the history of the West, but in the work of its greatest dramatist we see that these evils are not integral to its civilization, and that, in its critical spirit, is the means of its continual reform.

4

Shakespeare's History Plays and the Erasmian Christian Prince

The role of Catholicism in Shakespeare's life and writing has long been a topic of intense controversy. Investigations of the "lost years" have kept the issue alive over recent decades, while the efforts of historians to describe the persistence of pre-Reformation custom and belief in the face of persecution by successive Tudor regimes have described a rich cultural context in which Catholic habits of mind would have been available to the developing dramatist.[1] Although the personal convictions

---

[1]. An especially provocative work on Shakespeare's youth is E. A. J. Honigmann, *Shakespeare: The Lost Years* (Totowa, N.J.: Barnes and Noble, 1985). Honigmann is anticipated by John Henry de Groot, *The Shakespeares and "The Olde Faith"* (1946; repr. Fraser, Mich.: Real-View, n.d.). Sams, *Real Shakespeare*, esp. 11–16, makes much of the influence of Shakespeare's boyhood Catholicism on his imagination as it appears in the plays and poems. Richard Wilson, *Secret Shakespeare: Studies in Theatre, Religion and Resistance* (Manchester, UK, and New York: Manchester University Press, 2004), Clare Asquith, *Shadow Play: The Hidden Beliefs and Coded Politics of William Shakespeare* (New York: Public Affairs, 2005), and Joseph Pearce, *The Quest for Shakespeare* (San Francisco: Ignatius Press, 2008) all argue that the playwright was an active Catholic and that his plays and poems reflect his commitment to Catholicism beneath the surface of their literal meaning. On the persistence of Catholic loyalty and cultural practices in Reformation England, see such works as J. J. Scarisbrick, *The Reformation and the English People* (Oxford: Basil Blackwell, 1984); David Cressy, *Bonfires and Bells: National Memory and the Protestant Calendar in Elizabethan and Stuart England* (Berkeley

of an author of such power and influence will always be a source of endless fascination and illumination, Shakespeare's intimate religious beliefs are likely to remain to some extent inaccessible. What is certainly available for inspection is the evidence of the plays and poems, which reveal at least one mode in which the heritage of Catholic thought furnished a means of discreetly criticizing the dominant ethos of the highly political Protestantism of Queen Elizabeth's reign. The history plays, especially those of the second tetralogy, according to a longstanding tradition that is by no means defunct, offer a patriotic celebration of the burgeoning English nationalism of the Tudor era. If these plays are considered in relation to the political ideals advanced by the humanist Catholicism associated with Desiderius Erasmus and Sir Thomas More, however, the heroic tone may be rendered problematic, or is at least qualified. Shakespeare's treatment of English history takes on a coloration of subtle irony that comments obliquely on the political goals of the Elizabethan regime without implying a partisan commitment in the religious conflict of the sixteenth century. The Catholic humanism that was flourishing at the threshold of the Reformation provides a contrast less to Protestantism in the strict doctrinal sense than to the pragmatic secularism that was unleashed by the fierce political conflicts of the Reformation era. Shakespeare's drama, again, illustrates the capacity of Western civilization to entertain sharply divergent perspectives with the attendant intellectual and moral tension generated by the clash of competing ideals.

---

and Los Angeles: University of California Press, 1989); and, most notably, Eamon Duffy, *The Stripping of the Altars: Traditional Religion in England, 1400–1580* (New Haven, Conn., and London: Yale University Press, 1992). For an insightful example of how the Catholic doctrine of Purgatory pervades a play by Shakespeare in an equivocal but crucial fashion, see Anthony Low, "*Hamlet* and the Ghosts of Purgatory: Intimations of Killing the Father," in *Aspects of Subjectivity: Society and Individuality from the Middle Ages to Shakespeare and Milton* (Pittsburgh: Duquesne University Press, 2003), 98–128. See also Stephen Greenblatt, *Hamlet in Purgatory* (Princeton, N.J.: Princeton University Press, 2001). For the persistence of Catholic moral thought from pre-Reformation dramatic sources, see Phoebe Spinrad, "'Too Much Liberty': *Measure for Measure* and Skelton's *Magnificence*," *MLQ* (1999): 431–49.

Shakespeare's History Plays and the Erasmian Christian Prince

In a biographical study of John Donne's young manhood, Dennis Flynn maintains that this poet, descended from Sir Thomas More on his mother's side, was reared in a circle of "Erasmian English Catholics" who "put up resistance on their own terms, trying to survive both the English Reformation and the Council of Trent."[2] The same conjecture may reasonably be ventured about Shakespeare's "lost years," when the documentary record is blank, between the birth of his twin babies by his wife, Anne Hathaway, in 1585 and his emergence in the London theatrical world in 1592. The kind of Catholicism that Flynn has in mind takes its tone from the irenic humanism that preceded the Protestant Reformation in reformist Catholic circles. Among these pre-Reformation reformers, Erasmus was the central figure; although his works were put on the Index of Forbidden Books after the Council of Trent, and although he was regarded as insufficiently zealous—a kind of "lost leader"—by the more militant Protestants, he remained an important figure throughout the sixteenth and into the seventeenth century, a beacon to both Catholics and Protestants who clung to the hope of religious reconciliation.

In retrospect, it is evident that the generation of Erasmus and More was the last for whom the ideal of a reformed and united Christendom remained a not-implausible goal. After the fateful events of 1517, the prospect of a commonwealth of European *catholicity* was swept away in a flood of nationalism and religious dissension that rushed into the space opened up by the Roman Catholic / Protestant split. It is unlikely that those two quintessentially humanist works, More's *Utopia* (1516) and Erasmus's *Praise of Folly* (1511), would have been written after Luther's Ninety-five Theses were nailed (figuratively, if not literally) on the door of the castle church in Wittenberg, and subtlety and irony had become hopelessly suspect. *The Education of a Christian Prince*, which Erasmus first published in 1516, the same year as *Utopia*, provides a more revealing account of the concrete features of the

---

2. Dennis Flynn, *John Donne and the Ancient Catholic Nobility* (Bloomington and Indianapolis: Indiana University Press, 1995), 53.

reform program of the Catholic humanists, because it is not slyly ambiguous and because it has continuing influence on Protestant reformers as well. When it is set against Shakespeare's second tetralogy of history plays, the *Education* provides a context for the political orientation of dramas that are as elusive in their own way as *Utopia* and *Praise of Folly*. This comparison highlights Shakespeare's remarkable insight into the paradoxes of Western political institutions and attitudes.

"Where there is no power of choosing a ruler," writes Erasmus, "the man who is going to educate the future ruler ought to be chosen with suitable care."[3] When these words first appeared in *The Education of a Christian Prince*, most European realms were in fact hereditary monarchies that lacked the "power of choosing a ruler." Erasmus takes this state of affairs for granted. His short book, dedicated to the grandson of Spain's Ferdinand and Isabel, who would soon be one of Europe's most powerful monarchs as the Holy Roman Emperor Charles V, is devoted to the formation of a ruler whose reign is just and salutary rather than arbitrary and tyrannical. Erasmus recommends good government to Charles and other Renaissance princes by an appeal to duty based on the precepts of classical philosophy and the demands of Christian discipleship. "While wisdom in itself is an estimable thing," he advises, "Aristotle deems no kind of wisdom more excellent than that which teaches a beneficent prince how to conduct affairs, even as quite rightly Xenophon decides in his book *Oeconomicus* that to rule those who are free and willing is something beyond a man and plainly divine."[4] Obviously, Erasmus perceives the tension between the increasing absolutism of

---

3. Desiderius Erasmus, *Institutio Principis Christiani* (1516), vol. 4, part 1, ed. O. Harding, in *Opera Omnia Desiderii Erasmi* (Amsterdam: North Holland, 1974), 137: "Vbi potestas non est deligendi principem, ibi pari diligentia deligendus erit is, qui futurum instituat principem."

4. Erasmus, *Institutio Principis Christiani*, 133: "Cum per se res eximia quaedam est sapientia, Carole principum amplissime, tum vero nullum sapientiae genus excellentius existimat Aristoteles quam quae doceat salutarem agere principem, vt optimo iure Xenophon in libro, quem inscripsit Oeconomicon arbitretur esse quiddam homine maius planeque diuinum imperare liberis ac volentibus."

sixteenth-century monarchies and the classical ideal of the citizen whose submission to the state is voluntary. In addition to his invocation of the Greek concept of liberty under a lawful ruler, the humanist scholar reminds Renaissance princes of their subjects' equal dignity as Christians: "Since nature brought forth all men free and slavery was imposed contrary to nature, as even the laws of the heathen admit, think how unseemly it is for a Christian to seize dominion over Christians, whom the laws have not intended to be slaves and Christ has redeemed from all servitude."[5]

Although a straightforward, even a cautious work, *The Education of a Christian Prince* holds an equivocal place in the political thought of the era. The fact that the work is addressed to a dynastic ruler and assumes hereditary monarchy as the governmental norm places Erasmus in the camp of the centralized national kings whose ascent had begun in the later Middle Ages, and whose power would culminate in the Gallican royal absolutism of Bourbon France. Still, as Lisa Jardine observes, "His closely argued case for government by consent exerted an important influence on later-sixteenth and early-seventeenth-century treatments of the rights of subjects to resist imposed rule."[6] His relationship to modern political thought is similarly problematic. While his insistence on consent can be regarded as an anticipation of contract theories of government, for Erasmus politics remains a branch of morality, a view that links him to medieval thinkers such as St. Thomas Aquinas as well as the political philosophy of ancient Greece and Rome.[7]

The effect of Erasmus on Renaissance political thought is

---

5. Erasmus, *Institutio Principis Christiani*, 165: "Cum natura genuerit omneis homines liberos et praeter naturam inducta sit seruitus, quod ethnicorum etiam leges fatentur, cogita quam non conueniat Christianum in Christianos vsurpare dominium, quos nec leges seruos esse voluerunt et Christus ab omni seruitute redemit."

6. Lisa Jardine, "Introduction," in Erasmus, *The Education of a Christian Prince with Panegyric for Archduke Philip of Austria* (Cambridge: Cambridge University Press, 1997), xiv.

7. See Lester K. Born, "Introduction," in Erasmus, *The Education of a Christian Prince*, trans. Lester K. Born (1936; repr. New York: Norton 1968), 94–130.

further complicated by the relationship of his work to another—now far more famous—sixteenth-century book, Niccolò Machiavelli's *The Prince*, actually written three years before *The Education of a Christian Prince*, although not printed until 1532, after the author's death. In northern Europe, and especially in England, Erasmus remained a respected and widely acknowledged humanist authority throughout the century; that is, political writers and moralists could admit his influence. The term "Machiavel," however, became a bugbear with which to frighten naughty children and a term of political abuse—much as "Hitlerite" or "Stalinist" or "McCarthyite" in the twentieth century. In John Donne's anti-Jesuit satire *Ignatius His Conclave*, for example, Machiavelli competes with other "innovators" like Paracelsus, Copernicus, and St. Ignatius Loyola in challenging Satan for the rule of hell. In the English drama of the Elizabethan and Jacobean period, the scheming cynical "stage Machiavel" becomes a familiar figure—whether comic, like Ben Jonson's Sir Politic Would-Be in *Volpone*, or tragic, as in John Marston's *The Malcontent* or George Chapman's *Bussy D'Ambois*.

The antithesis established in the contrast between Erasmus and Machiavelli is neatly summed up in two quotations: "The tyrant," the former maintains, "is eager to be feared, the king to be loved."[8] In contrast, Machiavelli is notorious for asserting that "it is much safer to be feared than loved, if one of the two must be lacking."[9] Yet Machiavelli was finally more influential as a political thinker, and not just in the obvious sense that governmental power usually tends to operate cynically and amorally. The growth of nationalism and centralized national governments was both a cause and a result of the Protestant Reformation, and the rise of nationalism was inevitably accompanied by the secularization of politics. Machiavelli's *Prince* is the embodiment of

---

8. Erasmus, *Institutio Principis Christiani*, 156: "Tyrannus metui studet, rex amari."
9. Niccolò Machiavelli, *Machiavelli's "The Prince": A Bilingual Edition*, ed. and trans. Mark Musa (New York: St. Martin's Press, 1964), 138–39: "È molto piu sicuro essere temuto che amato, quando si abbi a mancare dell'uno de dua."

nationalistic, secular government. By contrast, despite his effect among Tudor churchmen, Erasmus represents the politics of the Catholic past; and his example shows how in Elizabethan England a Catholic presence was possible that was not furtive or marginalized but assimilated as part of the moral and cultural tradition that not only furnished the backdrop for the forces of change unleashed in the wake of the Reformation, but that also in some measure mitigated them.

An aspect of the genius of Shakespeare's history plays is to show how this moral polarity represented by Erasmus and Machiavelli is blurred in practice and thus embodies the unique combination of critical realism and deferential traditionalism of the Western world. By the 1590s, when Shakespeare wrote his great dramatic cycles on fourteenth- and fifteenth-century English history, Erasmus and Machiavelli had come to represent, respectively, the established moral norm of political conduct and its destructive, immoral counterpart. The remainder of this chapter could easily be devoted to showing how this standard assessment was fair neither to Erasmus nor to Machiavelli, but Shakespeare had already made this point in his history plays.

The second—and by far the greater—of Shakespeare's two tetralogies, which comprises *Richard II*, the two parts of *Henry IV*, and *Henry V*, might borrow a phrase from Erasmus and be entitled "the Education of Prince Hal." The drama—the conflict in the plays—emerges from the questions that Shakespeare raises about the kind of education that Hal receives and the kind of ruler that he becomes. In this intensely theatrical representation of human experience, Shakespeare challenges us to ask ourselves what kind of man ought to rule, and whether Hal is that man. Is he a "Christian Prince" in Erasmus's sense of the term or a Machiavellian opportunist? A true king or a tyrant? The Erasmian ideal prince might be designated a Christian absent presence: to fulfill the role Hal has recourse to a number of rather questionable devices. He must be very devious in order to seem a "Christian Prince," rather than a Machiavellian opportunist like his father. We may tentatively surmise that the consummate Machiavellian turns out to be the man who is best at seeming an Erasmian idealist; still, the ideal remains in place at least as a silent admonition.

Some sense of Shakespeare's achievement in the second tetralogy can be attained by a comparison with the first tetralogy, comprising the three parts of *Henry VI* and *Richard III*. The two kings who give these plays their titles are drawn as such extreme embodiments of ineffectual piousness and malevolent cruelty that they serve as caricatures of the Erasmian and Machiavellian rulers. When we first see Henry VI as a boy king, he is distraught over the conflict between his uncles, the Bishop of Winchester and the Duke of Gloucester, and admonishes them with sententious wisdom that could have been gleaned from a humanist book on statecraft:

> I would prevail, if prayers might prevail,
> To join your hearts in love and amity.
> O, what a scandal is it to our crown
> That two such noble peers as ye should jar!
> Believe me, lords, my tender years can tell,
> Civil dissension is a viperous worm
> That gnaws the bowels of the commonwealth.
> (*1 Henry VI* 3.1.67–73)

As a child, Henry is shocked especially at the wrath of the Bishop, which is so unbecoming in a Christian pastor:

> O, how this discord doth afflict my soul!
> Can you, my Lord of Winchester, behold
> My sighs and tears, and will not once relent?
> Who should be pitiful, if you be not?
> Or who should study to prefer a peace,
> If holy churchmen take delight in broils? (106–11)

The culmination of this youthful idealism and piety comes even as Henry, years later as a grown man and dispossessed king, is stabbed to death by Richard of Gloucester, who will become the infamous Richard III. Henry upbraids Richard for his cruelty and violence and prophesies that he will be a source of misery for countless Englishmen, but his final words are all contrition and forgiveness: "O God forgive my sins and pardon thee!" (*3 Henry VI* 5.6.60). Henry thus has the piety, the love of peace, and the concern for the commonwealth that are the marks of a good king in the humanist tradition modeled on Erasmus, but he is incapable of governing the ferociously ambitious barons who plunge England into continual warfare in the course of his ineffectual reign and its aftermath.

Richard, on the other hand, admits with great satisfaction that he is Henry's antithesis as he stabs him a second time to be sure that the job is done:[10]

> If any spark of life be yet remaining,
> Down, down to hell, and say I sent thee thither—
> I that have neither pity, love, nor fear.
> Indeed, 'tis true that Henry told me of;
> For I have often heard my mother say
> I came into the world with my legs forward.
> Had I not reason, think ye, to make haste,
> And seek their ruin that usurp'd our right?
> The midwife wonder'd and the women cried,
> "O, Jesus bless us, he is born with teeth!"
> And so I was, which plainly signified
> That I should snarl, and bite, and play the dog.
> Then since the heavens have shap'd my body so,
> Let hell make crook'd my mind to answer it.
> I have no brother, I am like no brother;
> And this word "love," which greybeards call divine,
> Be resident in men like one another,
> And not in me: I am myself alone. (66–83)

---

10. A further connection with earlier Catholic humanism is the ultimate origin of Shakespeare's portrayal of Richard in More's unfinished *Richard III*, which he began in 1513, "when the subject of tyranny was much on the minds of More and Erasmus," according to E. E. Reynolds, *The Field Is Won: The Life and Death of St. Thomas More* (Milwaukee: Bruce, 1968), 86.

Richard turns the grisly trauma of his birth and his crooked back into a matter of perverse pride: blaming "the heavens" for his physical deformity, he commits himself to the spiritual deformity of hell. Although at first he proclaims himself an avenger of "the downfall of our house" (65) vowed to "seek their ruin that usurp'd our right," it quickly becomes clear that the exaltation of the white rose of the dynasty of York is for Richard a means, not an end. In denying that he has brothers, he is revealing his intention to betray and murder those brothers he does in fact have and any of his other kinsmen who stand in the way of his self-aggrandizement. In Richard, who claims "I am myself alone," Shakespeare offers an extreme depiction of the ultimate amoral individualist—the most unsavory version of Renaissance "self-fashioning." He is also typical of the playwright's villains who (as we have seen already) are so often characterized by nominalist singularity.

The association between such a character and the Machiavellian notion of a prince is easy to understand. While Erasmus writes with the assumption of a well-established ruling house in place, Machiavelli writes in the more volatile context of the Italian city-state where, during the fifteenth and sixteenth centuries, assorted military adventurers and political schemers came in and out of power with considerably more frequency. Indeed, much of *The Prince* is addressed to men who have newly "acquired" the government of a state. Shakespeare's Henry VI, on the other hand, resembles Machiavelli's version of an idealistic humanist ruler whose virtuous principles have failed in the rough-and-tumble of political reality:

And many have imagined republics and principalities that have never been seen or known to exist in reality; for there is such a gap between how one lives and how one should live that he who neglects what is being done for what should be done will learn his destruction rather than his preservation: for a man who wishes to profess goodness at all times must fall to ruin among so many who are not good. Whereby it is necessary for a prince who wishes to maintain his position to learn how not to be good, and to use it or not according to necessity.[11]

Richard certainly is a man who has learned "how not to be good, and to use it" to his own advantage.

That he is a Machiavellian, at least in the sense of the term operative in Shakespeare's theatrical world, Richard himself makes clear in the third act of *3 Henry VI*:

> Why, I can smile, and murther whiles I smile,
> And cry "Content" to that which grieves my heart,
> And wet my cheeks with artificial tears,
> And frame my face to all occasions ...
> I can add colors to the chameleon,
> Change shapes with Proteus for advantages,
> And set the murtherous Machevil to school.
> Can I do this, and cannot get a crown?
> Tut, were it further off, I'll pluck it down.
> (182–85, 191–95)

"The murtherous Machevil" is more than a little harsh as an appellation (not to mention anachronistic) for a scholarly bureaucrat whose only firsthand experience with "Machiavellian" political practices was to have been tortured for his supposed connection with a plot against the restored Medici oligarchs in 1512. The composition of *The Prince* in the following year was in part intended to regain their favor and thus to secure for the author a place in Florentine government once again.

Machiavelli's image in Tudor literature, however, especially on the stage, was indelibly formed: in addition to murderous cruelty and violence, the Elizabethan "stage Machiavel" is char-

---

11. Machiavelli, *The Prince*, 127–28: "E molti si sono imaginati republiche e principati che non si sono mai visti nè consciuti essere in vero; perchè egli è tanto discosto da come si vive a come si doverrebbe vivere, che colui che lascia quello che si fa per quello che si doverrebbe fare impara piuttosto la ruini che la perservazione sue; perchè uno uomo che voglia fare in tutte le parte professione de buono, conviene ruini infra tanti che non sono buoni. Onde è necessario a uno principe, volendose mantenere, imparare a potere essere non buone, e usarlo e non l'usare secondo la necessità."

acterized by hypocrisy and deceit. He not only murders; he murders with a smile. In the course of his ruthless drive to the throne in *Richard III*, the title character usually deludes and manipulates his victims before he dispossesses and kills them. An element of the play's manic exuberance is Richard's nimbleness in setting "to school" all the would-be "murtherous Machevils" who populate the cast. Apart from the little princes murdered in the tower, there are few strictly innocent victims, and the audience experiences, if not sympathy, a certain fascination with Richard's sheer energy in foiling rivals who are somewhat less adept at unprincipled violence and unbridled wickedness.

Eventually, however, "Machiavellianism" fails as catastrophically as the feckless idealism of Henry VI. It turns out that all the apparently autonomous machinations of the human actors are episodes in a plot scripted by Divine Providence. Richard III is just the last and most terrible scourge sent by a just God to avenge the moral and political evils that have swept through the English commonwealth for nearly a century. The terrible bloodletting unleashed by Richard's ambition and malice is the final stage of the purge of the body politic, which is restored to order, peace, and prosperity by Richard's defeat at the hands of Henry Tudor, Earl of Richmond, who assumes the throne as Henry VII. His role as founder of the Tudor dynasty, deftly complimented by Shakespeare's first tetralogy of history plays, marks him as a providential figure, and it hardly matters that, as a character, he is considerably less interesting than the "bloody tyrant" whom he overcomes.

The second tetralogy displays a great advance in both dramatic and political sophistication. It moves back in time to take up those events that sowed the seeds of the dynastic strife culminating in the Wars of the Roses. The first play, *Richard II*, introduces another pair of antithetical rulers, but with the names reversed and the contrasts more subtle and problematic. While Shakespeare's Henry VI is a gentle, moral man whose failing is that, in Machiavelli's terms, he does not know how to be evil when exigency requires it, Richard II is hardly a model of virtue. He takes the privileges and authority of his crown as a given, as if his power were an unchangeable fact of nature. He rules England not for the sake of the common good, but for his own interests, favoring the cronies who are his companions in guilty pleasures and taking advantage of his enemies, not only by expropriation of property, but even murder. In the play's most frequently quoted speech, the dying John of Gaunt, who is the drama's voice of conscience, proclaims that Richard has turned "This blessed plot, this earth, this realm, this England" into "a tenement or pelting farm" (2.1.50, 60).

When Richard, however, refuses to let a trial by combat between Gaunt's son, Henry Bullingbrook, and Thomas Mowbray proceed—presumably to cover up the king's own complicity in the murder of the Duke of Gloucester—and banishes both combatants instead, John of Gaunt admonishes his son to bear patiently the sentence of his lawful master, even though it be unjust (1.3.253ff). Likewise, John refuses the entreaties of his widowed sister-in-law, the Duchess of Gloucester, to avenge the death of her husband. In John's view, it is not the place of a subject to punish a king:

> God's is the quarrel, for God's substitute
> His deputy anointed in His sight,
> Hath caus'd his death, the which if wrongfully,
> Let heaven revenge, for I may never lift
> An angry arm against His minister. (1.2.37–40)

According to this view, the person of the King is sacred because of his divinely ordained office no matter how evil or incompetent he may be: the recourse of the persecuted subject is to the power of God, the only judge of kings.

This is an understanding of monarchy associated less with the historical John of Gaunt than with the absolutist propaganda of the Tudor establishment. First promulgated in 1570, just a year after the abortive Northern Rebellion on behalf of Mary

Queen of Scots, *An Homily Against Disobedience and Wylful Rebellion* maintains that "all sins I say against GOD and all men heaped together nameth he, that nameth rebellion." The homilist warns Englishmen "that GOD placeth as well evyll princes as good," and explains why:

> But what if the prince be undiscrete, and evyll in deede, and it also evident to all men's eyes that he so is? I ask agayne, what if it be long of the wickednesse of the subjectes, that the prince is undiscrete or evyll? Shall the subjectes both by their wickednesse provoke God for their deserved punishment to geve them an undiscrete or evyll prince, and also rebell against hym, and withal against God, who for punishment of their sinnes dyd geve them suche a prince?[12]

One can certainly see a parallel between the Northern Rebellion of 1569, the immediate occasion of this homily, and the rebellion of the Northern Percy clan in *1 Henry IV*,[13] but the condemnation applies quite as readily to Henry's initial rebellion against Richard and the usurpation of his throne in *Richard II* (or Henry Tudor's rebellion against Richard III in the culminating play of the first tetralogy). Presumably, Henry would have met with disapproval from his own father, John of Gaunt, whose death, along with the spoliation of his property by Richard, provides the pretext for Bullingbrook's early return from exile. Certainly, he is reproved by his uncle, the Duke of York (*Richard II*, 2.3.81ff),[14] and it seems that Henry Bullingbrook's seizure of his cousin's crown sets in motion the entire dreadful history of murder and civil wars dramatized in the remaining plays of the tetralogy, as well as the Wars of the Roses that Shakespeare depicts in his earlier cycle. It takes all seven plays to set forth the fulfillment of the Bishop of Carlisle's grim prophecy regarding the consequences of

---

12. Ronald B. Bond, ed., *Certain Sermons or Homilies* (1547) *and A Homily Against Disobedience and Wilful Rebellion* (1570), ed. Ronald B. Bond (Toronto: University of Toronto Press, 1987), 225, 214.

13. The point is made by Barbara Hodgdon, ed., *The First Part of King Henry IV: Texts and Contexts* (Boston: Bedford, 1997), 171.

14. Once Henry is crowned, however, York displays extravagant loyalty to the new King by denouncing is own son for treason; see *Richard II*, 5.2–3.

Bullingbrook's usurpation: "The blood of English shall manure the ground, / And future ages groan for this foul act" (4.1.137–38).

The contrast between Richard II and Henry IV is thus more complicated than that between Richard III and Henry VI. Unlike the pious Henry VI, Richard II is not merely an inept ruler, he is personally vicious and is responsible for outrages against his subjects, including against Bullingbrook himself, who in turn overthrows Richard. By the same token, Bullingbrook is hardly a monster of depravity like Richard III. He has legitimate complaints against the King and makes a good show of the legality of his proceedings when he first returns to England before the term of his exile is finished. In justifying himself to his uncle, the Duke of York, he stakes his case upon the feudal rights of a peer of the realm by maintaining, "If that my cousin be King of England, / It must be granted I am Duke of Lancaster" (*Richard II* 2.3.123–24); and he argues that it is the King who has first undermined the nation's legal foundations:

> What would you have me do? I am a subject,
> And I challenge law. Attorneys are denied me,
> And therefore personally I lay my claim
> To my inheritance of free descent. (133–36)

Of course, Bullingbrook does not remain content with being Duke of Lancaster, and he is as much responsible for the death of Richard II as Richard III is for the death of Henry VI. Nevertheless, Bullingbrook kills out of what he regards as grim necessity—he never would have been safe while his royal cousin lived—not with Richard III's demonic relish. Bullingbrook even makes a plausible show of remorse over the murder of the king whom he dispossessed: "They love not poison that do poison need," he tells the actual perpetrator, Sir Pierce of Exton, "Nor do I thee. Though I did wish him dead, / I hate the murtherer, love him murthered" (5.6.38–40).

Still, in the most profound sense, Henry IV is finally a more destructive figure than Richard III. The latter is merely a fiend, a man whose twisted body inspires his twisted mind with bitterness toward the world growing out of self-loathing. He comes at the end of almost a century of betrayal, assassination, and civil war—the climactic instrument of Providential wrath. It is Bullingbrook, however, who commits the primal sin. As Dain Trafton points out, "Henry subverts not only the rule of a particular king, but also a fundamental principle of the realm. He violates, and thus undermines, the sanctity of monarchy itself, the belief that kings are God's deputies and that rebellion is a sin."[15] If Henry is a less horrifying character than Richard III, there is also a sense in which he makes Richard possible.

What is more, as Trafton further observes, Henry's assault on traditional political virtues is based on a consistently secular and materialistic vision of life: "To Henry, obviously, his father's and Carlisle's views of kingship are nothing more than pious myths. If the world is ruled by 'chance's mocks,' traditional religious restraints possess no more force than credulous minds are willing to give them."[16] Trafton calls attention to the exchange between John of Gaunt and his son after the latter's banishment has been proclaimed. While Gaunt urges Bullingbrook to be master of a bad situation by means of the virtue of his mind, his son denies that thoughts and words can be a match for material reality: "O, who can hold a fire in his hand / By thinking on the frosty Caucasus?" (1.3.294–95). As Trafton explains, Henry "reduces what his father regards as a moral issue, involving a necessity imposed by divine law, to a matter of avoiding personal pain. Gaunt's advice violates nature as Henry understands it. Gaunt assumes a world informed by divine purpose, but Henry takes his bearings by the body."[17] Ironically, Henry, in many ways a better man than Richard, is more of a Machiavellian—a man for whom "goodness" is a mere empty word compared to the hard, material reality of

---

15. Dain Trafton, "Shakespeare's Henry IV: A New Prince in a New Principality," in *Shakespeare As a Political Thinker*, ed. John Alvis and Thomas G. West (Durham, N.C.: Carolina Academic Press, 1981), 84.
16. Trafton, "Shakespeare's Henry IV," 86.
17. Trafton, "Shakespeare's Henry IV," 87.

staying in power. However flawed King Richard's personal character, his turn for poetic phrasing is a verbal and dramatic manifestation of his affinity for Erasmian moral idealism, insofar as he is forced to withdraw from the wielding of power and reflect upon its cost in personal terms.[18]

These are the moral and political tensions that shape the context of the education of Prince Hal, who, according to the "Chorus" at the beginning of Act 2 of *Henry V*, will become "the mirror of all Christian kings" (6). In other words, Prince Hal, as he develops into King Henry V, becomes, apparently, the embodiment of the Christian prince whom Erasmus and his English Tudor disciples, like Sir Thomas Elyot and Roger Ascham, sought to mold by laying out the proper form of princely education. The qualification *apparently* acknowledges the extent to which Hal's transformation would seem to be suspect to scholars and educators, both in Shakespeare's day and ours. Renaissance humanists could hardly approve the means of Hal's "education." From the time he is first mentioned in *Richard II* (5.31–22)—he is not a character onstage in that play—until the final scene of *2 Henry IV*, Hal displays a taste for dubious company and questionable activities. To all appearances, he is on the way to becoming another Richard II—this is his father's chief fear—dissolute and corrupt, surrounded by flattering parasites. If humanist educators would have cause for skepticism regarding Hal's capacity for personal reformation, many modern scholars have also cast doubt on the extent to which he is a genuine exemplar of the Christian ruler. Whether Hal is not just a more subtle and effective Machiavellian than his father, and whether this ought to be a matter for celebration or disapproval, are pressing questions for the interpretation of the second *Henriad*.

18. Raphael Falco, *Charismatic Authority in Early Modern English Tragedy* (Baltimore and London: Johns Hopkins University Press, 2000), 65–100, argues that the conflict between Richard and Henry is a clash between different kinds of charisma, understood in the terms laid out by Max Weber's *Economy and Society* (1922). Despite Falco's useful and original insights, he neglects Shakespeare's essentially moral perspective on the political struggle.

Shakespeare's History Plays and the Erasmian Christian Prince

The opening of *1 Henry IV* seems designed to set Erasmus's teeth on edge. In the first scene the King and his counselors—including one of his younger sons, John of Lancaster—deliberate about the prospects of a crusade to recover the Holy Land in the face of new uprisings among the Welsh and the Scots. In the third scene, the King confronts the recalcitrant Hotspur about the prisoners he has failed to hand over. Hotspur is left on the stage with his father and uncle, the Earls of Northumberland and Worcester, to plot the King's overthrow. In between these scenes of men on the battlefield, engaged in determining the fate of the realm, we find Prince Hal, the heir apparent, carousing with his low-born cronies, exchanging witticisms with the disreputable Sir John Falstaff, and plotting highway robbery.

The company of a young prince must be chosen very carefully, Erasmus warns; "the crowd of lechers, drunks, scoundrels, and above all flatterers must be kept far away from the eyes and ears of youths, while the mind is not yet established with principles."[19] Falstaff seems to fit the Dutch humanist's observation about the man who corrupts a prince: "As there is no punishment not deserved by one who poisons the common well from which everyone drinks, just as pernicious is someone who infects the mind of the prince with vicious opinions, which will soon result in the harm of so many men."[20] Erasmus could not well countenance Prince Hal's complacent amusement with such speeches as this:

> Marry, then, sweet wag, when thou are king, let not us that are squires of the night's body be call'd thieves of the day's beauty. Let us be Diana's foresters, gentlemen of the shade, minions of the moon, and let men say we be men of good government,

---

19. Erasmus, *Institutio Principis Christiani*, 139: "Lasciuorum iuuenum ebriosorum turpiloquorum, in primis autem adulatorum turba procul ab huius auribus atque oculis erit arcenda, dum nondum praeceptis confirmatus animus."
20. Erasmus, *Institutio Principis Christiani*, 141–42: "Quemadmodum non vno supplicio dignus sit, qui fontem publicum, vnde bibant omnes, veneno inficiat ita nocentissimus est, qui principis animum prauis infecerit opinionibus, quae mox in tot hominum perniciem redundent."

being govern'd, as the sea is, by our noble and chaste
mistress the moon, under whose countenance we steal.
 (1.2.23–29)

Like Prince Hal, modern audiences are inclined to find Falstaff so entertaining that they tend to overlook the fact that he is not merely gluttonous, cowardly, and generally dissolute—but actually harmful. "I have misus'd the King's press damnably" (4.2.12–13), he admits later in the play after Hal has procured him a commission. If we forget that human lives are at stake in Falstaff's manipulation of forced military recruitment to line his own pockets, then we miss the sharp edge of Shakespeare's comedy. Falstaff is as much an object of reproof as the "Captane" in Donne's *Satyre* 1, "Bright parcel-guilt, with forty dead mens pay" (17, 18).[21]

Set over against Falstaff is the man whom King Henry and the nobles allied with him would most wish to see his son emulate: Henry Percy, known as Hotspur, son of the Earl of Northumberland. The King admires Hotspur's valor and ambition for military glory despite the threat these aggressive virtues pose to the realm and overtly expresses his envy of Northumberland for his son:

O that it could be prov'd
That some night-tripping fairy had exchang'd
In cradle-clothes our children where they lay,
And call'd mine Percy, his Plantagenet!
Then I would have his Harry and he mine.
 (1.1.86–90)

---

21. John Donne, *The Variorum Edition of the Poetry of John Donne*, vol. 3, *The Satyres*, ed. Gary Stringer et al. (Bloomington and Indianapolis: Indiana University Press, 2016), 5. Donne here provides a context that puts in doubt the ingenious argument that Falstaff ought to be regarded as an anti-monarchical puritan hero proffered by Grace Tiffany, "Puritanism in Comic History: Exposing Royalty in the Henry Plays," *Shakespeare Studies* 26 (1998): 256–67. Falstaff certainly exposes royalty, but it is improbable that Elizabethan puritans—or anyone else except for Harold Bloom—would care to identify with him.

But in fact, Hal is his father's son through and through, yet he is even shrewder, having sense enough to recognize that Hotspur is not a very good model for an aspiring prince. To be sure, he is fighting and taking part in great affairs of the realm while Hal is drinking and joking in the Boar's Head Tavern. But although Hotspur is a formidable warrior, he is neither a prudent leader nor a reliable follower. He vexes his father and his uncle by continually interrupting their plotting with outbursts of wrath toward the King (1.3). He annoys his cousin Mortimer by insulting the pretensions of Mortimer's father-in-law, the Welshman Own Glendower, who, while assuredly a pompous bore, is also essential to the success of the Percy rebellion against King Henry (3.1.1–190). Finally, it is Hotspur, out of impatience as well as to enhance his own glory, who insists that the rebels give battle before their forces are all gathered, ensuring their defeat and Hotspur's own death.

The obvious interpretation of the Falstaff/Hotspur dichotomy—an interpretation that has been widely accepted and that is by no means without plausibility—is to see Hal attaining the Aristotelian ethical golden mean of virtue by moderating between the extremes represented by his poltroonish friend and his fiery enemy.[22] In *1 Henry IV* he demonstrates his standing as a courageous soldier by defeating and killing Hotspur in single combat on the battlefield at Shrewsbury, and in *2 Henry IV* he proves himself a just ruler by confirming the Lord Chief Justice in his position and dismissing Falstaff and the Eastcheap hooligans from his retinue. Thus the ground is laid for the triumphant confirmation in *Henry V* of Hal's metamorphosis into "the mirror of all Christian kings" in his conquest of France, highlighted by the grand victory of Agincourt. But this reading is not only too neat and tidy; it also leaves unanswered questions about Hal, both as a man and as a king. In the political perspective, an aggressive

---

22. For a thorough exposition of this view, see E. M. W. Tillyard, *Shakespeare's History Plays* (1944; repr. Harmondsworth Middlesex: Penguin, 1962), 264–314, esp. 265–66.

war is a problematic undertaking for the ideal Christian prince in the eyes of both medieval and Renaissance moralists. In personal terms, Shakespeare seems to be at pains to make us conscious of a certain callousness in Hal.

The question of Hal's political probity arises most pointedly when we come to assess his greatest triumph, the conquest of France and reestablishment of the Plantagenet claim to the French throne. The last chapter of Erasmus's *Education of a Christian Prince*, "On Undertaking War," begins by asserting that the virtuous prince, who ought to make all decisions circumspectly, will never be more cautious and steadier than in considering war; and though Erasmus never denies outright the traditional teaching that in proper circumstances waging war can be just, he asks the prince to wonder "if any war ought to be called altogether just."[23] In going to war with France, Hal seems to be following the deathbed advice of his father, although one suspects that the son probably could have arrived at the same scheme on his own:

> I cut them off, and had a purpose now
> To lead out many to the Holy Land,
> Lest rest and lying still might make them look
> Too near my state. Therefore, my Harry,
> Be it thy course to busy giddy minds
> With foreign quarrels, that action, hence borne out,
> May waste the memory of former days.
> (*2 Henry IV* 4.5.209–15)

It is indeed questionable whether a war undertaken to "busy giddy minds," to distract them from looking too closely into the doubtful legitimacy of the regime, could be called "altogether just." Also worth noting is the fact that Hal chooses not a crusade to the Holy Land, but an invasion of France—a nearer and richer

---

23. Erasmus, *Institutio Principis Christiani*, 213, 214: "Cum nusquam oporteat principem praecipiti esse consilio, tum haud alibi contantior erit aut cicumspectior quam in suscipiendo bello"; "E diuerso, quam calamitosa simul et scelerata res bellum, quantumque malorum omnium agmen secum trahat, etiam si iustissimum sit, si quod omnino bellum iustum vocari debet."

prize that will bring something more materially rewarding than the honor of shedding blood in a religious cause.

At the beginning of *Henry V*, as he deliberates about the invasion of France, Hal demands that two of the most eminent bishops of his realm convince him that the war is just. The charge he gives them suggests that he has taken into account all the calamities and horrors that Erasmus associates with war and is reluctant to proceed without utter certainty that his action will be morally and religiously upright:

> My learned lord, we pray you to proceed,
> And justly and religiously unfold
> Why the law Salique, that they have in France,
> Or should, or should not, bar us in our claim;
> And God forbid, my dear and faithful lord,
> That you should fashion, wrest, or bow your reading,
> Or nicely charge your understanding soul
> With opening titles miscreate, whose right
> Suits not in native colors with the truth;
> For God doth know how many now in health
> Shall drop their blood in approbation
> Of what your reverence shall incite us to.
> Therefore take heed how you impawn our person,
> How you awake our sleeping sword of war—
> We charge you, in the name of God, take heed;
> For never two such kingdoms did contend
> Without much fall of blood, whose guiltless drops
> Are every one a woe, a sore complaint,
> 'Gainst him whose wrongs gives edge unto the swords
> That makes such waste in brief mortality.
> Under this conjuration speak, my lord;
> For we will hear, note, believe in heart,
> That what you speak is in your conscience wash'd
> As pure as sin with baptism. (1.2.9–32)

A noble speech seeming to echo the words of Erasmus himself: "How fleeting, how short, how fragile is human life and subject to so many disasters—it is vigorously assaulted by so many accidents and diseases: collapsing buildings, shipwrecks, earthquakes, lightning. There is no point, then, in fetching more evils through wars and yet there are more evils here than in all the others."[24]

Or at least Hal's speech would seem as noble as Erasmus's, if in the previous scene the audience had not just heard the Archbishop of Canterbury and the Bishop of Ely, to whom the King's words are addressed, discussing how best to enlist their sovereign in averting a bill before Parliament that would strip the bishops of "the better half of our possession" (1.1.8). "I have made an offer to his Majesty," the Archbishop says, and it involves a large sum of money and "causes now in hand.... As touching France" (1.1.75–81). What appears to be a noble utterance by a young ruler ingenuously seeking counsel from the lords spiritual turns out, upon inspection, to be a piece of cynical manipulation by which a king, who has already made up his mind about what he wants to do, pressures corrupt clergymen to furnish a rationalization—indeed to take responsibility—for a war of doubtful legitimacy.

A genuine Christian humanist counselor, instead of finespun lucubrations on the application of the "law Salique," would have given the same advice that Raphael Hythlodaeus, the chief speaker in St. Thomas More's satire *Utopia*, offers a fictitious King of France bent on conquering Italy: "Let him love his people and be loved by them, let him live among them, and govern them gently, and let him allow other kingdoms to thrive, since the one belonging to him now is large enough and then some."[25] And the evils of war are not merely theoretical in *Henry V*: one

---

24. Erasmus, *Institutio Principis Christiani*, 218: "Quam fugax quam breuis quam fragilis est hominum vita et quot obnoxia calamitatibus, quippe quam tot morbi tot casus impetunt assidue: ruinae naufragia terremotus fulmina. Nihil igitur opus belli accersere mala et tamen hinc plus malorum quam ex omnibus illis."
25. Sir Thomas More, *Utopia*, ed. Edward J. Surtz, SJ, and J. H. Hexter, in vol. 4 of *Complete Works of Thomas More*, ed. Richard Sylvester et al. (New Haven, Conn.: Yale University Press, 1965), 90: "Amet suos & ametur a suis, cum his una uiuat, imperetque suauiter, atque alia regna ualere sinat, quando id quod nunc ei contigisset, satis amplum superque esset."

need only consider such disquieting incidents as King Henry's threat of massacre and rapine to the citizens of Harfleur if he were forced to take the city by storm (3.3.1–43), or the mutual exchange of atrocities by the English and the French at Agincourt (4.7.1–65). As for the motivation for the conflict, it is perhaps best summed up by one of Hal's old tavern cronies, Pistol: "Let us to France, like horse-leeches, my boys, / To suck, to suck, the very blood to suck" (2.3.55–56).

It would be a mistake, however, to read the play simply as an antiwar satire, the very antithesis of Sir Laurence Olivier's 1944 film version, which is so heavily marked by World War II patriotism. John Alvis provides a useful caution:

> By introducing the witch's kitchen of *Realpolitik* in his opening scene, Shakespeare seems rather abruptly to deflate the expectations of high epic decorum voiced by the Chorus. However, when they take these ironies as definitive indications of Shakespeare's disapproval, Henry's critics may tell us more about their own political tenderness than about the tough-minded understanding of politics which characterizes the histories generally and the present play in particular. The ironies raise rather than settle questions, and to the extent that he is at all conscious of these obliquities, Henry might feel that they are exonerated by his situation.[26]

To be sure, Alvis proceeds to construct a detailed, and to my mind convincing, argument "that the testimony of the history plays inclines against the assumption that would approve the Chorus and Henry."[27] At this point, however, it is more to my purpose to leave the question to one side and turn to what might be called Hal's personal relationships. What makes Shakespeare a great poet and dramatist—a great creator of literary fictions rather than a political theorist—is that he embodies ideas about politics and morals (and everything else) in concrete situations

---

26. John Alvis, "A Little Touch of the Night in Harry: The Career of Henry Monmouth," in *Shakespeare as a Political Thinker*, ed. John Alvis and Thomas G. West (Durham, N.C.: Carolina Academic Press, 1981), 111.

27. Alvis, "Little Touch of the Night," 121.

peopled by individual characters, who seem so real and alive that we discuss them as if we knew them. One might even maintain that, in some ways, we do know them better than many of the actual men and women in our lives.

At the end of the first tavern scene in *1 Henry IV*, Hal is left alone on the stage for a soliloquy, and he apostrophizes Falstaff and his other departed drinking companions:

> I know you all, and will a while uphold
> The unyok'd humor of your idleness,
> Yet herein I will imitate the sun,
> Who doth permit the base contagious clouds
> To smother up his beauty from the world,
> That when he please again to be himself,
> Being wanted, he may be more wond'red at
> By breaking through the foul and ugly mists
> Of vapors that did seem to strangle him.
>
> So, when this loose behavior I throw off
> And pay the debt I never promised,
> By how much better than my word I am,
> By so much shall I falsify men's hopes,
> And like bright metal on a sullen ground,
> My reformation, glitt'ring o'er my fault,
> Shall show more goodly and attract more eyes
> Than that which hath no foil to set it off.
> I'll so offend, to make offense a skill,
> Redeeming time when men think least I will.
>
> (1.2.195–203, 208–17)

It is fairly easy to turn this speech into an allegory out of the tradition of the morality play: the sun imagery may suggest Christ, and Falstaff makes for a fairly plausible devil. Or one can see Hal following the advice of *The Boke Named the Gouernour* (1531) by the Tudor humanist, Sir Thomas Elyot:

But certes the very cause of decay, nor the true mean to cure it, may never be sufficiently known of gouernors, except they themselves will personally resort and peruse all parts of the countries under their governance, and insearch diligently as well what be the customs and manners of people good and bad, as also the commodities and discommodities, how the one may be preserved, the other suppressed, or at the leastways amended.[28]

Apart from the fact that Sir Thomas would undoubtedly have balked at the "governor" joining the knaves in their knavery for the sake of experience, there is finally a more pressing issue: Shakespeare will not allow his characters to be reduced to symbols or literary devices. Falstaff and his companions in the Boar's Head Tavern are certainly scoundrels, and Hal is certainly right to dismiss them from his company once he becomes King Henry V; nevertheless, they are also human beings, and Hal is using them as objects in an extremely callous fashion—largely for the purpose of creating a spectacle with himself at the center.[29] Indeed, the cold-blooded efficiency with which Hal goes about "doing the right thing" is among the more disturbing aspects of the second tetralogy. An extremely charming and witty man, there is also something in Hal of the ruthless egoism that we nowadays associate with celebrity entertainers and—more to the point—politicians.

And it is this personal element that Shakespeare never lets us forget that adds a sense of poignant reality to his mature dramas. Hal's great triumph in *1 Henry IV* is killing Hotspur on the battlefield at Shrewsbury, but our pleasure in the hero's triumph must be muted somewhat by a facet of the defeated Percy that Shakespeare did not find in Raphael Holinshed's *Chronicles* and made a point of adding: the tenderly comic and intimate scenes

---

28. Sir Thomas Elyot, *The Book Named the Governor*, 3.26, ed. S. E. Lehmberg (1907; repr. London: Dent, and New York: Dutton, 1962), 232. The connection has been noticed by Larry S. Champion, *Perspective in Shakespeare's English Histories* (Athens: University of Georgia Press, 1980), 116. Duke Vincentio going among the people in disguise as a friar in *Measure for Measure* is probably nearer what Elyot had in mind. The *locus classicus* is, of course, Haroun al Rashid, the eighth-century Caliph of Bagdhad.

29. See Alvis, "Little Touch of the Night," 95, passim.

between Hotspur and his wife, Kate. Shakespeare's invention of these scenes teaches us to know and take delight in the disconsolate widow left behind by Hal's victory, and this is all of a piece with the rejection of Falstaff, whom we have also enjoyed immensely. Robert Ornstein points out how favorably Hotspur's gentle teasing of Kate (2.3) compares with Hal's cruel baiting of the tapster Francis in the scene that follows immediately (2.4).[30]

The relationship between Kate and Hotspur also casts an ironic light forward onto the affectedly bumptious "wooing" scene (*Henry V* 5.2) between the triumphant Henry V and the French princess Katherine—also "Kate"—whose nuptial fate has already been decided by what in our day we call "the peace process." The irony deepens when this political marriage is set against Erasmus's general comment on such dynastic arrangements: "Meantime I shall say nothing about how altogether inhumanly in this way the girls are treated, who are often handed over to men who are completely unlike them in language, appearance, habits, and interests in distant inaccessible regions just as if they were in exile."[31] It is just because the fate of individual men and women never disappears from his view that Erasmus's political prescriptions are always touched by moral considerations—as are Shakespeare's.

These moral considerations are also quite complex, even perplexing, as we see with regard to Prince Hal, latterly King Henry V. We may doubt the sincerity of his going among the troops disguised as a common soldier on the eve of the battle of Agincourt in *Henry V* (4.1), if we recall the soliloquy in which he admits that he is merely shamming in the tavern; yet it remains a magnani-

---

30. Robert Ornstein, *A Kingdom for a Stage: The Achievement of Shakespeare's History Plays* (Cambridge, Mass.: Harvard University Press, 1972), 134. Tillyard, *Shakespeare's History Plays*, 274–77, mounts a remarkable display of casuistry in trying to excuse Hal's contemptuous treatment of Francis.

31. Erasmus, *Institutio Principis Christiani*, 209: "Vt ne dicam interim, quod hac via non admodum humaniter agitur cum ipsis puellis, quae nonnunquam in procul semotas regiones ad homines lingua specie moribus ingeniis dissimillimos velut in exilium relegantur."

mous gesture splendidly brought off. The speech to the bishops ostensibly requesting spiritual counsel is chillingly cynical, and yet Hal remains an engaging man whom most theatregoers like. It is a measure of Shakespeare's greatness and of the advance in his dramatic art between *Richard III* and *Henry V* that he can show us a man capable of remorseless Machiavellian calculation who is not, in the conventional Elizabethan sense, a "Machiavel."[32]

Is he, then, as the Chorus at the beginning of the second act maintains, "the mirror of all Christian kings"? As a possible answer I should suggest a "no" and a qualified "yes." He certainly fails to live up to the Erasmian prescription for a Christian prince; nevertheless, as Erasmus himself well knew, the idealized image he presented was a model to be emulated but rarely if ever attained by men of flesh and blood in real historical situations.[33] If we consider all the kings and would-be kings in Shakespeare's two tetralogies dealing with fifteenth-century English history, Henry Monmouth—Prince Hal—is probably the best of the lot as a ruler. It is the tragedy of the human condition that he may have done as much damage to the English commonwealth as men far worse than he in gifts and character.

There is no need to suppose that an explicit reference to Erasmus is an integral part of Shakespeare's dramatic treatment of English politics. The reforming humanism of which Erasmus was the chief exponent had long been assimilated to Tudor education and literary culture. A pre-Reformation Catholic presence thus functioned as a voice of conscience and ironic skepticism in a society that was growing increasingly nationalistic and self-consciously Protestant in the face of the militancy of Counter-Reformation Spain. *Henry V* was undoubtedly as much a spectacle of English patriotism to its original Elizabethan audiences as Olivier's film of the play was to the war-weary English

---

32. A. D. Nuttall, *A New Mimesis: Shakespeare and the Representation of Reality*, 2nd ed. (1983; repr. New Haven, Conn., and London: Yale University Press, 2007), 147, defines Prince Hal as a "White Machiavel."

33. See Jardine, "Introduction," in Erasmus, *Education of a Christian Prince*, xix–xx.

at the end of World War II; nagging questions about the triumphant King's character and methods, however, are evidence of the residual influence of Catholic humanism in the national consciousness, although the Catholic Church had been formally rejected. Despite the efforts of successive English governments to isolate Catholic recusants and banish them from the mainstream of English life, eventually with great effect, a Catholic presence perdured in the mind of Protestant England, because Catholicism was intrinsic to the Christian civilization out of which England grew. In this respect, the Catholic/Protestant tension of early modern England is analogous to the perennial tension within Western civilization as a whole between a reverence for tradition and a critical spirit that perpetually questions its own assumptions. As for the playwright himself, it is more rewarding to appreciate his ability to balance traditional Christian wisdom with a keen awareness of the questing mind of the Renaissance than to worry about his particular doctrinal orientation or religious practice at specific moments in his life. Such equipoise bespeaks a profoundly generous imagination or, in Dryden's words, his "comprehensive soul."

5

Freedom and Tyranny in *Julius Caesar* and *Hamlet*

In his brief treatise on the writing of letters, Justus Lipsius maintains that not only the style but also the content of a letter, especially a letter to a friend, ought to radiate simplicity: "As for the thought, I take it that a kind of simplicity and forthrightness should shine throughout the composition and disclose the special candor of a free mind."[1] Such a personally revealing comment in the midst of a work ostensibly aimed at youthful students indicates the manner in which "the pursuit of eloquence," in Hannah Gray's fine phrase, had begun to develop.[2] While it had always involved far more for Renaissance humanists than mere stylistic adornment, eloquence eventually began to constitute their sense of self and personal identity. As Lipsius adds, "For in nothing do the nature and individuality of anyone more clearly shine forth

---

1. Justus Lipsius, *Principles of Letter-Writing: A Bilingual Text of Justi Lipsi Epistolica Institutio* (1591), ed., trans. R. V. Young and M. Thomas Hester (Carbondale and Edwardsville: Southern Illinois University Press, 1996), 30–31: "At de Mente: ita intellego; ut simplex quiddam et ingenuum in tota scriptione eluceat, et aperiat candorem quemdam liberae mentis."

2. Hannah H. Gray, "Renaissance Humanism: The Pursuit of Eloquence," in *Renaissance Essays from the Journal of the History of Ideas*, ed. Paul Oskar Kristeller and P. P. Wiener (New York: Harper and Row, 1968), 199–216. See also Marc Fumaroli, "Rhetoric, Politics, and Society: From Italian Ciceronianism to French Classicism," in *Renaissance Eloquence: Studies in the Theory and Practice of Renaissance Rhetoric*, ed. James J. Murphy (Berkeley: University of California Press, 1983), 253–73.

...than in a letter."[3] The Flemish scholar thus furnishes an example of the increasing importance to many of the later humanists of private integrity as distinct from the political concerns and ambitions that were the preoccupation of the earlier generations of humanist scholars. By the end of the sixteenth century, disillusionment had arisen in the wake of the religious struggles of the Reformation: the great expectations of earlier generations for peaceful, enlightened reform of social and religious institutions driven by humanist learning and education no longer seemed probable.[4] Indeed, public engagement—marked by peril, caution, and secrecy—seemed subject to inevitable moral compromise. Sincerity, the "special candor of a free mind," is made possible by that liberty and liberality of thought that attaches to the private individual and his relations with kindred spirits.

Among the specifically tragic developments of a number of Shakespeare's mature tragedies is the threat to this "special candor of a free mind." The tragic heroes of *Julius Caesar* and *Hamlet*, both after their own fashion, find their freedom of mind—their candor as men of integrity—imperiled or impaired by an entanglement of one kind or another with tyranny. Even at its most overtly political, Shakespearean tragedy is concerned with the corruption of moral character, with the defilement of pure intentions, as much as with political institutions. While Shakespeare was fully aware of the power politics of his own day—of the means Queen Elizabeth used to maintain her shaky authority, of the clash between Parliamentary aspirations to independence and Stuart pretensions to royal absolutism—and shadows these

---

3. Lipsius, *Principles of Letter-Writing*, 30–31: "Nulla enim ex re magis natura cujusque et certa indoles elucet...quam ex epistola."

4. The classic work here is, of course, Hiram Haydn, *The Counter-Renaissance* (New York: Scribner's, 1950). On Lipsius's specific role, see R. V. Young, "Lipsius and Imitation as Educational Technique," in *Iustus Lipsius Europae Lumen et Columen: Supplementa Humanistica Lovaniensia* XV, ed. G. Tournoy, J. de Landtsheer, and J. Papy (Leuven: Leuven University Press, 1999): 268–80; and Young, "*Constantia Nos Armat*: Lipsius and the Trials of Constancy," in *Syntagmatia: Essays on Neo-Latin Literature in Honour of Monique Mund-Dopchie and Gilbert Tournoy*, ed. Dirk Sacré and Jan Papy (Leuven: Leuven University Press, 2009), 547–55.

contemporary issues by dramatizing the political conflicts of the past, what finally drives Shakespeare's tragic vision is the spiritual destiny of individual human beings. What is ultimately *tragic* about tyranny is less the use of force to suppress public or political freedom than the spiritual deterioration, the diminished mental candor, that afflicts not only tyrants and their supporters but also those who resist them.

An implication of this approach is that tragic possibilities lurk in political engagement as such, just insofar as the pursuit of political power inhibits rather than enhances more fundamental human goods of actual persons—goods that are prior to and more permanent than any particular political arrangement. The heart of Shakespearean tragedy thus escapes the intensely political formulations that dominate academic literary study nowadays, whether they sail under the flag of cultural materialism or new historicism, whether the pressing agenda are feminist or Marxist. By way of explaining cultural materialism, Jonathan Dollimore says, "'Materialism' is opposed to 'idealism': it insists that culture does not (cannot) transcend the material forces and relations of production." At the same time, he avers, "Cultural materialism does not pretend to political neutrality.... On the contrary, it registers its commitment to the transformation of a social order which exploits people on grounds of race, gender and class."[5] Jean Howard and Marion O'Connor likewise deprecate the notions "that Shakespeare depicts a universal and unchanging human nature," "that the meaning of a Shakespearean text is ineluctably *in* the text," and "that the Shakespearean text resides in an aesthetic zone above ideology." Howard and O'Connor also resemble Dollimore in urging that critics "*take a position on* ... the political uses of texts" and refrain from "laying claim to an Olympian disinterestedness."[6]

---

5. Jonathan Dollimore, "Foreword," in Dollimore and Sinfield, *Political Shakespeare*, viii.
6. Jean Howard and Marion O'Connor, "Introduction," in Howard and O'Connor, *Shakespeare Reproduced*, 4.

These are no longer even extreme expressions of the current received wisdom; any convention of the Modern Language Association or the Shakespeare Association of America would yield a bumper crop of similar pronouncements. The general viewpoint has become so routine that hardly anyone notices that it is self-contradictory and, more to the present point, incompatible with the basic virtues of Shakespearean drama, which treasures above all *disinterestedness* (though not of an "Olympian" kind) and a "zone above ideology" (though not necessarily an "aesthetic" zone). There is no small irony in the relentless campaign of the current managers of the academic "Shakespeare industry"—a campaign that resembles nothing so much as a "public relations blitz"—to manufacture a Shakespeare who resembles the most egregious villains of his own tragedies. To the contrary, there is no more distinctive feature of Shakespearean tragedy than its subtle depiction of the pitfalls of ideology, of the abandonment of disinterestedness, of "taking sides."

One of Shakespeare's earliest and most straightforward representations of the ideological threat to personal integrity in the pursuit of power comes in *Julius Caesar*. In excusing his recent coldness toward Cassius, Brutus, perhaps unconsciously, reveals the affliction that marks him throughout the play and defines his tragic fall:

> But let not therefore my good friends be griev'd
> (Among which number, Cassius, be you one),
> Nor construe any further my neglect,
> Than that poor Brutus, with himself at war,
> Forgets the shows of love to other men. (I.ii.43–47)

"The Tragedy of Poor Brutus, with Himself at War" could serve admirably as an alternate title for this play. Yet, while Schlegel is certainly right in the main that Brutus rather than Caesar himself is the central tragic figure,[7] it is important to take note

---

7. August Wilhelm von Schlegel, excerpt in *The Globe Illustrated Shakespeare*, ed. Howard Staunton (1979; repr. New York: Greenwich House, 1983), 1991.

of how Caesar likewise manifests an inner division with tragic consequences.

Our first sight of him at the beginning of the second scene is not promising: he appears with lordly mien among his entourage, dispensing commands and contemptuously dismissing the soothsayer who warns him, "Beware the Ides of March" (I.ii.18, 23). Mark Antony, the eager protégé, dances obsequious attendance: "When Caesar says, 'Do this,' it is perform'd" (I.ii.10). Further along in the same scene, however, this initial, less than edifying impression is both modified and reinforced. Caesar's perceptive assessment of Cassius reveals the shrewd political insight required for his rise to power and eminence: "Yond Cassius hath a lean and hungry look, / He thinks too much; such men are dangerous" (I.ii.194–95). Caesar's admonition contrasts pointedly with Antony's bland assumption that Cassius is "not dangerous," "a noble Roman, and well given" (196–97). Moreover, there is at least a hint of affection for Antony, howbeit patronizing, in the distinction Caesar draws between his follower and Cassius:

> Yet if my name were liable to fear,
> I do not know the man I should avoid
> So soon as that spare Cassius. He reads much,
> He is a great observer, and he looks
> Quite through the deeds of men. He loves no plays,
> As thou dost, Antony; he hears no music;
> Seldom he smiles, and smiles in such a sort
> As if he mock'd himself, and scorn'd his spirit
> That could be mov'd to smile at any thing.
> Such men as he be never at heart's ease
> Whiles they behold a greater than themselves,
> And therefore are they very dangerous.
> I rather tell thee what is to be fear'd
> Than what I fear; for always I am Caesar.
> Come on my right hand, for this ear is deaf,
> And tell me truly what thou think'st of him. (I.ii.198–214)

This speech displays both Caesar's prudent knowledge of other men and his diminishing knowledge of himself. Although he is perfectly aware of the threat posed by Cassius, the unique position of absolute political superiority that he has assumed requires him to feign an equally absolute moral superiority over other men. In modern parlance, Caesar has an image to maintain in order to sustain his preeminence; in order to convince others he must, in some measure, believe in his own divinity and is thus oblivious to the irony that gods do not age and go deaf. Decius Brutus instinctively recognizes the flaw of Caesar's susceptibility to flattery (II.i.202–11) and fulfills his promise to bring him to the Capitol on the fatal day despite Calpurnia's ominous dreams and Caesar's own misgivings (II.ii).

Caesar's most impressive appearance in the play comes after his assassination, toward the end of Act IV, as a ghost in Brutus's tent. When this apparition, which resembles Caesar,[8] identifies itself as "Thy evil spirit, Brutus" (IV.iii.282), it signifies the failure of the conspirators, who have murdered the man Julius Caesar, but not the political development that he symbolized. This outcome is the opposite of what Brutus had hoped, and he acknowledges as much as the republican cause falls apart in the final act:

> O Julius Caesar, thou are mighty yet!
> Thy spirit walks abroad, and turns our swords
> In our own proper entrails. (V.iii.94–96)

The pompous self-delusion that is so regrettable a feature of the character whom we see in the first three acts represents the degeneracy of a genuinely formidable and admirable man. That he has attained the loyalty of Antony, the friendship of Brutus, even the envy of Cassius—all witness to a man of extraordinary character and gifts. Caesar the man of worthy human qualities has sacrificed himself, however, to the quasi-divine image. Allan Bloom sums up the dilemma nicely:

---

8. The apparition is identified as "the Ghost of Caesar" in the First Folio stage direction and finally by Brutus in V.v.17.

Caesar required honor upon honor in order to live; universal empire was the fulfillment of his ambitions. Only the situation of a god could satisfy his thirst, and he did achieve this satisfaction—eternal fame and worship. But, humanly, he wanted the free and honest admiration of the best men of his time, and this he did not get. As a man, he was a failure; his tragedy is consummated in seeing the Roman senators—and particularly the most virtuous of them all, Brutus—he had so sedulously courted attack him. To be Caesar is no solution to the problem of leading a noble political life that is not tragic, not rooted in fundamental contradictions.[9]

By becoming a tyrant, Caesar has become incapable of friendship. Whatever one thinks of Mark Antony, it becomes obvious as soon as Caesar is dead that he is a capable man, not the cipher he appears as Caesar's client. The alienated Brutus joins the conspiracy because he sees the fundamental contradiction in Caesar: the man he counted a friend, for whom he still feels love, has become a tyrant in aspiring to honor beyond a man's lot. "O that we could come by Caesar's spirit," Brutus cries, "And not dismember Caesar!" (II.i.169–70). But as he ruefully admits on the field of Philippi, it is the spirit of tyranny that lives on after the death of the man Caesar. "The conspirators prevented Caesar from making the final error of allowing himself to be called king," says Allan Bloom epigrammatically. "Instead, they made it possible for kings to be honored to be called 'Caesar.'"[10]

Brutus sees the tragic contradiction in his friend Julius Caesar, but he fails to see a similar tragic flaw opening up as a moral abyss within himself. The play is tragic precisely because Brutus finds himself in a politically impossible situation, one "rooted in fundamental contradictions," as Bloom puts it, but one in which Brutus still feels compelled to act. He allows Cassius to convince him that the fate of Rome is completely in the hands of the individuals involved in the struggle to dominate her: "The fault, dear

---

9. Allan Bloom, "The Morality of the Pagan Hero: *Julius Caesar*," in Bloom and Jaffa, *Shakespeare's Politics*, 91.

10. Bloom, "Morality of the Pagan Hero."

Brutus, is not in our stars, / But in ourselves that we are underlings" (I.ii.140–41). But in a soliloquy Cassius reveals his disdain for the impassivity of Brutus's Stoic rationality:

> Well, Brutus, thou art noble; yet I see
> Thy honorable mettle may be wrought
> From that it is dispos'd; therefore it is meet
> That noble minds keep ever with their likes;
> For who so firm that cannot be seduc'd? (I.ii.308–12)

In mistaking Cassius for a true friend, a man who shares the same ideals of virtue and who can be trusted completely,[11] Brutus reveals the limitations of his own wisdom and insight. Cassius's profession of Epicureanism ought to have been a warning (V.i.76) that he would not share or even wholly respect Brutus's convictions. When Brutus explains his anger with Cassius by saying, "I am sick of many griefs," Cassius at first rather smugly reminds him of the failure of his Stoicism: "Of your philosophy you make no use, / If you give place to accidental evils"; but when Brutus discloses that the "grief" in question is the death of Portia, Cassius's conciliatory response suggests that he has no belief at all in the efficacy of philosophical principles to confront genuine sorrow: "How scap'd I killing when I cross'd you so? / O insupportable and touching loss!" (IV.iii.144–46, 150–51). Cassius may mean well, but he has no real sense of Brutus's interior life.

Brutus's mistake about Cassius is not so grave, however, as his mistake about his own motivations. At the very end of Act I, Casca and Cassius agree that it is absolutely necessary that Brutus be brought into their conspiracy to assassinate Caesar because

---

11. See Marcus Tullius Cicero, *De Amicitia* VI.20, in *Complete Works of Cicero* (Hastings, East Sussex: Delphi Classics, 2014), Kindle ed. loc. 148452: "Qui autem in virtute summum bonum ponunt, praeclare illi quidem, sed haec ipsa virtus amicitiam et gignit et continet, nec sine virtute amicitia esse ullo pacto potest"; and Lucius Annaeus Seneca, *Epistulae Morales* III.2, *Ad Lucilium Epistulae Morales*, ed. Richard Gummere (1912; repr. Cambridge, Mass.: Harvard University Press, 1989), 1:10: "Sed si aliquem amicum existimas, cui non tantundem credis quantum tibi, vehementer erras et non satis nosti vim verae amicitiae."

> He sits high in all the people's hearts;
> And that, which would appear offense in us,
> His countenance, like richest alchymy,
> Will change to virtue and to worthiness. (I.iii.157–60)

The opening of the next act, on the heels of these words, is pointedly ironic: in a soliloquy Brutus decides upon the murder of his friend Julius Caesar, although he admits, "for my part, / I know no personal cause to spurn at him" (II.i.10–11). It is Brutus's reputation for unblemished, disinterested virtue that makes his participation so crucial to the plot's success, but his determination to kill Caesar *without actual cause* calls the purity of that virtue into question:

> Th'abuse of greatness is when it disjoins
> Remorse from power; and to speak truth of Caesar,
> I have not known when his affections sway'd
> More than his reason. (II.i.18–21)

For our understanding of Brutus, his own deliberations are more important than any independent knowledge we may have or opinions we may form about Caesar's real nature.[12] Admitting that he has witnessed no concrete offense that should cost his friend his life, Brutus must substitute a political abstraction for a personal relationship in order to rationalize the murder:

> And since the quarrel
> Will bear no color for the thing he is,
> Fashion it thus: that what he is, augmented,
> Would run to these and these extremities;
> And therefore think him as a serpent's egg,
> Which, hatch'd, would as his kind grow mischievous,
> And kill him in the shell. (II.i.28–34)

---

12. Coleridge expresses bafflement at Brutus's exoneration of Julius Caesar's personal character and lists all the reasons a good republican would loathe Caesar, but Coleridge is mistaken in attempting to import the actual historical facts into a fictional representation of history; see Coleridge, *Coleridge's Writings on Shakespeare*, 244–45.

Katharine Eisaman Maus speculates, not altogether implausibly, that in the light of the "flattering messages" that Cassius has had thrown through his windows, "Brutus is swayed by a personal ambition of which he may not be entirely aware."[13] But the text of the play provides little evidence for this notion—indeed, it follows the same logic that Brutus applies to Caesar. What we see in Brutus is less a hypocrite than an ideologue.

Ideology is, fundamentally, a set of preconceptions about how the world ought to be that displace any genuine perception of the world itself. Brutus's conduct as a dominant partner in the conspiracy reflects just such a proclivity to substitute abstract notions for concrete realities, as well as a penchant for assuming that ordinary men and women do the same. It is Brutus who dissuades the other conspirators from including Cicero (II.i.150–52), who might well have strengthened their cause and who would at least have provided an orator to counter the rhetoric of Antony's funeral speech. Likewise, it is Brutus who—having agreed to the unjust assassination of Caesar—becomes scrupulous and fails to see that political exigency requires Antony's death as well. Even as Antony misjudges Cassius, so Brutus underestimates Antony. The latter, however, manifests the capacity to learn from experience, which is occluded for Brutus by ideological abstractions. This is never more apparent than in Brutus granting Antony permission to make, unsupervised, a highly rhetorical speech over Caesar's bleeding corpse. Brutus takes it for granted that the crowd, which has long idolized Caesar, will be reconciled to his murder by the recitation of a list of republican political principles. The contrast between Brutus's laconic prose and Antony's resonant blank verse tells practically the entire story. Finally, it is Brutus who insists that the republican forces march to Philippi and meet Antony and Octavian in battle

---

13. Katharine Eisaman Maus, introduction to *Julius Caesar*, in Greenblatt et al., *Norton Shakespeare*, 1,528.

without adequate preparation.[14] "There is a tide in the affairs of men," he admonishes Cassius,

> Which taken at the flood, leads on to fortune;
> Omitted, all the voyage of their life
> Is bound in shallows and in miseries. (IV.iii.218–21)

These stirring words are often quoted without attention to context, in which they indicate Brutus's impatience and unrealistic expectations and portend disaster.

But the most intense tragedy for Brutus is the deterioration of his personal life and character. Brutus rationalizes his involvement in the murder of Caesar by dehumanizing a man whom he has counted a friend, regarding him as a serpent in its egg. The result is immediate: toward the end of the long first scene of the second act, in which he makes his fateful decision and commits himself to the conspiracy, there is an exchange between Brutus and his wife, Portia, that reveals their growing estrangement. Portia demands of him precisely that he regard her not merely as a conventional wife of convenience, but as a friend, as someone to whom he will reveal his "forthrightness" and the "candor of a free mind":

> Within the bond of marriage, tell me, Brutus,
> Is it excepted I should know no secrets
> That appertain to you? Am I yourself
> But, as it were, in sort or limitation.
> To keep with you at meals, comfort your bed,
> And talk to you sometimes? Dwell I but in the suburbs
> Of your good pleasure? If it be no more,
> Portia is Brutus' harlot not his wife. (II.i.280–87)

Brutus, it would seem, has lost the gift of friendship, and he has difficulty rekindling it with his new comrade, Cassius.

"The contention and reconcilement of Brutus and Cassius,"

---

14. This entire paragraph has benefited from the analysis by Bloom, in "Morality of the Pagan Hero," 92–105.

writes Dr. Johnson, "is universally celebrated; but I have never been strongly agitated in perusing it and think it somewhat cold and unaffecting in comparison with some other of Shakespeare's plays."[15] The coldness is a result of a friendship based on dissimulation on the part of Cassius and misjudgment by Brutus; the "reconcilement" is more along the lines of patching up a quarrel, not really settling it. The immediate source of the quarrel is Brutus's complaint about Cassius over money:

> I did send to you
> For certain sums of gold, which you denied me;
> For I can raise no money by vile means.
> By heaven, I had rather coin my heart
> And drop my blood for drachmaes than to wring
> From the hard hands of peasants their vile trash
> By any indirection. I did send
> To you for gold to pay my legions,
> Which you denied me. (IV.iii.69–77)

"For I can raise no money by vile means"—this is the key line. Allan Bloom comments shrewdly, if perhaps too severely:

> Brutus himself is too good to squeeze the poor peasants. But he still needs the money, and he is perfectly willing to use Cassius' vice for his needs. He is unwilling to face the implications of his own situation and is forced into a rather ugly form of hypocrisy. Brutus remains pure by allowing others to perform the immoral acts which are the conditions of his purity. Then he can attack Cassius for being immoral.[16]

While it is difficult to deny any of the specifics of Bloom's indictment, it does not really do justice to Brutus's character. We are not inclined, after all, to sneer at Antony's final judgment of Brutus or regard it as cynical; when Antony addresses the corpse of Brutus, saying "This was the noblest Roman of them all" (V.v.68), he lacks the motive for deceit that animated him in his funeral

---

15. Johnson, *Samuel Johnson on Shakespeare*, 105–6.
16. Bloom and Jaffa, *Shakespeare's Politics*, 100.

speech for Caesar. What makes Brutus a *tragic* figure is precisely that he retains his nobility even as he fails to come to terms with "the implications of his own situation."

In this play, Julius Caesar represents the spirit of tyranny—of illicit, unchecked political power—and his ghost speaks truly in Brutus's tent when he identifies himself as "Thy evil spirit" (IV.iii.282). Antony correctly credits Brutus with acting without envy and "in a general honest thought / And common good to all" (V.iii.70–71), but his preoccupation with thwarting tyranny leads him to compromise his own principles in a dubious alliance with Cassius and to destroy authentic nonpolitical goods, his friendship with Caesar, and his marriage to Portia. In a letter to Cicero, written out of disillusionment over his hero's failings of pettiness and ambition, Petrarch pens words that may well be applied to Brutus: "Yet I do not demand anything in your life beyond constancy and the eagerness for quiet owed to the philosophical profession, and a withdrawal from civil strife once liberty is extinct and the Republic already buried and mourned."[17] Allan Bloom says that Brutus "is so completely a political man that he cannot conceive of a virtuous life which is not the life of a Roman senator,"[18] but the play *Julius Caesar* shows, above all, that the resources of politics are limited and political solutions often unavailable. Insistence upon a nonexistent political ideal leads Brutus into an abyss of futile and immoral political assassination and civil war; in more general terms it bespeaks a descent into ideology.

Shakespeare recognizes political futility as well as Petrarch and dramatizes this moral reality even more acutely in *Hamlet*, which draws additional depth from its Christian setting. From its opening line, "Who's there?," until its final catastrophe, the entire play broods upon the mystery of human identity, and its

---

17. *Familiarum reum libri* XXIV.4, *Opere*, ed. Mario Martelli (Firenze: Sansone Editore, 1975) I, 1252: "Neque tamen in vita tua quicquam preter constantiam requiro, et philosophicae professioni debitum quietis studium, et a civilibus bellis fugam, extincta libertate ac sepulta iam et complorata republica."

18. Bloom and Jaffa, *Shakespeare's Politics*, 95.

title character is in anguish over the candor and freedom of his mind, of his inner being. The action of the play arises out of the appearance of a ghost, whose nature, purpose, and provenance are of crucial concern to Hamlet:

> Be thou a spirit of health, or goblin damn'd,
> Bring with thee airs from heaven, or blasts from hell,
> Be thy intents wicked, or charitable,
> Thou com'st in such a questionable shape
> That I will speak to thee. (I.iv.40–44)

A pensive young man of saturnine wit, who asserts his personal integrity and yet questions his self-worth, who contemplates suicide and yet later entrusts himself to Providence—Hamlet is thrust into turmoil and forced to confront the soul's ultimate destiny by this confrontation with a mysterious emissary from another realm. The fundamental problem that the Prince confronts is how to maintain constancy—his sense of individual meaning and purpose—amidst threatening and morally doubtful political circumstances.

Thus among all Shakespeare's plays *Hamlet* most explicitly addresses the reductionist treatment of individual human identity that characterizes new historicism and cultural materialism. Oddly enough, *Hamlet* had taken a generally minor role in the scholarly production of literary materialists. As John Lee observed, "*Hamlet* ... plays the ghost in New Historicism's drama, but it is a ghost to which New Historicism has not spoken."[19] As fortune would have it, Lee's detailed critique of the New Historicism's neglect of *Hamlet* had hardly attained print in 2000, when Stephen Greenblatt published *Hamlet in Purgatory* the following year. This book calls for a brief consideration, because, even as it seems to challenge Lee's contention, closer inspection reveals that it confirms his negative assessment. In fact, Greenblatt's work epitomizes the incapacity of the materialist assumptions of

---

19. John Lee, *Shakespeare's "Hamlet" and the Controversies of Self* (Oxford: Clarendon, 2000), 51.

New Historicism to come to terms with literature as such. Much the same could be said about cultural materialism, except that it cheerfully accepts the admonition and takes it for praise.

Hamlet in Purgatory arrived on the crest of a wave of speculation regarding Shakespeare's Catholic boyhood and youth and its effects on his subsequent career.[20] A Catholic element in the play cannot be ignored, though numerous critics have tried, because there is no other explanation for the ghost of Hamlet's father except as a spirit come back from Purgatory, or at least as a spirit who claims in all but use of the word itself to have come back from Purgatory. Now Greenblatt exerts himself mightily to exhibit sympathy for the idea of Purgatory, or at least for the benighted souls who have believed in it, but he musters almost no understanding of the religious experience of the Communion of the Saints. After more than 250 pages, the Protestant view of Purgatory, which turns out to be the postmodernist view of literature, prevails:

> The Protestant attack on the "middle state of souls" and the middle place those souls inhabited destroyed this method for most people in England, but it did not destroy the longings and fears that Catholic doctrine had focused and exploited. Instead, as Gee [a Protestant polemicist] perceives, the space of Purgatory becomes the stage where old Hamlet's Ghost is doomed for a certain term to walk the night. That term has now lasted some four hundred years, and it has brought with it a cult of the dead that I and the readers of this book have been serving.[21]

In other words, Catholic beliefs and practices make for wonderful theatre—don't those Papists know how to put on a good show! What may be less apparent is the implication about the

---

20. See note 1 of chapter 4 for a representative sample of such works, which continued after the publication of *Hamlet in Purgatory*.

21. Greenblatt, *Hamlet in Purgatory*, 256–57. See the withering review of this book by William Kerrigan, *Ben Jonson Journal* 8 (2001): 385–90, who points out that "Greenblatt begins with the welcome admission that he has felt, and means to explain in some measure, the literary power of *Hamlet*" (385), but leaves us with the observation that "cultural poetics is here, as elsewhere, more cultural than poetic" (390).

play itself: Shakespeare's representation of the ghost in *Hamlet* is not a representation even of a phenomenon, much less of a reality; it is rather a representation of dramatic representation itself. For new historicism, as for deconstruction, there is no *hors de texte*. At least it is an equal-opportunity insult: literature and religion are both trivialized, since both are merely "theatrical."

Fortunately, Greenblatt does not exhaust the possibilities of making sense of *Hamlet's* purgatorial ghost. Anthony Low shows that Shakespeare makes a serious representation of Purgatory and dramatizes it as an issue in Reformation England. He also provides a portal into Prince Hamlet's soul and his anxiety about sincerity and integrity—a condition that seems to arise at least in part from the unsettled conditions of the fictional Danish court, which seems as religiously ambiguous as the Tudor court of Shakespeare's day. As Low points out, the ghost of old Hamlet demands revenge, but he also says, "remember me" (I.v.91). This injunction could be taken—would have been taken by Englishmen of an earlier generation—as a request for prayers, but the Prince seems oblivious. Acknowledging the peril of arguing from absence about Shakespeare's motive, Low adds,

> What we can say with greater certainty is that even though the Ghost plainly comes from Purgatory, and says so in terms as explicit as may be, short of an open declaration, neither Hamlet nor any of the younger Danes ever openly reveals that he has heard of such a place as Purgatory. As was the case in England, so in Hamlet's Denmark. Purgatory is not just abolished but effectively forgotten, as if it never were.[22]

This great occlusion in Hamlet's consciousness, his inability to come to terms with the situation of his father's soul, also marks

---

22. Anthony Low, "*Hamlet* and the Ghost of Purgatory: Intimations of Killing the Father," *English Literary Renaissance* 29 (1999): 458, 459. A revised version of this essay appears in Low's *Aspects of Subjectivity*, 98–128. Jan H. Blitz, *Deadly Thought: "Hamlet" and the Human Soul* (Lanham, Md.: Lexington, 2001), 1, also sees the religious tension in the play, but he assumes that it takes place "in the early sixteenth century," when "Denmark is still a Catholic country." Much as I admire many elements in this book, I am skeptical of Blitz's attempt to align the fictional world of *Hamlet* with specific historical realities.

an emptiness in the young man's own soul. Like Brutus, Hamlet is ensnared by a situation in which he feels compelled to confront tyranny; his moral and spiritual integrity is imperiled by his very efforts to deal with corruption: "The time is out of joint— O cursed spite, / That ever I was born to set it right!" (I.v.189).

When the Prince first appears in the second scene of Act I, he is visibly estranged from a court of which he does not approve, although he does not as yet have evidence—or even a suspicion— that his uncle is in fact a tyrant rather than merely a scoundrel. It is immediately clear to the audience, however, that Claudius is an accomplished politician, in both the Elizabethan and the contemporary sense of the term. A modern officeholder could learn a good deal about how to conduct a press conference from his rationalization of the blending of "mirth in funeral" with "dirge in marriage" (I.ii.12), which is a masterly piece of evasive rhetoric. Claudius appears to handle the crisis involving young Fortinbras with shrewd diplomacy and the petition of Laertes with aplomb. It is only the young Hamlet with his "inky cloak," ostentatious sighs, and grieving countenance who strikes a discordant note in the harmonious transfer of power from the deceased king to his brother. When both his mother and uncle accuse Hamlet of excessive mourning, his response is an assertion of sincerity and integrity that brings to mind the Lipsian ideal of the candor of a free mind: "I have that within which passes show" (I.ii.85). Noble as these words sound, they settle nothing. Jan Blitz notes that Hamlet severs the connection between "the internal and the external, the mind and actions, of a man. His identification of actions and playacting serves to deny the moral significance of actions as such."[23] Anthony Low provides an explanation: "When Hamlet's mother as well as his uncle accuses him of unusual excess in his grief, and therefore of dangerous impiety"—a viewpoint typical of Protestant sermons of the Tudor period—"he cannot grapple with the theological questions

---

23. Blitz, *Deadly Thought*, 55.

implied. Instead, he is driven inward, into the most famous of all early-modern gestures of radical individualist subjectivity."[24]

If we accept Low's thesis, that lying behind *Hamlet* is a cultural crisis of conscience occasioned by the Tudor abolition of Purgatory, then the anguished doubts and hesitations that beleaguer the Prince throughout much of the play show more consistency with his character and situation. Maynard Mack points out that from its opening scene, *Hamlet* "creates a world where uncertainties are of the essence," which stresses "the problematic nature of reality and the relation of reality to appearance."[25] Lying firmly at the base of this general haze of uncertainties, however, is the particular uncertainty of how to regard the dead. Elsinore implicitly seems to be a court that has moved from Catholicism to Protestantism between the death of old Hamlet and the accession of his brother. Discreetly declining to specify a clear analogue to the actual facts of history, Shakespeare succeeds in suggesting a situation that would be uncomfortably familiar to an Elizabeth audience. The new king has hastily and incestuously married his brother's widow, presumably for reasons of state. How could Shakespeare's audience *not* think of Henry VIII, the man who, in order to free himself from a marriage to his brother's widow, initiated the Reformation in England that outlawed prayers for the dead and confiscated the wealth of the institutions founded for the remembrance of departed souls? The resemblance is strengthened when this king promptly reproves his nephew and now stepson for dwelling impiously on his deceased father—an act of impiety only to someone who denies the existence of Purgatory and hence the efficacy of remembering the dead. And young Hamlet seems to be a part of this new, reformed world: surely it is no coincidence that he is a student at Wittenberg, Luther's university, and that he makes a punning reference to the Diet of Worms—"Your worm is your only emperor for diet" (III.iv.21)—after killing Polonius.

---

24. Low, "*Hamlet* and the Ghost of Purgatory," 463.
25. Mack, *Everybody's Shakespeare*, 111–12.

But the death of his father and the debauchery of his mother change everything. Hamlet exhibits a certain bravado in his scarcely veiled insults and defiance of Claudius and Gertrude, but his soliloquies reveal that what he has "within which passes show" are disillusion and despair:

> O that this too too sallied flesh would melt,
> Thaw, and resolve itself into a dew!
> Or that the Everlasting had not fix'd
> His canon 'gainst self-slaughter! O God, God,
> How weary, stale, flat, and unprofitable
> Seem to me all the uses of this world!
> Fie on't, ah fie! 'tis an unweeded garden
> That grows to seed, things rank and gross in nature
> Possess it merely. (I.ii.129–37)

The famous "To be, or not to be" speech, which likewise broods upon suicide, discloses a similar disgust with life and fearful bewilderment in the face of death. Life is the realm of the "slings and arrows of outrageous fortune," of the "whips and scorns of time," and a host of ills spelled out in morbid detail; but death is the realm of "dread," "The undiscover'd country, from whose bourn / No traveler returns," which "puzzles the will, / And makes us rather bear those ills we have, / Than fly to others that we know not of" (III.i.55–81). Beginning at least with Coleridge, critics have often wished to gloss over the inconsistency of this speech, which seems to deny the Prince's very recent encounter with the ghost of his dead father.[26] Inconsistency it surely is, but an inconsistency consistent with Hamlet's character and situation. The abolition of Purgatory has *made* death "an undiscover'd country" and explicitly denied the connection between the living and the dead that was so important in medieval Catholic piety.[27]

---

26. Coleridge, *Coleridge's Writings on Shakespeare*, 150. See also, e.g., the note on the passage by G. R. Hibbard, ed., in *Hamlet* (Oxford and New York: Oxford University Press, 1987), 241.

27. The most compelling work on this subject remains Duffy, *The Stripping of the Altars*.

Hamlet has simply reverted to his usual mode of thinking, a mode of thinking encouraged by the Tudor authorities of Reformation England, a mode of thinking that has become typical of the modern, secular world, a mode of thinking that discourages reflection upon death, a topic that "puzzles the will." The invasion of this world by a spirit from that nonexistent place, that "undiscover'd country," who takes leave of his son with the injunction, "remember me," is understandably an occasion for confusion and emotional turbulence, for inconsistency.

Like Brutus, Hamlet longs for Stoic mastery of himself. Such is the burden of his praise of Horatio: "Give me that man / That is not passion's slave, and I will wear him / In my heart's core, ay, in my heart of heart, / As I do thee" (III.ii.71–74). Likewise he is a man who has been recognized for his virtues, both an exemplar and an exponent of the humanist vision of excellence at its most optimistic. He expresses his disillusionment with this vision to Rosencrantz and Guildenstern: "What a piece of work is man, how noble in reason, how infinite in faculties, in form and moving, how express and admirable in action, how like an angel in apprehension, how like a god! the beauty of the world; the paragon of animals; and yet to me what is this quintessence of dust?" (II.ii.303–08). His lapse from the exemplary status he once held is manifest in Ophelia's lament over his apparent madness:

> O, what a noble mind is here o'erthrown!
> The courtier's, soldier's, scholar's, eye, tongue, sword,
> The expectation and rose of the fair state,
> The glass of fashion and the mould of form,
> Th' observ'd of all observers, quite, quite down!
>   (III.i.150–54)

In the face of the death of his father and the degradation of his mother, the self-assurance of courtly humanism and of Stoic rational autonomy has crumbled. With the suppression of participation in the Communion of the Saints made possible by the doctrine of Purgatory, there is nothing on which Hamlet may rely.

Cast adrift in "a sea of troubles," beset all around by a world of uncertainties, Hamlet enters into a deadly struggle of wits with Claudius; like Brutus, he attempts to defeat tyranny by its own means, in Hamlet's case by deviousness and deception, by staying one step ahead of a nimble adversary in a psychological guessing game. To his credit, Hamlet is not very adept at court intrigue; for that matter, he is not very adept at revenge. As Claudius recognizes and tells Laertes, as the two of them plot Hamlet's death in an ostensibly friendly fencing match, Hamlet "being remiss" will not check the foils because he is "most generous and free from all contriving" (IV.vii.134–35).

Like Brutus again, however, his innocence and honor are stained by the effort. In a remarkable sequence of events on the heels of his evidently successful "Mouse-trap" play, Hamlet demonstrates a total inability as a schemer and avenger—had he been in Prince Hal's place, Hotspur would probably have become king of England. Having been summoned by his mother, Hamlet comes upon Claudius at prayer and refrains from killing him lest his soul be saved, so Hamlet says, thus affording no true vengeance (III.iii.73–96). "This speech," writes Dr. Johnson, "in which Hamlet, represented as a virtuous character, is not content with taking blood for blood, but contrives damnation for the man he would punish, is too horrible to be read or to be uttered."[28] Now if we mistake Hamlet for Vindice of *The Revenger's Tragedy*, with his elaborate scheme and poisoned skull, Dr. Johnson has a point; but surely Coleridge is correct in finding here "the marks of reluctance and procrastination" rather than "impetuous, horror-striking fiendishness."[29] Hamlet is a "virtuous character" with a natural reluctance to stab a defenseless man in the back, but having sworn vengeance he must devise for himself a satisfactory explanation for his hesitation.

Shakespeare's sly parody of the blood-curdling features of the typical revenge tragedy, including his own *Titus Andronicus*,

28. Johnson, *Samuel Johnson on Shakespeare*, 111.
29. Coleridge, *Coleridge's Writings on Shakespeare*, 153.

is in no way inconsistent with Hamlet's impulsive stabbing of Polonius through the arras. Despite his own doubts about himself, Hamlet is quite courageous and capable of vigorous action when threatened. Not only does he strike out at what he takes to be Claudius behind the arras, but he also acts decisively in dispatching Rosencrantz and Guildenstern and taking advantage of the opportunity afforded by the pirates. But the result of his exertions is the pointless, unjust death of men who are at worst merely meddlesome (we have no reason to believe that any of them were in on the plot to kill the old king), indirectly the death of Ophelia, and eventually the death of her brother, Laertes, and Gertrude, as well as his intended victim, Claudius. Although Hamlet is wittier than Claudius, he has not outwitted him; the death of the fratricidal usurper is a result of the failure of his own machinations, not the success of Hamlet's.

There is of course a difference of enormous significance between the destinies of Brutus and Hamlet. Although Hamlet's "deep plots do pall," he still becomes the providential instrument of Claudius's punishment: "There's a divinity that shapes our ends, / Rough-hew them how we will" (V.ii.9–11). Most important, because Hamlet lives under the Christian dispensation, he grows in a knowledge that is closed to Brutus:

> There is special providence in the fall of a sparrow.
> if it be now, 'tis not to come; if it be not to come,
> it will be now; if it be not now, yet it will come—the
> readiness it all. (V.ii.219–22)

This is an anti-ideological conclusion to Hamlet's ideological efforts to avenge his father. Like Brutus, Hamlet faces the impossible political predicament of dealing with an apparently invincible tyranny, and, like Brutus, he attempts to confront the tyrant on his own political terms. The ghost warns his son, "Taint not thy mind" (I.v.85); the impossible task, however, leads to an inevitable taint: in his efforts to bring a murderer to heel Hamlet becomes, ironically, an indiscriminate killer. His acknowledgment of Providence prepares him for a far more hopeful death than Brutus suffers: Hamlet is concerned not only about his own reputation, in exhorting Horatio to "draw thy breath in pain / To tell my story" (V.ii.348–49), but also with the future of his country in giving Fortinbras his "dying voice" (V.ii.356).

But despite such gleams of affirmation, *Hamlet* remains tragic; its ending is ambiguous. Hamlet's admonition applies to critics as well as to Guildenstern: "You would pluck out the heart of my mystery" (III.ii.365); and we must accede to the force of his final words: "—the rest is silence" (V.ii.358). He dies with a great deal of bloodshed troubling his conscience—consider his extraordinary behavior at Ophelia's grave (V.i.218ff.) and his mention of his "conscience" twice within ten lines in the following scene. Although Hamlet claims that Rosencrantz and Guildenstern "are not near my conscience" (V.ii.58), his mother's words about the player queen apply here as well: he "doth protest too much" (III.ii.230). And Fortinbras is, at best, an unknown quantity: how optimistic should we be about the fate of Denmark in the hands of "a delicate and tender prince" whose spirit is, nonetheless, "with divine ambition puff'd" (IV.iv.48–49). Yet *Hamlet*, like all the great Shakespearean tragedies and unlike most Elizabethan revenge tragedies, ends with a sense of exultation. The "taint" in the candor of Hamlet's mind, the threat to his inner freedom, the sense that something precious had been damaged—all point to the existence of nobility. While it is true that "Something is rotten in the state of Denmark" (I.iv.90), rottenness implies a prior condition of wholeness and health. Hamlet is tainted by this rottenness, but, in the end, he seems to recover spiritually. He learns that the answer of a free mind to tyranny is not to imitate the violence and deceit of the tyrant, nor is it resignation. It is rather what he calls "readiness."

6

"Light Thickens"

Freedom and Tyranny
in *Macbeth*

As we have seen in chapter 5, the tragic heroes of *Julius Caesar* and *Hamlet* find their freedom of mind—their candor as men of integrity—imperiled or impaired by an entanglement of one kind or another with tyranny. Both Brutus and Hamlet are, to some extent, tainted by the tyranny of their antagonists, Caesar and Claudius, with whom they struggle. In the later play *Macbeth*, however, the perspective is reversed: the attention of the audience is more intimately concerned with the embodiment of tyranny himself; and, instead of witnessing the struggle of virtue to resist contamination by the vice it confronts, we observe with horror the utter deterioration of virtue and the protagonist's descent into an abyss of evil. The result is that the tyrant, who threatens the freedom and integrity of his subjects, destroys the freedom and candor of his own mind by enslaving himself to his passions. It is again apparent that in his mature drama, even at its most overtly political, Shakespeare is concerned with the corruption of moral character, with the defilement of pure intentions, as much as with political institutions.

The heart of Shakespearean theatre thus escapes the single-minded political preoccupations of every variety of postmodernism that dominates academic literary study nowadays. Nevertheless, the conception of literature as an exercise in power politics can have especially baneful results for the interpretation of a play such as *Macbeth* precisely because of its superficial plausibility. The tragedy is, after all, about politics. Stephen Orgel, for example, recommends the postmodernist power-politics interpretation of the play by pointing out that the playwright altered his historical sources in ways calculated to please King James I.[1] Orgel's assumption is not unreasonable, but to approach the play in this fashion is analogous to considering Velázquez's masterpiece *Las Meninas* in terms of its appeal to the painter's royal patron, an interesting enough inquiry in itself, but surely not a sound means of determining why the picture is counted among the glories of baroque art.

Orgel further maintains, however, that the playwright's undoubted deference to his sovereign fails to result in a play that ought, after careful consideration, to be agreeable to an advocate of submissive loyalty to royal power, because Duncan fails as a king:

> Duncan's rule is utterly chaotic, and maintaining it depends on constant warfare—the battle that opens the play, after all, is not an invasion, but a rebellion. Duncan's rule has never commanded the deference it claims for itself—deference is not natural to it. In upsetting the sense of deference Macbeth feels he owes to Duncan, maybe the witches are releasing into the play something the play both overtly denies and implicitly articulates: that there is no basis whatever for the values asserted on Duncan's behalf; that the primary characteristic of his rule, perhaps of any rule in the world of the play, is not order but rebellion.[2]

---

1. In fact, the only recorded production of the play was in the Globe in 1611, as witnessed and described by Simon Forman, who was later implicated in the murder of Sir Thomas Overbury and executed.

2. Stephen Orgel, "*Macbeth* and the Antic Round," in William Shakespeare, *Macbeth: A Norton Critical Edition*, ed. Robert S. Miola, 2nd ed. (New York and London: W. W. Norton, 2014), 258–59 [Kindle edition]. In his (mostly sensible) introduction to *Macbeth* in Shakespeare, *Norton Shakespeare*, Greenblatt also says, "Shakespeare may have set out to please the king, but it is difficult to see how the king, if he paid any attention to the tragedy that the King's Men offered him, could be reassured. The

As an account of the plot, this assessment is not strictly accurate, neglecting not only the consistency of Shakespeare's modifications of the historical sources of *Macbeth*, but also the religious and political context of the Jacobean era.

In the first place, there is no indication in the play that "Duncan's rule is utterly chaotic," that its maintenance requires constant warfare. So far as we can ascertain from the text of *Macbeth*, the attack upon Duncan's throne that opens the drama was not typical but an unexpected interruption of a peaceful reign of unspecified duration. Moreover, one of the rebels, "the merciless Macdonwald," drew upon mercenary help from Ireland (I.ii.9–15), and the second, "that most disloyal traitor, the Thane of Cawdor," is described as *assisting* an invasion by the King of Norway (I.ii.49–58). While Orgel's description of Duncan's situation in the play is thus simply wrong, it applies reasonably well to the account of the eleventh-century Duncan in Shakespeare's historical sources. Duncan was a much younger man of Macbeth's generation, and the latter had a fairly strong claim upon the crown. The historical Duncan was, in fact, an ineffectual ruler, who damaged his country by a series of military defeats. The Scottish thanes seem not to have been much troubled by Macbeth's assassination of Duncan and usurpation of the throne, because they regarded Macbeth as a just, competent king.[3]

Rather than trying to rewrite Shakespeare's tragedy according to the "real" history, it makes more sense to consider the significance of the substantial changes that the playwright made to the historians' record. Shakespeare's only plausible reason for making Duncan into an elderly, effective king respected,

---

ambiguities of demonic agency are never resolved, and its horror spreads like a mist through a murky landscape."

3. Bullough, *Narrative and Dramatic Sources of Shakespeare*, 7:432ff. Orgel and other new historicist commentators of the 1990s treat the discrepancies between the plot of *Macbeth* and the historical sources as a great revelation of contemporary theoretical scholarship, but the historical background has been known for centuries and, since Bullough's landmark compilation, easily available in moderate-sized university libraries for decades.

even revered, by all the other characters would be to darken the character of his murderers; and this is certainly the effect of the change on stage. To be sure, the sharp contrast between a tyrant and a good king would appeal to James I, since this was a principal theme of his treatise on monarchy, *Basilikon Doron*; and Duncan's excessive trust of Macdonwald and the Thane of Cawdor and subsequently of Macbeth would doubtless strengthen James's cautious measures against rebellion and assassination.

But a change more obviously aimed at pleasing his sovereign was Shakespeare's treatment of Banquo, who, according to the historical sources, was Macbeth's accomplice in Duncan's murder. Since the Stuarts traced their lineage back to Banquo, it behooved the playwright to convert him into a decent, loyal subject. Still, what is evidently an appeal for the King's continued patronage is also an effective dramatic device: like Macbeth, Banquo has also heard an ambiguous prophecy regarding his relation to the crown of Scotland; but unlike his comrade in arms, Banquo resists the temptation to assure that the prophecy will be fulfilled, trusting instead to Providence. Just as Shakespeare's modification of the historical character of Duncan sharpens the dramatic contrast between a good king and a tyrant, so the playwright's improvement of the character of Banquo emphasizes the difference between the integrity of a loyal subject and the deceit of a traitor.

While the pointed contrasts between Duncan and Macbeth, between Macbeth and Banquo, resulting from Shakespeare's revision of his sources, serve to remind us that we are dealing with drama, not historiography, these contrasts ought also to disabuse us of a more subtle misprision of the tragedy equally driven by the urge to reduce the play to terms amenable to postmodern ideology. Such is the motive of Stephen Orgel's attempt to judge Shakespeare's dramatic simplification of the tale of Macbeth against the "real Macbeth" of history. To drive his point home, Orgel invokes, finally, not history, but Edmund's invocation of Nature as a goddess in *King Lear*:

It is a Nature that is not the image of divine order, but one in which the strongest and the craftiest survive—and when they survive, they then go on to devise claims about Nature that justify their success, claims about hierarchies, natural law and order, and the divine right of kings. Edmund is a villain, but if he were ultimately successful he would be indistinguishable from the Duncans and Malcolms (and James I's) of Shakespeare's world.[4]

As I have pointed out elsewhere, postmodernist interpretations of Shakespeare take a contrarian approach to his plays because, for the most part, they share the moral and political views of his villains.[5] In order to recruit Shakespeare to their party, however, it is necessary to dismantle the careful distinctions among his characters that are the source of his vibrant moral realism.

Orgel offers no evidence, for example, that a successful Edmund would be no different from Duncan or Malcolm: Edmund's counterpart in *Macbeth*, the eponymous villain, institutes a reign of terror, which Duncan had not done, and which Malcolm shows no signs of doing. Hence the preoccupation with the historical Macbeth, who was, ostensibly, an effective ruler with as good a claim to the throne as Duncan. Even so, he *did* murder Duncan and perpetuate the cycle of violence that too often attended transitions of power in medieval Scotland. While the theme of governmental stability provided by the institution of hereditary monarchy would, doubtless, appeal to King James, it is not, therefore, a negligible or contemptible theme. Examples of the perils of uncertain measures for moving from one regime to the next abound in our time.

But Shakespeare is keenly interested not in the institutional procedures of government, but in the character of men and women. The dramatic thrust of *Macbeth* depends upon the audience's experience of the disintegration of the usurper's character in contrast to men who maintain their loyalty and integrity. At the

---

4. Orgel, "*Macbeth* and the Antic Round," 260.
5. Young, *At War with the Word*, esp. chapter 4, "The New Historicism and the Will to Power," 85–114.

very beginning of the tragedy, a "bleeding Sergeant" describes for Duncan and his attendants how "brave Macbeth" encountered "the merciless Macdonwald" and "unseam'd him from the nave to the chaps" (I.ii.21–26). It's just as well that action takes place offstage. Macduff's killing of Macbeth at the play's conclusion likewise takes place offstage, but the victor brings the head of the vanquished tyrant onstage to the acclaim of Malcolm and his supporters. Both of these slayings are grisly, violent acts that would elicit a shudder in most of us; but unless they are accepted as works of valorous patriotism, essentially different from Macbeth's killing of Duncan and his contriving the murders of Banquo and the wife and children of Macduff, the play is rendered meaningless.

Such, however, is the point of postmodern interpretations. An unvarnished assertion of the moral equivalence of these various killings is nonetheless difficult to sustain, so the usual ploy is to digress deep into the weeds of ideological irrelevance. Stephen Orgel, for instance, leads us on a puzzling excursion into the characters of Macduff and Malcolm as he assays the scene in England in which the former seeks to persuade Duncan's exiled son to lead the discontented Scots in a campaign to overthrow Macbeth (IV.iii). Malcolm at first suggests that Macduff may intend to entrap and betray the rightful heir on behalf of "the tyrant." Next Malcolm condemns himself as lustful, avaricious, and utterly devoid of virtue. At this point, Macduff throws up his hands in despair. It is only then, when he has tested Macduff's virtue, discretion, and resolve, that Malcolm denies his self-condemnation and accepts Macduff's offer to lead a military campaign against Macbeth:

>   I am yet
> Unknown to woman, never was forsworn,
> Scarcely have coveted what was mine own;
> At no time broke my faith, would not betray
> The devil to his fellow, and delight

> No less in truth than life; my first false speaking
> Was this upon myself. (142–48)

This is a powerfully moving and edifying scene in which a young, inexperienced man in an equivocal, perilous situation carefully assesses what seems an emissary of hope with understandable caution. As Malcolm reminds Macduff, "This tyrant, whose sole name blisters our tongues, / Was once thought honest: you have lov'd him well" (16–17). Here is what Stephen Orgel makes of this interchange:

> Why is it so important ... at the end of the play, that Malcolm is a virgin? Malcolm insists that he is utterly pure, "as yet / Unknown to woman" (4.3.126–27), uncontaminated by heterosexuality—this is offered as the first of his qualifications for displacing and succeeding Macbeth. Perhaps this bears too on the really big unanswered question about Macduff: why he left his family unprotected when he went to seek Malcolm in England—this is what makes Malcolm mistrust him so deeply.

Orgel answers this innuendo with an insinuating rhetorical question:

> It really is an astonishingly male-oriented and misogynistic play, especially at the end, when there are simply no women left, not even the witches, and the restored commonwealth is a world of heroic soldiers. Is the answer to Malcolm's question about why Macduff left his family, "Because it's *you* I really love"?[6]

We might begin to answer these questions with a couple of common-sense observations; first, that the absence of women in the play's final scene is not evidence of misogyny but of the fact that women were not usually active on battlefields in eleventh-century Scotland; and, second, that Shakespeare probably kept the number of women's parts in all of his plays to a minimum, because the stage conventions of the era required that they be

---

6. Orgel, "*Macbeth* and the Antic Round," 264–65.

played by boys, who may have been hard to recruit and had the notorious habit of growing up into men with beards and deep voices.

Whatever the motivations of Orgel and the numerous others who have read "feminist" and "gender" issues into *Macbeth*, the actual effect of their ruminations is to obscure the obvious significance of the tragedy's treatment of character. Macduff does, to be sure, imprudently leave his wife and children unprotected in Scotland, and Malcolm does mention it as a possible indication that Macduff is deceitfully in league with Macbeth. Nevertheless, the implied inference that Macduff's intention was that his family be butchered in order to free himself from any inhibition to express his passion for Malcolm seems a trifle far-fetched. A more plausible explanation for Macduff's lapse in judgment is that as yet it had not occurred to him that even Macbeth was so depraved as to murder undefended women and children. This view has the additional virtue of dovetailing with the central theme of the tragedy: the deterioration of a man's character, the perdition of his soul, the besmirching of "the special candor of a free mind."

It is candor that endows the testing scene between Macduff and Malcolm with such poignancy. Both the youthful Malcolm and the veteran warrior Macduff are, in their differing ways, sincere, even ingenuous, men. Each wishes desperately to believe in the sincerity of the other, but, as Malcolm admonishes Macduff, Macbeth "was once thought honest," a remark that looks back tellingly on Duncan's observation about the disgraced Thane of Cawdor:

> There's no art
> To find the mind's construction in the face:
> He was a gentleman on whom I built
> An absolute trust. (I.iv.15–18)

When Duncan is again deceived in the "absolute trust" that he proceeds to "build" on Macbeth, postmodern critics find a rationale for maintaining that no one can be trusted, that power is everyone's only motivation, that there is no difference between Edmund and Malcolm, between Macbeth and Macduff—and that they are all representations of James I.

Millicent Bell argues that *Macbeth*, like Shakespeare's other tragedies, embodies an absolute skepticism, which the playwright derives from Montaigne, undermining not only the stability of human nature, but even the consistency of individual human identity:

> The play invites a glance at the void over one's shoulder, challenging skeptically those conventions that govern our negotiations with reality—those fictions without which we cannot live. I am reminded, as I have been before, of Montaigne's insistent denial of the constancy—even the reality—of human character.[7]

Similarly, she maintains, "What kind of king Malcolm could prove in the future beyond the play remains an open question."[8]

But a play is a self-contained world; as a dramatic character, Malcolm has no "future beyond the play." Bell is leading us into such questions as "How many children had Lady Macbeth?" Further, her skeptical deconstruction of Shakespeare's characters essentially undermines the notion of tragedy, which requires conflict not only *between* characters, but also *within* the protagonist. There can be no conflict, however, within a character lacking minimal consistency. In classical tragedy, the protagonist is confronted with intractable fate: an ineluctable, external force drives him into an abyss that conflicts with his concept of himself. In Shakespeare's essentially Christian tragedy, the conflict is between the protagonist's knowledge of what he ought to be and what his sinful will desires. The moral deterioration of a man's character requires, in either case, the existence of a consistent

---

7. Bell, *Shakespeare's Tragic Skepticism*, 206.
8. Bell, *Shakespeare's Tragic Skepticism*, 232. For the "complexity and coherence" of Shakespearean characters as well as of Montaigne's view of human nature, see Ellrodt, *Montaigne et Shakespeare*; English version by the author: *Montaigne and Shakespeare*. In the latter version see esp. 108, 110, 144–72.

self that is vulnerable to ruin, and the process is nowhere better exemplified than in *Macbeth*.

Hence postmodern skepticism, which reduces all characters to common incoherence, grotesquely oversimplifies the play. As Malcolm tells Macduff, in the crucial scene that we have been considering:

> Angels are bright still, though the brightest fell;
> Though all things foul would wear the brows of grace,
> Yet grace would still look so. (IV.iii.27–29)

Macbeth is thus a tragedy of the spiritual contingency of human life, and Shakespeare's alterations to Scottish history are designed to highlight the contrasts that result from the divergent decisions men make confronting the crises of their lives. While the elevating of the characters of Duncan and Banquo may have pleased King James, the dramatic effect of the changes is to provide a context of normal, decent behavior for Macbeth's moral and spiritual deterioration.

The prospect of royal honor is suggested to both Macbeth and Banquo by the witches on the heath, but the ultimate responses of these two men are strikingly different. Both are, quite naturally, puzzled, disturbed, and fascinated; and there is nothing that we learn about the pair as they are described by their king and their comrades in arms that would indicate that either of them would succumb to the demonic suggestion that Duncan's crown might be seized through treason and murder. It is evident that Shakespeare has designed the tragedy with the aim of highlighting the dissimilar choices that two similar and similarly circumstanced men make in the face of similar temptations.

The contrast begins as soon as Macbeth and Banquo learn that one of the witches' prophecies has come true, that the former has in fact been named Thane of Cawdor. "What, can the devil speak true?" Banquo exclaims (I.iii.107); and as soon as the new title is explained, he admonishes Macbeth:

> That, trusted home,
> Might yet enkindle you unto the crown,
> Besides the Thane of Cawdor. But 'tis strange;
> And oftentimes, to win us to our harm,
> The instruments of darkness tell us truths,
> Win us with honest trifles, to betray's
> In deepest consequence. (I.iii.120–26)

In an aside, however, while he is, in Banquo's word, "rapt," Macbeth has already begun to rationalize an inclination that he knows intuitively to be evil:

> This supernatural soliciting
> Cannot be ill; cannot be good. If ill,
> Why hath it given me earnest of success,
> Commencing in a truth? I am Thane of Cawdor.
> If good, why do I yield to that suggestion
> Whose horrid image doth unfix my hair
> And make my seated heart knock at my ribs
> Against the use of nature? (I.iii.130–37)

Notice the trifling argument that a proposition that is factual is, therefore, "good." Our Lord warns us that to harbor lust in our heart is tantamount to adultery; to nurse anger is morally no different than murder. Macbeth is here analogous to a man who has been aroused by the allure of another man's wife and fantasizes about committing adultery with her.

The powerful final scene of Act I (vii), in which Lady Macbeth urges her husband to hasten the diabolical prophecy's fulfillment, reveals that his acquiescence in the murder violates his natural inclination and his better judgment. Before she enters, he admits to himself that he has "no spur / To prick the sides of my intent, but only / Vaulting ambition, which o'erleaps itself" (I.vii.25–27). In laboring to overcome his reluctance to commit murder, his wife does not refute his argument; she challenges his masculinity:

> From this time
> Such I account thy love. Art thou afeard
> To be the same in thine own act and valor
> As thou art in desire? (I.vii.38–41)

Macbeth succumbs to her sexual taunting, but, as Dr. Johnson pointed out two and a half centuries ago, he knows better, "distinguishing true from false fortitude, in a line and a half"[9]: "I dare do all that may become a man, / Who dares do more, is none" (I.vii.46–47).

Having chosen to commit murder despite his moral reason, Macbeth still has natural qualms against the deed. The phantasmal dagger that he sees before him as he enters Duncan's bedchamber and his admission to his wife after he has committed the murder that he could not utter "Amen" when one of the sleeping grooms cried out "God bless us!" are indications of his revulsion against what he is doing. But Lady Macbeth also discloses her own inhibitions in saying, "Had he [Duncan] not resembled / My father as he slept, I had done't" (II.ii12–13). It seems that her invocation of the "spirits that tend on mortal thoughts" to "unsex" her and to infuse her "with direst cruelty" (I.v.38–54) and her boast that she would dash her nursing baby's brains against a wall before relinquishing her ambition (Ivii.54–59) are mostly bravado. Both killers have to overcome reason and repugnance to killing in order to carry out the assassination. What we ought to see in this inner conflict is a man and woman deliberately struggling to destroy their human nature.

Their willful dehumanization is, moreover, a result of a lack of faith. Millicent Bell is typical of contemporary critical opinion in asserting that "Shakespeare's play is sparing of religious reference,"[10] but this assertion is difficult to sustain. Macbeth's

---

9. Johnson, *Samuel Johnson on Shakespeare*, 102.
10. Bell, *Shakespeare's Tragic Skepticism*, 232. On the next page Bell says that Macbeth's speech about pity (I.vii.16–28) is "drenched in the imagery of religious revelation" but denies its religious significance. Similarly, she says, "In *Macbeth* [Shakespeare] invoked the most ancient and the most persistent dramatic idea in

incapacity to utter "amen" ought to recall an often overlooked remark as he ruminates over the King's murder:

> If it were done, when it is done, then 'twere well
> It were done quickly. If th'assassination
> Could trammel up the consequence, and catch
> With his surcease, success; that but this blow
> Might be the be-all and the end-all—here,
> But here upon this bank and shoal of time,
> We'ld jump the life to come. (I.vii.1–7)

Shakespeare's tragic protagonist pointedly considers "the life to come" and rejects it with Machiavellian insouciance; nevertheless, at the end of the speech, when Macbeth takes into account Duncan's goodness and all he owes him, his language betrays an explicitly Christian sense of the evil he is planning despite his earlier disclaimer:

> Besides, this Duncan
> Hath borne his faculties so meek, hath been
> So clear in his great office, that his virtues
> Will plead like angels, trumpet-tongu'd, against
> The deep damnation of his taking off;
> And pity, like a naked new-born babe,
> Striding the blast, or heaven's cherubin, hors'd
> Upon the sightless couriers of the air,
> Shall blow the horrid deed in every eye,
> That tears shall drown the wind. (I.vii.16–25)

It is difficult to conceive a purpose for this speech if not to apprise the audience of the intrinsically spiritual nature of Macbeth's inner conflict.

It is a commonplace of *Macbeth* commentary that the play is filled with images of darkness beyond any of Shakespeare's other works, but it ought to be noted as well that the protago-

---

the theatrical tradition, the idea that life is a contest between heavenly and demonic forces—and drains this idea of conviction." She makes no compelling argument for this claim.

nist and his wife are largely responsible for this imagery through their repeated invocation of darkness to hide their deeds. "Stars, hide your fires, / Let not the light see my black and deep desires" (I.iv.50–51), Macbeth cries upon hearing Duncan name his son Malcolm heir apparent. In the next scene, as Lady Macbeth is determining to strengthen her husband's resolve, she, too, calls upon the explicitly infernal powers of darkness:

> Come, thick night,
> And pall thee in the dunnest smoke of hell,
> That my keen knife see not the wound it makes,
> Nor heaven peep through the blanket of the dark
> To cry, "Hold, hold!" (I.v.50–54)

Even a casual perusal of the play will turn up a number of additional instances of their sinister supplication of the powers of night, and a modest acquaintance with the Christian scriptures will supply an even more plenteous array of passages associating darkness and night with sin, day and light with grace and virtue, as, for instance John 3.19: "And this is the judgment, that the light is come into the world, and men loved darkness rather than light, because their deeds were evil."[11]

The culmination of this imagery comes at what may be the tragedy's climactic scene, when Macbeth seizes the initiative from his wife and determines to do away with both Banquo and his son Fleance in order to thwart the witches' prophecy that Banquo's descendants will reign in the future:

> Come, seeling night,
> Scarf up the tender eye of pitiful day,
> And with thy bloody and invisible hand
> Cancel and tear to pieces the great bond
> Which keeps me pale. Light thickens, and the crow
> Makes wing to th' rooky wood;
> Good things of day begin to droop and drowse,

---

11. In *Macbeth* see, e.g., II.i.49–56, II.iii.54–61, II.iv.10–13 IV.i.48; for the New Testament see, e.g., Mt 4:13, Lk 11:34–36, Jn 8:12, Rom 13:12, Eph. 5:8–11, 1 Pt 2:9.

> Whiles night's black agents to their preys do rouse.
> Thou marvel'st at my words, but hold thee still:
> Things bad begun make strong themselves by ill.
> (III.ii.45–55)

"Light thickens." One editor glosses "thickens" as "dims";[12] this is accurate, but hardly adequate to convey the full horror of the phrase. It is as if the light itself were curdling and losing its luster; or "night's black agents" have succeeded in making "the good things of day" their prey. Macbeth has begun to see the night as the embodiment of the dark powers arrayed in his favor. Evil, he suggests, strengthens itself by repeated and intensified acts of evil.

At first nonplussed by the prophecies of the bearded "weird sisters" regarding his fate, Macbeth now tries to take hold of fate and manipulate it to his own advantage—a surpassingly irrational act. Having attained everything the witches have promised him, thus persuaded of their perspicacity, he is hardly consistent in thinking he can undo their promise to Banquo. When Fleance eludes the clutches of the hired assassins, the fruits of Macbeth's foul deeds turn to ash in his mouth. He has only just learned of the boy's escape, when the specter of Banquo appears at the banquet for the thanes and, in Macbeth's words, shakes his "gory locks" at him. Having gained his crown by murder, Macbeth has unleashed a reign of death. "If charnel-house and our graves," he exclaims, "must send / Those that we bury back, our monuments / Shall be the maws of kites" (III.iv.50, 70–72).

The new king and queen thought that supreme power would be the same as absolute freedom, but that is because they have never learned that true freedom is internal: *the special candor of a free mind*. Lady Macbeth cannot escape the imaginary blood stains on her hands and eventually takes her own life. Macbeth himself is trapped in the meaningless world that his tyranny has created, and he is increasingly isolated in the final two acts of the

---

12. Miola, *Macbeth: A Norton Critical Edition*, 41n49.

play. In a remark that reminds us of the practices of repressive governments in our day, Macbeth boasts that he spies on all his thanes: "There's not a one of them but in his house / I keep a servant fee'd" (III.iv.130–31); but Macduff still manages to steal away to England to seek help against the usurper. Macbeth, now dependent on their dubious counsel, returns again to the weird sisters, who will befuddle him with duplicitous ambiguities about moving forests and men not borne of women. Illegitimate power, he learns, enslaves its possessor: "I am in blood / Stepp'd in so far that, should I wade no more, / Returning is as tedious as go o'er" (III.iv.135–37). At the play's beginning he could choose between taking the forbidden fruit proffered by the witches or retaining his loyalty and virtue. Now, however, he feels that he acts under compulsion—"The very firstlings of my heart," he vows, "shall be / The firstlings of my hand" (IV.i.147–48). The result is the senseless slaughter of Macduff's wife and children, which brings down upon their killer the wrath of a man not born of woman.

Macbeth dies spiritually, however, before Macduff presents his severed head to the restored Malcolm. The tyrant has created his own hell on earth, which he expounds in the tragedy's most famous speech, delivered with a shrug of indifference upon the news of Lady Macbeth's death:

> To-morrow, and to-morrow, and to-morrow,
> Creeps in this petty pace from day to day,
> To the last syllable of recorded time;
> And all our yesterdays have lighted fools
> The way to dusty death. Out, out, brief candle!
> Life's but a walking shadow, a poor player,
> That struts and frets his hour upon the stage,
> And then is heard no more. It is a tale
> Told by an idiot, full of sound and fury,
> Signifying nothing. (V.v.19–28)

Such is the world that the character Macbeth has devised for himself, but it is not, despite much recent commentary, the world of the tragedy *Macbeth* devised by William Shakespeare. That thesis can only be maintained by smuggling in elements that are no part of the dramatic work: for example, the "real" history upon which the playwright drew for character and incident or unwarranted conjectures about the behavior of characters after the action of the play closes. It appears that many contemporary scholars share the grim view of life to which Macbeth is reduced—"It is a tale / Told by an idiot"—and are determined to foist it upon Shakespeare by confusing Holingshed's historical Duncan with the king in the tragedy or presuming that Malcolm will be as bad a king as Macbeth, or that Macduff, who shows such "violence" in dispatching the usurper, will turn usurper himself and assail Malcolm.

But to accept this nihilistic world as the world of Shakespeare's play is to deprive it of its status as a tragedy. Macbeth is a *tragic* figure only because he is in conflict with an order that transcends his own "devices and desires." If there are no moral distinctions to be made among the characters, if Macbeth is really no worse than the rest, then no *tragedy* is possible. He is tragic because, attempting to overturn the divinely ordained reality of the world that actually exists, he engineers a realm of meaningless chaos.[13] Shakespeare has thus derived from a seemingly random selection of historical details from an obscure period in Scottish history a parable of human pride, folly, and ambition disrupting the natural order of human life, but also the restoration of that order by the violent death of the tragic protagonist. In some ways Shakespeare's darkest and grimmest tragedy, in its dénouement *Macbeth* is the most hopeful.

---

13. See Mack, *Everybody's Shakespeare*, 190: "We are asked to sense that his crime is not simply a misdeed in the secular political society of a given time and place, but simultaneously a rupture in some dimly apprehended ultimate scheme of things where our material world of evil *versus* good and virtue *versus* vice gives way to a spiritual world of sin *versus* grace and hell *versus* heaven."

7

Hope and Despair in *King Lear*

The Gospel and the Crisis of Natural Law

King Lear has long been regarded as one of Shakespeare's greatest plays and is not infrequently judged to be the finest specimen of the Western dramatic tradition. Nevertheless, it has also been viewed as problematic both morally and aesthetically. The most powerful example of the discomfort caused by the play among audiences and critics is the revision by Nahum Tate, which has Cordelia surviving and marrying Edgar. This version was the basis of every theatrical production of *King Lear* from 1681 until 1838, and it was endorsed by no less a figure than Dr. Johnson:

> In the present case the public has decided. Cordelia, from the time of Tate, has always retired with victory and felicity. And, if my sensations could add anything to the general suffrage, I might relate, I was many years ago so shocked by Cordelia's death that I know not whether I ever endured to read again the last scenes of the play till I undertook to revise them as an editor.[1]

While a twenty-first-century revival of Tate's rewriting of Shakespeare is improbable and would be unlikely to find favor, at least

---

1. Johnson, *Johnson on Shakespeare*, 98.

among professional scholars and critics, Johnson's demurrer and the theatrical taste of more than a century and a half must not be lightly dismissed. Sharp disagreements over the import of the play's grim conclusion throughout the twentieth century and persisting even to the present are evidence of how terrible that ending seems even to the most cynical and sophisticated of readers and audiences.

Interpreters have generally sought to show either that the tragic close evinces a redemptive possibility, notwithstanding its horror, or that Tate was right—that *King Lear* in fact subverts a Christian or even Enlightenment worldview and anticipates the absurd universe of existentialism or postmodern materialism. The redemptive readings, which dominated the middle of the twentieth century, often seem to assume that the close of a Christian tragedy must be marked by an explicit affirmation of the human efforts of the more sympathetic characters. The relationship between Christian redemption and natural law, a theme obviously emphasized in the play, is regarded as unproblematic. The anti-Christian readings, which have predominated over the past four decades, have concentrated on refuting this "optimistic Christian" reading. This chapter is designed to show that "Christian Optimism," although promulgated by some "Christian" critics, reflects a misunderstanding of Christianity, which is not an optimistic religion, and that natural law and the meaning of "nature" are critical themes in *King Lear* because their relation to grace was a contested concept at the turn of the seventeenth century. Regarded in this perspective, *King Lear* may be understood as a profoundly Christian vision of human reality unfolding in a decidedly non-Christian setting among pagan characters. The play thus provides one of Shakespeare's most insightful embodiments of the paradoxical vision of reality that shapes Western civilization.

What might be called the *affirmative* view of the ending of *King Lear* goes back at least to some manuscript notes of Coleridge: "The affecting return of Lear to reason and the mild pathos preparing the mind for the last sad yet sweet consolation of his death."[2] In *A Study of Shakespeare* (1880), Swinburne countered by suggesting that the import of *King Lear* is summed up in the despair of the blinded Gloucester: "'As flies to wanton boys are we to the gods; / They kill us for their sport'. . . . the words just cited," Swinburne remarks, "are not causal or episodical; they strike the keynote of the whole poem, lay the keystone of the whole arch of thought."[3] A. C Bradley's *Shakespearean Tragedy* (1904), a work that would influence everyone who approached the subject for decades to come, qualifies Swinburne's "pessimistic" reading (see 228–30) by remarking that the tragedy "presents the world as a place where heavenly good grows side by side with evil, where extreme evil cannot long endure, and where all that survives the storm is good, if not great" (271–72). Bradley even suggests that we might as justly refer to the play as *"The Redemption of King Lear"* as accept Swinburne's view (235).[4] By the middle of the twentieth century, there were numerous accounts of *King Lear* maintaining that the final effect of the tragedy was exaltation at the spiritual transcendence of Cordelia and the redemption of her father, not despair over their suffering and death.

Robert Speaight puts the case rather forcefully in explicitly Christian terms:

Cordelia's death must remain as a redemption, but also as a reproach. For her there can be no felicity except at her father's side in the immunity of eternal sleep. The Fool is there already, and Kent will follow shortly. Albany feels no title to authority and only Edgar remains. But in a metaphysical sense, . . . Edgar and Cordelia are one. They are the male and female, the active and the passive counterparts of a single redemptive process. They answer, for those who have ears, the trag-

---

2. Coleridge, *Coleridge's Writings of Shakespeare*, 188.
3. Algernon Charles Swinburne, *The Complete Works of Algernon Charles Swinburne*, ed. Sir Edmund Gosse and Thomas James Wise, vol. 11, *Prose Works* (1925–27; repr. New York: Russell and Russell, 1968), 123. In the later "Four Plays," 11:232–41, Swinburne seems to mitigate the severity of his view and praises Coleridge.
4. A. C. Bradley, *Shakespearean Tragedy* (1904; repr. New York: Fawcett World Library, 1968), 228–30, 271–72, 235.

ic agnosticism of the play, although neither may fully understand the significance of their words and actions.

This solution sounds rather like Tate in "metaphysical" terms; Cordelia and Edgar are, in a sense, "married" after all. But Speaight maintains that Cordelia transcends even this kind of continued life "in Edgar"; "she lives on also," he says, "in her own right.... She is Nature redeemed and remade; she is mercy and reconciliation; she is the pole around which all the movement of *King Lear* revolves."[5] Speaight thus typifies readings of *King Lear* that answer the unease of Dr. Johnson by asserting that the conclusion of the play as Shakespeare originally wrote it is sufficiently happy insofar as it suggests that the death of Cordelia is an image of saving grace, not a revelation of meaninglessness.[6]

To be sure, some of the critics who present generally affirmative readings are more cautious and offer more qualifications than Speaight. Reflecting on the dying Lear's last words, "Look on her! Look her lips, / Look there, look there!" (V.iii. 311–12), Maynard Mack, for example, disparages "two ways of being sentimental" about the ending of the tragedy in *"King Lear" in Our Time*. "One is to follow those who argue that, because these last lines probably mean that Lear dies in the joy of thinking Cordelia lives, some sort of mitigation or transformation has been reached which turns defeat into total victory." This, Mack maintains, "is too simple"; and he might have added that these apparently hopeful lines do not occur in the quarto version of the play. He rejects more emphatically, however, the opposite view,

---

5. Robert Speaight, *Nature in Shakespearean Tragedy* (1955; repr. New York: Collier Books, 1962), 129–30.

6. Other redemptive interpretations of *King Lear* in generally Christian terms include those of John F. Danby, *Shakespeare's Doctrine of Nature: A Study of "King Lear"* (London: Faber and Faber, 1948); Oscar James Campbell, "The Salvation of Lear," *ELH* 15 (1948): 93–109; R. W. Chambers, *"King Lear,"* Glasgow University Publications 54 (1940): 20–52; G. Wilson Knight, *The Wheel of Fire: Interpretations of Shakespearean Tragedy* (1930; repr. London and New York: Routledge, 2001); Peter Milward, SJ, *Biblical Influences in Shakespeare's Great Tragedies* (Bloomington and Indianapolis: Indiana University Press, 1987); and Theodore Spencer, *Shakespeare and the Nature of Man*, 2nd ed. (New York: Macmillan, 1949), among many others.

Hope and Despair in *King Lear*

as presented by Judah Stampfer: "The other sentimentality leads us to indulge the currently fashionable existentialist *nausée*, and to derive from the fact that Lear's joy is mistaken, or, alternatively, from the fact that in the Lear world 'even those who have fully repented, done penance, and risen to the tender regard of sainthood can be hunted down, driven insane, and killed by the most agonizing extremes of passion,' the conclusion that 'we inhabit an imbecile universe.' Perhaps we do," is Mack's curt rejoinder, "—but Shakespeare's *King Lear* provides no evidence of it that till now we lacked."[7]

Certainly, Shakespeare's original audience would have not found profound suffering and pervasive evil to be proof of a godless world. In 1563 Alexander Neville prefaced a translation of Seneca's *Oedipus* with an explanation of its horrors that would serve nicely for Shakespeare's tragedy:

As in this present tragedy, and so forth in the process of the whole history, thou mayst right well perceive, wherein thou shalt see a very express and lively image of the inconstant change of fickle fortune in the person of a Prince of passing fame and renown, midst whole floods of earthly bliss, by mere misfortune (nay rather by the deep hidden judgements of God) piteously plunged in most extreme miseries. The whole realm for his sake in strangest guise grievously plagued; besides the apparent destruction of the nobility, the general death and spoil of the communalty, the miserable transformed face of the city, with an infinite number of mischiefs more.[8]

This stern view was not confined to poetry. Only a little more than twenty years before the composition of *King Lear*, Justus Lipsius, in his popular philosophical dialogue *De Constantia*, had subjected a youthful version of himself to the admonitions of an

---

7. Maynard Mack, *King Lear in Our Time* (Berkeley and Los Angeles: University of California Press, 1965), 114, 115. He is rebuking Judah Stampfer, "The Catharsis of *King Lear*," *Shakespeare Survey* 13 (1960): 1–10, who supplies the phrase "imbecile universe."
8. Alexander Neville, "Tragedy and God's Moral Judgments" (1563), in *English Renaissance Literary Criticism*, ed. Brian Vickers (Oxford: Clarendon, 1999), 125–26.

elder Stoic sage for presuming that the sufferings of his native Low Countries in the civil war of the late sixteenth century were in any way extraordinary or a cause to doubt divine providence.[9]

Still, when all the allowances and qualifications have been made, the closing scene of *King Lear* remains a terrible spectacle, and many commentators have maintained that it betrays an ultimate skepticism concerning a divine ordering of the universe or indeed any rational significance apart from what men and women can provisionally devise for themselves. Robert G. Hunter, who has investigated Shakespeare's encounter with Reformation theology quite thoroughly, finds in the close of *King Lear* a message "different from and rather worse even than" the "imbecile universe" rejected by Mack:

> It tells us nothing. It shows us that in a state of nature, without the knowledge or the grace of God, we are nothing—O's without a figure. And it suggests that perhaps we *are* in a state of nature. It suggests but does not say that our knowledge may be an illusion, that the faith and theology of the original audience, may, by analogy with the evasions within the play, be one more admirable evasion of whoremaster man. Indeed, any attempt to deal with the play's either/or statement of incomprehensibility and meaninglessness by resolving it in favor of one or the other is to evade the play's demonstration of our incertitude.

Hunter evokes Pascal's "wager"—after realizing that one can neither prove nor disprove the existence of God, *il faut parier*—only to dismiss it. "Of all the distractions," he says, "tragedy is the most nearly capable of confronting mystery without denying it. It can cope without evading and can take as its motto

---

9. *De Constantia libri duo* was first published in Leiden and Antwerp at the end of 1583 and went through numerous editions through the seventeenth century. It was translated into English by Sir John Stradling (London, 1594), and since Lipsius's work was well known to Shakespeare's theatrical colleague Ben Jonson, there is every reason to believe that the work would have been available to Shakespeare as well. The important point is, of course, that the consideration of the guidance of divine providence in the face of dreadful evil would not have been a shocking or unusual topic for Shakespeare's audience. See Lipsius's "Introduction" to *Justus Lipsius Concerning Constancy*, ed., trans. R. V. Young, Medieval and Renaissance Texts and Studies 389 (Tempe, Ariz.: ACMRS, 2011), xxiv.

'le juste est de ne point parier.' Art is above nature in that respect." Hunter seems to arrive at the same conclusion as Mack: "Tragedy never tells us what to think; it shows us what we are and may be."[10] While their tone is very different, both critics finally excuse the playwright from any obligation to define a theological—or "atheological"—position.

The determined skeptics, however, are as insistent about recruiting Shakespeare to their company as their Christian counterparts who find a parable of regeneration in the conclusion of *King Lear*. In *The Structure of Complex Words* William Empson provides less a refutation of A. C. Bradley than subdued ridicule by incredulity. Bradley suggests that we are reconciled to Cordelia's death because "The 'gods,' it seems, do *not* show their approval by 'defending' their own from adversity or death, or by giving them power and prosperity. These, on the contrary, are worthless, or worse; it is not on them, but on the renunciation of them, that the gods throw incense."[11] Empson at first admits that Bradley does not apply the remark about the corrupting effect of power and prosperity to Cordelia, but this concession is quickly dismissed:

The main thing about this argument, no doubt, is that it succeeds in turning the blasphemies against the gods into the orthodox view held by Mrs. Gamp, that the world is a Wale. I do not know how seriously he took his last little twist of piety, the view that Cordelia was sure to become corrupt. It is curious how often the puritan high-mindedness can be found interlocked with an almost farcical cynicism.[12]

10. Robert G. Hunter, *Shakespeare and the Mystery of God's Judgments* (Athens: University of Georgia Press, 1976), 190–91, 196. He is quoting Blaise Pascal, *Pensées* II.418, in *Oeuvres Complètes*, ed. Henri Gouhier and Louis Lafuma (Paris: Éditions du Seuil, 1963), 550. See Mack, *King Lear in Our Time*, 117.

11. Speaight, *Nature in Shakespearean Tragedy*, 270–71.

12. William Empson, *The Structure of Complex Words*, 3rd ed. (Totowa, N.J.: Rowman and Littlefield, 1979), 153–54. Mrs. Sarah Gamp is a disreputable, drunken nurse in Charles Dickens's *Martin Chuzzlewit* (1843–44). She is given to making fatuously sentimental remarks. Empson also says (8) that "the attempts to fit Christian sentiments onto it [*Lear*] seem to me to falsify the play." In addition to Empson, other skeptical accounts from around the middle of the twentieth century include G. B. Harrison, *Shakespeare's Tragedies* (London: Routledge and Kegan Paul, 1951); D. G. James,

Bradley, who sometimes wins Empson's praise, and who hardly qualifies as a champion of the "Christian Right," is nonetheless chided in derisory fashion for insufficient stress upon the grimly subversive features of Shakespeare's tragedy.

Fifty years after the first edition of *The Structure of Complex Words*, the skeptical view of *King Lear* is still prominent and even more explicit, as attested by the example of Millicent Bell's *Shakespeare's Tragic Skepticism*:

> But their [Lear's and Cordelia's] own loving reconciliation before death does not look toward the heavenly afterlife religion promises. In his madness Lear had had a vision of himself in hell, "on a wheel of fire," and of Cordelia in heaven—but when he dies at last it is only the condition of recovered selfhood and sanity that can replace despair and confusion in a purely secular way.[13]

Like Empson, Bell attributes to Shakespeare a sardonic, modern vision that sees through all traditional pieties, and she is able to invoke Stephen Greenblatt and the New Historicists as further witnesses to her claim; in fact, Greenblatt becomes for her virtually a model for the playwright himself: "Shakespeare, one might almost propose, is an early-seventeenth- [*sic*] century New Historicist of sorts, bounded by his own time and place yet enabled by his skepticism to view his culture with detachment."[14] High praise for the Bard indeed! He is enlisted among the ranks of knowing postmodern theorists, who alone seem to escape the fate they ascribe to ordinary mortals of being helpless puppets of the currently regnant ideological hegemony.

The most important attack upon the redemptive view of *King Lear*, the work that presents the most relentless and scholarly ref-

---

The Dream of Learning: An Essay on "The Advancement of Learning," "Hamlet," and "King Lear" (Oxford: Clarendon, 1951); John Peter, *Complaint and Satire in Early English Literature* (Oxford: Clarendon, 1956); John Rosenberg, "King Lear and His Comforters," *Essays in Criticism* 16 (1966):135–46; Arthur Sewell, *Character and Society in Shakespeare* (Oxford: Clarendon, 1951); and Stampfer, "Catharsis of *King Lear*" (see n. 197).

13. Bell, *Shakespeare's Tragic Skepticism*, 189
14. Bell, *Shakespeare's Tragic Skepticism*, xiv.

utation of what it calls "the currently widespread view that *Lear* is an optimistically Christian drama," is W. R. Elton's *"King Lear" and the Gods*, which first appeared in 1966.[15] Since its appearance, this book has been what might be called the "Unholy Writ" of the school of Shakespeare criticism that regards *King Lear* as a skeptical, radically subversive play, calling into question all the norms and pieties of the "Elizabethan World Picture," now perceived as a self-interested ideological imposition of the ruling classes of early modern England. Among its advocates Elton's work appears to be not merely definitive, but simply irrefutable. In *Radical Tragedy* Jonathan Dollimore maintains, "As William R. Elton has demonstrated in an important study, the Elizabethan-Jacobean period witnessed 'the skeptical disintegration of providential belief,'" and he later declines to "argue again the case against the Christian view [of *King Lear*] since, even though it is still sometimes advanced, it has been effectively discredited by writers as diverse as Barbara Everett, William R. Elton, and Cedric Watts."[16] According to Bell, "William Elton, in his learned *King Lear and the Gods* (1966) buried the idea that *King Lear* was optimistically Christian.'"[17] As these sample remarks show, Elton has been thought to have overwhelmed opposition so decisively that the matter requires no further investigation.

It is true that Elton's massive volume makes a formidable display of learning and, unlike many of its scholarly beneficiaries and supporters, delves deeply into the religious thought of Shakespeare's day. In some respects, however, the mountain of theological and philosophical details that Elton has so painstakingly amassed seems to occlude his vision of its significance, and his refutation of "Christian" readings of *King Lear* often accepts as "Christian" accounts of human nature and man's relation to

---

15. W. R. Elton, *"King Lear" and the Gods* (San Marino, Calif.: Huntingdon Library, 1968), 3.

16. Jonathan Dollimore, *Radical Tragedy: Religion, Ideology and Power in the Drama of Shakespeare and His Contemporaries*, 3rd ed. (Durham, N.C.: Duke University Press, 2004), 38, 190.

17. Bell, *Shakespeare's Tragic Skepticism*, xi.

providence that dubiously fit under that rubric. Further, his religious taxonomy of the various characters, especially his effort to show that Lear himself is not saved, tends to treat them as symbols for religious ideas rather than as agents of a tragic action in Aristotle's sense. Finally, although his argument stresses the rising current of skepticism, he pays little attention to the specific associations of the various characters with what we may call the crisis of natural law in the era of Elizabeth and James. Critics who rely on Elton's work to dismiss Christian interpretations of *King Lear* are thus heaping disdain on a sentimental, insubstantial version of Christianity. The Christian import of the play can only be grasped in terms of its complex relation to natural law.

In order to understand the play both as a product and an assessment of Western civilization, a fresh look at the theme of natural law in *King Lear* will be helpful. Although this topic has been dealt with extensively in the critical literature for many decades, it will not be amiss to reconsider natural law as it interacts in a Christian culture with the doctrine of original sin and redemption through grace, as well as in relation to the notion of God's providential ordering of the creation. Moreover, it is important that the play be treated as a tragic drama, not a treatise. In Aristotelian terms, the διάνοια or "thought" or "theme" will emerge more clearly and persuasively if we begin with the representation of "a piece of action, of life, of happiness and unhappiness" (*Poetics* 1450a) rather than with the ideas as such. Regarded in this perspective, *King Lear* is most assuredly *not* an exposition of "Christian optimism," a phrase that is not even a paradox, but a contradiction in terms. What Shakespeare offers us is an embodiment of the social disintegration that results when the philosophical and cultural foundations of a Christian community are undermined by radical skepticism about the nature and purpose of human life. Elton is very perceptive in remarking the crisis of belief figured forth in the play, but he treats the characters schematically in terms of fixed theological categories rather than attending to the overall effect of the drama. The "redemptive" interpretations are surely correct in seeing that our sympathy remains with the characters who adhere to natural law. They fail to see, however, that a crisis of natural law leaves only the naked gospel, a "Good News" that offers a stark choice of hope and despair and reveals *optimism* to be a shallow presumption.

It is a critical commonplace that "natural," "unnatural," and their cognates are used more in *King Lear* than in any other play by Shakespeare. Theodore Spencer avails himself of a concordance in his 1942 study, and Leon Harold Craig still is counting word occurrences almost sixty years later.[18] The point of these observations is stated most plainly by Danby: "*King Lear* can be regarded as a play dramatizing the meanings of the single word 'Nature.'" These meanings are effectively reduced to two by a dichotomy between internal headings of the first chapter: "The Benignant Nature of Bacon, Hooker, and Lear" and "The Malignant Nature of Hobbes, Edmund, and the Wicked Daughters." "The idea of Nature, then, in orthodox Elizabethan thought, is always something normative for human beings." This is the view of "the Lear party" with Cordelia as its "limiting expression." It is the view that the moral law arises *naturally* out of the constitutive rationality of the souls of human beings situated in an intelligible created order. It is the practical antithesis of the "mechanical necessity" associated with modern scientifically determined "laws of nature":

> The law it [Reason] observed was felt more as self-expression than as external restraint. It was a law, in any case, which the creature was most itself when it obeyed. And rebellion against this law was rebellion against one's self, loss of all nature, lapse into chaos.[19]

The opposite vision of nature and the law of nature is voiced in Edmund's famous soliloquy at the beginning of the play's

---

18. Theodore Spencer, *Shakespeare and the Nature of* Man, 2nd ed. (New York: Macmillan, 1949), 142n8; Leon Harold Craig, *Of Philosophers and Kings: Political Philosophy in Shakespeare's "Macbeth" and "King Lear"* (Toronto, Buffalo, and London: Toronto University Press, 2001), 133.

19. Danby, *Shakespeare's Doctrine of Nature*, 15, 20, 31, 21, 20, 25.

second scene, "Thou, Nature, art my goddess, to thy law / My services are bound" (I.ii.1–2). Edmund's notion of nature is individual rather than communal: "nature" for him means what distinguishes him as a particular being rather than what unites him to mankind by participation in a common human nature. What is "natural" is, in romantic fashion, opposed to what is social, traditional, conventional, or artificial—"the plague of custom" and "the curiosity of nations" (I.ii.3–4). Finally, his "nature" is defined by passion rather than reason, which is passion's servant. Edmund relishes his illegitimate status, asserting that the transgression of conventional morality involved in begetting a bastard is likely to produce more vigorous and aggressive sons:

> Who, in the lusty stealth of nature, take
> More composition and fierce quality,
> Than doth within a dull, stale, tired bed
> Go to th'creating a whole tribe of fops....
> (I.ii.11–14)

Danby catches the tone of this quite well: "Edmund is not a devil. He is, on the contrary, a normal, sensible, reasonable fellow; but emancipated. His knowledge of what Nature is like is a real knowledge of what she is really like" (34–35). And Danby likewise quite shrewdly observes that "the dualism of Reason *versus* the Passions is useless to explain Edmund. Though Edmund is Appetite, he is also a rationalist" (36–37). Noting that Shakespeare has presciently anticipated in Edmund the philosophy of Thomas Hobbes, he observes, "Reason is no longer a normative drive but a calculator of the means to satisfy the appetites with which we were born" (38).

Danby finds in the dramatic unfolding of the clash between the traditional classical and Christian view of natural law and the modern, Hobbesian view "not only our profoundest tragedy" but even "our profoundest expression of an essentially Christian comment on man's world and his society, using the terms and benefiting by the formulations of the Christian tradition"

(204–5). His interpretation (especially in a summary) is rather schematic and seems vulnerable to Elton's disdainful disparaging of "Shakespearean neo-Christianizers" (263); it cannot be maintained, however, that Danby has simply failed to see the subversive tendencies toward skepticism that Elton finds proliferating at the end of the sixteenth century: "New orientations between man and the heavenly powers were, in several directions, formed during the Renaissance, disintegrating the relative medieval sense of security."[20] Nearly twenty years before the appearance of Elton's book, Danby, arguing the opposite case, makes the same basic observation about the growing prevalence of the subversive outlook expressed in Edmund's soliloquy:

> The sentiments of Edmund's speech must have been fairly widespread in Shakespeare's society. There is no doubt that similar ethical views were implicit in the eminent generality of public conduct at any time during the sixteenth and seventeenth centuries. It was not, however, an acceptable view.[21]

The issue, then, is not whether *King Lear* dramatizes powerful doubts about the traditional orthodox doctrine of natural law and divine providence, but, rather, what the import of the play is regarding the contemporaneous challenge to orthodoxy.

If the usual "orthodox" interpretation is to be faulted, it is not for tying the debate about nature too closely to Christian doctrine, but for attributing too much latitude to natural law as such. As Russell Hittinger points out, "It is true that modern philosophy abandoned the metaphysics of participation, and thus wrestled with the problem of whether law belongs properly to physical states of affairs or mental constructs, but it is entirely anachronistic to impose this dilemma on the older tradition."[22] In summing up his own argument Danby seems torn between the urge to see the natural law embodied in a "physical state of

---

20. Elton, *"King Lear" and the Gods*, 9.
21. Danby, *Shakespeare's Doctrine of Nature*, 32.
22. Russell Hittinger, *First Grace: Rediscovering the Natural Law in a Post-Christian World* (Wilmington, Del.: ISI, 2003), xxii.

affairs" and the regret that it seems finally only a "mental construct":

> It has been argued that Shakespeare began by seeing a new thrustful godlessness attacking the pious medieval structure represented by the good King Henry VI. Regretfully, Shakespeare then comes to terms with "the times" such as he saw them to be under Elizabeth. Last, he recognized the iniquity of the times and of the machiavel's rule. To these he opposed the society that Lear's and Gloster's prayers demand, a transcendent society adequated to the necessity for a community of goodness in which Lear's regeneration and Cordelia's truth might be completed: a Utopia and a New Jerusalem.²³

Writing half a century after Danby, R. S. White is even more explicit about how *King Lear* demands that the natural law be embodied in a specific political order: "Lear's sentiments in this part of the play [III.iv] are as communitarian, anti-individualistic, and anti-authoritarian as More's in his fictional version of Utopia." White suggests that Shakespeare, like a seventeenth-century Jean-Jacques Rousseau, maintains that the norms of natural law could be realized by a kind of communitarian socialism that is prevented only by deeply established vested interests:

> The logic of *King Lear*, with its decisive celebration of virtue over vice and its equally decisive extinction of virtue, folds back to catch in its snare those who would impose any kind of positive law, literary or legal, over Natural Law. As in *Utopia*, no matter how splendid is the prospect of a world based on reason and conscience, that world may not be achievable, because human greed and power-seeking are too deeply entrenched in the existing structures of authority and power: but the effort of trying should still go on.²⁴

This sounds more like the liberation theology of the twentieth century than what St. Thomas Aquinas or Richard Hooker would recognize as natural law. Hobbes is, quite reasonably, the villain

---

23. Danby, *Shakespeare's Doctrine of Nature*, 202.
24. R. S. White, *Natural Law in English Renaissance Literature* (Cambridge: Cambridge University Press, 1996), 210, 215.

waiting in the wings to provide philosophical cover for the Edmunds of the world in both Danby and White, but in their insistence that natural law be embodied in a particular program that will somehow guarantee the poetic justice that Shakespeare's version of *King Lear* denies, they are to some degree embracing Hobbes's instrumental version of reason, much as Rousseau did in the eighteenth century, and endorsing Nahum Tate's revision of the play.[25]

It is important to bear in mind that the most explicit and thorough exposition of natural law in Shakespeare's time, Richard Hooker's *Of the Laws of Ecclesiastical Polity* (1593, 1597), was composed with the express purpose of refuting the Puritan view that the Church of England ought to be governed strictly according to scriptural norms, identified with the Presbyterian form of church governance established by Calvin in Geneva. Taking continental Anabaptists as a negative exemplum, Hooker warns the Puritans against attempting to establish the realm of divine perfection on earth:

> Nothing more clear unto their seeming, than that a new Jerusalem being often spoken of in Scripture, they undoubtedly were themselves that new Jerusalem, and the old did by way of a certain figurative resemblance signify what they should both be and do.[26]

Natural law is thus invoked, not as a template for the New Jerusalem or Utopia, but as a constraint upon the imprudent effort to embody these ideals literally in human institutions:

---

25. White, *Natural Law in English Renaissance Literature*, 267n11, tries to distance himself from Danby by citing an unconvincing distinction between his own treatment of "Natural Law" and Danby's preoccupation with "what I have called 'natural philosophy.'" For a persuasive demonstration that Lear's and Gloucester's attacks upon privilege and inequity in the middle of the play are considerably less radical or subversive than many critics claim, see Judy Kronenfeld, *King Lear and the Naked Truth: Rethinking the Language of Religion and Resistance* (Durham, N.C., and London: Duke University Press, 1998), esp. 170–229. For the view that "in the point of doctrine, Christianity reverses the tragic view and makes tragedy impossible," see Richard B. Sewall, *The Vision of Tragedy* (New Haven, Conn., and London: Yale University Press, 1959), 50–56, 68–79.

26. Richard Hooker, *Of the Laws of Ecclesiastical Polity*, introduction by Christopher Morris (London: J. M. Dent, 1907), 1:139.

These men, in whose mouths at the first sounded nothing but only mortification of the flesh, were come at the length to think they might lawfully have their six or seven wives apiece; they which at the first thought judgment and justice itself to be merciless cruelty, accounted at the length their own hands sanctified with being embrued in Christian blood; they who at the first were wont to beat down all dominion, and to urge against poor constables, "Kings of nations"; had at the length both consuls and kings of their own erection amongst themselves. (1:139–40)

Natural law is not, according to Hooker, the basis for an absolutely just polity or community, but rather a set of norms guiding the admittedly diverse and contingent political arrangements of fallen men in an uncertain world: "The case of man's nature standing therefore as it doth, some kind of regiment the Law of Nature doth require; yet the kinds thereof being many, Nature tieth not to any one, but leaveth the choice as a thing arbitrary" (1:191–92).

"The case of man's nature" raises a second point: Christians at the end of the sixteenth century were under no illusions about the character of fallen men. Human beings, along with angels, are rational agents and fulfill the law of their nature voluntarily: "God which moveth mere natural agents as an efficient only, doth otherwise move intellectual creatures" (1:161). The result of this freedom is that men's apprehension of their good, of the object of their nature, may vary:

There is in the Will of man naturally that freedom, whereby it is apt to take or refuse any particular object whatsoever being presented unto it. Whereupon it followeth, that there is no particular object so good, but it may have the show of some difficulty or unpleasant quality annexed to it, in respect whereof the Will may shrink and decline it; contrariwise (for so things are blended) there is no particular evil which hath not some appearance of goodness whereby to insinuate itself. (1:171–72)

What is more, in actual human history, from the perspective not merely of Hooker but all Christians, the indeterminacy of the human will had led not merely to contingency, but to the depravity of original sin. Men may know by nature—even the heathen—"the shewe & effect of the Law written in their hearts" (Rom 2:15), but this knowledge serves only to justify their condemnation. The estate of men under merely natural law is described grimly by St. Paul in the Epistle to the Ephesians: "That ye were, I say at that time without Christ, & were aliantes from the commune welth of Israel, & were strangers from the covenants of the promes, & had no hope, & were without God in the worlde" (Eph 2:12).[27] Natural law may provide a pattern for the positive laws of commonwealths, but Hooker insists that the human legislator must take into account the effects of original sin:

> Law politic, ordained for external order and regiment among men, are never framed as they should be, unless presuming the will of man to be inwardly obstinate, rebellious, and averse from all obedience unto the sacred laws of his nature; in a word, unless presuming man to be in regard of his depraved mind little better than a wild beast. (1:188)

Hooker's account of natural law owes a good deal to St. Thomas Aquinas, and in his baleful view of human nature with its aversion "from all obedience unto the sacred laws of his nature," he differs from the Angelic Doctor not at all. R. S. White contrasts "Aquinas' idealism about people and the scepticism of Calvin and Hobbes,"[28] but this view is rather short-sighted. In the first place, like Hooker, St. Thomas realizes that mankind is subject to original sin. Particular human laws are necessary, since fallen human beings are incapable of grasping the natural law completely "because human reason is unable to participate in the full order of divine reason, but only in its own capacity and imperfectly" (ST I-II, q. 91, a. 3, ad 1); "hence it was necessary for the peace and virtue

---

27. Unless otherwise specified, I quote scripture from *The Geneva Bible*, but I have modernized punctuation and typographical conventions.
28. White, *Natural Law in English Renaissance Literature*, 185.

of men that laws be imposed ... ; because man has the weapons of reason for carrying out his concupiscence and his savagery, which other animals do not have" (I-II, q. 95, a. 1).[29] Most important, the "optimistic" St. Thomas denies that "anyone can be happy in this life." And it is not just that the goal "in which happiness specially consists, namely the vision of the divine essence,"[30] is unattainable in this life, but even the good of natural life:

> Now happiness, since it would be a perfect and sufficient good, excludes every evil and fulfills every desire. In this life, however, it is not possible that every evil be excluded. For the present life is subject to many evils, which cannot be avoided: to ignorance on the part of the intellect, to inordinate longing on the part of the appetite, and to many pains on the part of the body.[31] (*ST* I-II, q. 5, a 3)

Both Aquinas and Hooker, then, in expounding the natural law that St. Paul says is written in the hearts of all, are constantly aware that this inherent moral sense is of no avail to men and women under the curse of original sin and without grace—"who had no hope, & were without God in the worlde."

Such is precisely the situation that Shakespeare imagines in *King Lear*. The characters are pagans whose knowledge and understanding of natural law are real but imperfect or distorted. Edmund's view of human nature and the law that governs it is perverse according to the traditional standards of Shakespeare's

---

29. The work is quoted throughout from *Summa Theologiae*, 5 vols. (Madrid: Biblioteca de Autores Cristianos, 1961–65), with standard references given parenthetically in the text. The Latin of the first quotation reads, "Ad primum ergo dicendum quod ratio humana non potest participare ad plenum dictamen rationis divinae, sed suo modo et imperfecte"; and the second, "Unde necessarium fuit ad pacem hominum et virtutem, ut leges ponerentur ... ; quia homo habet arma rationis ad explendas concupiscentias et saevitias, quae non habent alia animalia."

30. The article is "Utrum aliquis in hac vita possit esse beatus." St. Thomas maintains, "Si consideretur id in quo specialiter beatitudo consistit, scilicet visio divinae essentiae, quae non potest homini provenire in hac vita."

31. "Nam beatitudo, cum sit *perfectum et sufficiens bonum* (see a. 2, n. 5), omne malum excludit et omne desiderium implet. In hac autem vita non potest omne malum excludi. Multis enim malis praesens vita subiacet, quae vitari non possunt: et ignorantiae ex parte intellectus, et inordinatae affectioni ex parte appetitus, et multiplicibus poenalitatibus ex parte corporis."

society—or progressive, if one takes the modern view, first fully articulated, perhaps, by Hobbes.[32] Opposing Edmund's position most explicitly are the utterances of Lear and Gloucester, who both condemn their children for a failure of the filial love and loyalty required by natural law. Just as Edmund calls upon the "gods" associated with the "goddess" Nature to "stand up for bastards" (I.ii.1, 22), thus giving shape to his ruthlessly individualistic and self-serving idea of human nature, so Lear calls upon the "dear goddess" Nature to punish Goneril for her transgression of natural *moral* law with a failure or defect of her *physical* nature:

> Suspend thy purpose, if thou didst intend
> To make this creature fruitful.
> Into her womb convey sterility,
> Dry up in her the organs of increase,
> And from her derogate body never spring
> A babe to honor her! (I.iv.276–81)

Or, alternatively, he demands that she be repaid in kind for ingratitude with a "child of spleen ... that she may feel, / How sharper than a serpent's tooth it is / To have a thankless child!" (I.iv.282, 287–89). Although he *knows* that his paternal obligations are as binding as his daughter's filial obligations, his practical conduct is as selfish as Edmund's without the latter's explicit rationalization of selfishness as only "natural." Even when his rage and frustration with Goneril lead him to regret his treatment of Cordelia, he does not yet acknowledge the extent of his injustice:

---

32. See, for example, Dollimore, *Radical Tragedy*, 196: "Plays like *Lear* precisely disallow 'transcendence'; in this at least they confirm Edmund's contention that 'men / Are as the time is.'" And again: Edmund's "revolutionary scepticism is discredited by the purpose to which it is put. How are we to take this? Are we to assume that Edmund is simply evil and therefore so is his philosophy? I want to argue that we need not" (198). Dollimore is opposing a straw man. From the traditional Christian natural law perspective, nothing is "simply evil." As St. Thomas Aquinas says, "Evil is not an entity, but the subject that evil befalls is, since evil is only the privation of a particular good" (*De Malo* I.1: "Malum non est aliquid, sed id cui accidit esse malum est aliquid, in quantum malum priuat nonnisi aliquod particulare bonum"). In this he follows St. Augustine's refutation of Manichaeanism in *Confessions* VII.x–xiii.

> O most small fault,
> How ugly didst thou in Cordelia show!
> Which, like an engine wrench'd my frame of nature
> From the fix'd place, drew from my heart all love,
> And added to the gall. (I.iv.266–70)

It is a "most small fault," but it is still Cordelia's *fault* that caused the displacement of his "frame of nature." Lear's conduct provides some basis for Regan's assertion that "he hath ever but slenderly known himself" (I.i.294).

Gloucester provides an equally clear example of how, in St. Thomas's view, human reason can grasp the requirements of the natural law "only in its own capacity and imperfectly." The ease with which Edmund deceives his father into believing that Edgar wrote the forged letter suggests that Gloucester does not know the character of either of his sons at all well, and that the younger bastard has become adept at exploiting his father's weaknesses. The audience is likely to infer, for example, that Edmund's ostentatiously awkward attempt to hide the letter was devised to exploit the curiosity of a man he knows to be officious and overbearing. Given Gloucester's obvious relish in the memory of the illicit copulation that resulted in Edmund's begetting at the very beginning of the play ("yet was his mother fair, there was good sport at his making" [I.i.22–23]), it is reasonable to suppose that the old man's judgment is clouded by the presence of the young man who is the living image of gratified lust.[33] When Gloucester has left the stage, Edmund sneers at his attributing disturbances in human society to dislocations among celestial phenomena—"An admirable evasion of whoremaster man, to lay his goatish disposition to the charge of a star!" (I.ii.126–28)—and it is not improbable that at least some members of a Jacobean audience would have found here evidence of superstition. But more alarming than Gloucester's predilection for astrology is his

---

33. See *ST* II-II, q. 153, a. 5, on "mental blindness" (*caecitas mentis*) as the first "daughter of lust" (*filia luxuriae*). In the reply to the first objection in the same article, he quotes Aristotle saying that "intemperance above all corrupts prudence."

lack of self-knowledge; while he has a lucid comprehension of the King's foolish and unjust anger as a "scourge" of nature, he is blind—ominous word in relation to Gloucester—to his own:

> This villain of mine comes under the prediction; there's son against father: the King falls from the bias of nature; there's father against child. We have seen the best of our time. Machinations, hollowness, treachery, and all ruinous disorders follow us disquietly to our graves. Find out this villain, Edmund, it shall lose thee nothing, do it carefully. And the noble and true-hearted Kent banish'd! his offense, honesty! 'Tis strange. (I.ii.109–17)

While Gloucester seems to Edmund, and perhaps to us, merely a foolish old man waxing nostalgic over the "good old days," his judgment of Lear's conduct and its likely consequences is sound enough. He has insight and prudence, but they are darkened when his own pleasure, comfort, and vanity are at stake.

Lear and Gloucester, the defenders of the classical tradition of natural law, seem hypocritical and even deluded at the outset of the play; and Edmund is a far more persuasive and impressive spokesman for his self-centered but "realistic" perspective. But before the two old men are judged too severely, it is necessary to take stock, for they are easy to identify with. At least that would be Aristotle's dictum: Lear, and Gloucester in a lesser but parallel fashion, are very much "like us": they are neither absolutely good nor absolutely bad. Of course, they are also, in a sense, "better" than we are; that is, they are tragic figures. Tragedy, Aristotle says, is designed to elicit pity (ἔλεος) "for the man who does not deserve his misfortune" and fear (φόβος) "for the man who is like ourselves." Hence a particular kind of character is called for at the center of a tragedy:

This is the sort of man who is not pre-eminently virtuous and just, and yet it is through no badness or villainy of his own that he falls into the misfortune, but rather through some flaw ('ἁμαρτία) in him, he being one of those who are in high station and good fortune, like Oedipus and Thyestes and the famous men of such families as these. (1453a)

A bit further on in the *Poetics* (1454a), Aristotle says that of the four elements of character in tragedy, "the first and most important is that the character should be good" (χρηστός).

Lear and Gloucester both correspond well to this account of tragic character. Their behavior in the first scene is embarrassingly selfish and short-sighted, and there is hardly any improvement until the climactic third act. Nevertheless, the play provides ample evidence that both have earned better reputations in the past and that they remain capable of decency and courage and, finally, of wisdom. The action is tragic precisely because their realization of their moral failings, which suggests Aristotle's notion of "discovery" (αναγνώρισις) and is properly coupled with a "reversal" (περιπέτεια), comes too late to avert the catastrophic arc of the action (*Poetics* 1452a). Both men are basically "good," although neither comes near the luminous virtue of Cordelia. Both of them cause their own suffering and that of others not because of depraved intentions or utterly corrupt character, but because of an *error* or *piece of ignorance* arising from understandable if reprehensibly foolish vanity. In a bleak mood, Gloucester attributes his misery to "an imbecile universe": "As flies to wanton boys are we to th'gods, / They kill us for their sport" (IV.i.36–37). Edgar's observation to his dying brother in the final scene is in strict logic an undeniable refutation of their father's complaint:

> The gods are just, and of our pleasant vices
> Make instruments to plague us:
> The dark and vicious place where thee he got
> Cost him his eyes. (V.iii.171–74)

Since Gloucester's moral "blindness" is the source of his personal irresponsibility and misjudgment of his sons' characters, there is an ironic, even "poetic" justice in the loss of his eyes, as he himself admits: "I have no way, and therefore want no eyes; / I stumbled when I saw" (IV.i.18–19). But of course we find his suffering completely out of proportion to his guilt, since it arises from human frailty—vanity and sensuality—rather than malice and cruelty; and it is important to remember that Edgar utters his harsh verdict *not* to his father, but in reproof of the vicious brother with whom he has just struggled in mortal combat.[34]

Gloucester's conduct is certainly bad enough. One can only shudder to imagine what Edmund must experience in hearing his aged father crow about the "good sport" he enjoyed in begetting his "whoreson" (I.i.23–24). His obliviousness to the consequences of his indulgence in "pleasant vices" (V.iii.171) is ironically underscored in subsequent scenes by his ill-tempered and credulous rage at the suggestion that his older son may not be true to *his* natural obligations to his father. Most audiences will surely feel a great deal of disdain for Gloucester and sympathy for his illegitimate son at the outset of the play. On the other hand, Gloucester has not abandoned the bastard: he has educated him, he introduces him to a powerful nobleman at court in the first scene, and he has evidently treated him with love, even though he never lets Edmund forget his origins. More important, Gloucester, while lacking adequate self-knowledge and knowledge of his sons, shows genuine insight into the characters of Lear and Kent and a healthy suspicion of the King's older daughters and Cornwall. Finally, when the action comes to a crisis, Gloucester displays great courage in remaining loyal not just to Lear, but to the cause of justice. At the beginning of the tragedy, Gloucester behaves contemptibly, but it soon becomes clear that he is by no means a contemptible man and is indeed admirable in many respects.

Much the same is a fortiori true of Lear himself. The ritual abasement of his daughters that he stages in the opening scene is, like Gloucester's salacious reminiscing about his youthful sexual conquest, an embarrassment. Anyone who has suffered

---

34. Marilyn French, "The Late Tragedies," in *Shakespearean Tragedy*, ed. John Drakakis (London and New York: Longman, 1992), 259, thus misses the point in accusing Edgar of "mean-minded moralization" for this remark. What would have been unfeeling said to his father is properly said to the flagitious brother, who grants the justice of the remark and begins to feel stirrings of remorse. The sanctimony here is the critic's, not the character's.

through the antics of an overbearing relative demanding to be the center of attention at a family gathering will have a sense of what Lear is doing. The difference is that he is a long-reigning absolute monarch who can demand outrageous tributes to his own vainglory. An audience in Shakespeare's England would have no difficulty understanding the apprehension of a King with only daughters about the succession to the throne, and his anxiety on this score may at least suggest an explanation for his staging of a ceremony in which he both relinquishes and seeks to retain his power and royal prestige and puts his daughters through a mortifying charade of heaving their hearts into their mouths. Once again, however, ample evidence is provided that there is—or at least has been—more to Lear than this scene might imply, that Goneril's complaint, "The best and soundest of his time hath been but rash" (I.i.295), is self-serving hyperbole. Lear has the love and respect of most of the other important characters: Albany and Gloucester and, above all Kent and Cordelia, whose character is unimpeachable and whose regard worth having. Both of them are, apparently, used to speaking freely and candidly to the King and are shocked at his behavior. Gloucester is likewise nonplussed by the turn of events, and Albany will show no predisposition to take his wife's part in Lear's confrontation with Goneril: "My lord, I am guiltless as I am ignorant / Of what hath moved you" (I.iv.273–74). When Kent returns in disguise to serve Lear in spite of his banishment, he seems to speak for many of Lear's subjects in saying to the old King, "you have that in your countenance which I would fain call master"; namely, "Authority" (I.iv.27–30). *Authority* is plainly to be distinguished from the mere raw power seized by Edmund, Cornwall, Goneril, and Regan.[35]

35. Craig, *Of Philosophers and Kings*, 116–18, provides a good summary of various indications of Lear's virtue, but his argument that the love test is actually a shrewd political move, marred only by Cordelia's politically naïve failure to grasp his subtle maneuver, is unconvincing. Craig, following the lead of Harry Jaffa, constructs an elaborate Straussian political fable of Lear manipulating the elder daughters into accepting Cordelia's and Burgundy's dominance, with the idea that they will eventually control

Although he can with some justice claim, "I am a man / More sinn'd against than sinning" (III.ii.59–60), King Lear and the characters associated with him and with the traditional view of natural law, which maintains that objective moral norms are built into the structure of human nature and the reality of the human condition, by no means observe their own principles perfectly. Edmund, who claims that the law of nature is no more than the selfish pursuit of one's desire, has at least the virtue of relative consistency. Through the first two acts of the play, the wicked characters, the characters who follow Edmund's cynical assessment of human nature, are more vigorous and resourceful than their opponents who, when not causing their own troubles, are at best bemused and ineffectual. Having been placed in the stocks by the irate Cornwall for his assault on Oswald, "true-hearted Kent" admits the imprudence of his dealings with Goneril's steward, "Having more man than wit about me" (II.iv.42). His conduct provides at least a rationale for the punishment meted out by Cornwall and for Goneril's complaints about the unruliness of her father's train of 100 knights. There is some ambiguity about the extent to which the elder sisters are justified in condemning the behavior of the King's retinue and demanding a reduction in their numbers. Under the very best of circumstances, however, a long-term houseguest with his own armed retainers will present a problem. The innocent characters, on the other hand, appear indecisive. Edmund manages to make Edgar's modesty and candor seem mere timidity: "A credulous

---

the entire country, thus obviating the threat of Cornwall's ambition and Albany's weakness (118–33). It is a wonderfully ingenious scheme, but there is no indication in the text that such was Lear's intention, and no way that a theatre audience could possibly make the inference. While it is true, as Craig insists, that a play may not be "*only* a play," that it may "be intended to communicate something to a careful reader that goes well beyond what is accessible to even its most astute and attentive viewer" (8), what it "communicates" must, nonetheless, be compatible with the dramatic context, or the work ceases to be a play or work of literature and becomes an encoded political treatise. In principle, this approach is no different from the attempt to read the plays as encoded messages that their true author was not Shakespeare or, more recently, that their *real* import is veiled Catholic recusant propaganda, as in Wilson and Asquith.

father and a brother noble,/Whose nature is so far from doing harms/That he suspects none; on whose foolish honesty/My practices ride easy" (I.ii.179–82). Goneril takes the same line with her husband, Albany, a "Milk-liver'd man,/That bear'st a cheek for blows, a head for wrongs" (IV.ii.50–51).[36]

Marilyn French tells an anecdote about Robert Lowell reducing Harvard seminar students to shocked silence "by suggesting that maybe Goneril and Regan were right, maybe Lear's knights were rowdy and lecherous drunkards, and *were* disturbing the house." She goes on to enumerate the faults of Lear, Gloucester, and even Kent and complains that "these questions are not permitted within the terms of the play" (260). But not only are these questions "permitted"; they are essential to the full significance of the tragedy, which not only stages a conflict between two visions of human nature and natural law, but in fact dramatizes in the starkest terms the limitations of human knowledge of that law and the futility of man's attempt to save himself from his own worst instincts by means of moral behavior. It is not that the traditional moral vision is repudiated; it is certainly endorsed by the action of the play, and the effort to live merely according to self-interest is shown to be not only self-destructive but vile. The proponents of natural law do not, however, defeat their enemies by virtue of their superior morality. For the most part, the wicked characters destroy themselves and one another along with the most virtuous characters. *King Lear* stages not just a conflict between rival versions of natural law, but the crisis of natural law with respect to its role in the community—an actual crisis in Shakespeare's day, as intimated by Hooker's lengthy reflection

---

36. The vulnerability of sincerity and gentleness to the guile and violence of malice and ambition was obviously a preoccupation of Shakespeare's. Claudius assures Laertes that the Prince Hamlet is himself "Most generous, and free from all contriving," so it will be easy to kill him with a poisoned, unbated foil in the "friendly" fencing match (*Hamlet* V.i.134–39); and Iago counts on the "free and open nature" of the Moor in order to deceive him (*Othello* I.iii.399–402). Similar to Goneril, Lady Macbeth deprecates her husband's "nature" for being "too full o' th'milk of human kindness" (*Macbeth* I.v.16–17).

on the matter in *Ecclesiastical Polity*: "For my purpose herein is to shew, that when the minds of men are once erroneously persuaded that it is the will of God to have those things done which they fancy, their opinions are as thorns in their sides, never suffering them to take rest till they have brought their speculations into practice" (1:139). Edmund has this in common with Hooker's Puritan antagonists: a burning impatience with customary laws and practices fueled by a suspicion that there is nothing supporting them besides the arbitrary will of the established rulers. Shakespeare thus dramatizes precisely what Hooker feared: the vulnerability of social order when it is forced to explain itself. As St. Thomas concedes, since practical moral reason deals with singular and contingent affairs, "Human laws cannot possess the infallibility of the necessary conclusions of the sciences" (*ST* I-II, q. 91, a. 3, ad 3).[37]

The intractable complexity of the issue emerges most vividly in Lear's conflict with his daughters over the number of retainers he will be allowed to keep. For Goneril and Regan, of course, the argument is a means of cruelly humiliating their father as well as a stratagem for reducing him to helplessness by isolating him. Why do you need twenty-five followers, or ten, or five, Goneril demands, since so many of my servants and my sister's are there to serve you? "What need one?" (II.iv.263), is Regan's insolent, though logical, conclusion to this economic train of reasoning. Lear's reply, while self-serving, nonetheless gropes toward an important truth:

> O, reason not the need! our basest beggars
> Are in the poorest thing superfluous.
> Allow not nature more than nature needs,
> Man's life is cheap as beast's. Thou art a lady;
> If only to go warm were gorgeous,
> Why, nature needs not what thou gorgeous wear'st,

---

[37]. "Ratio practica est circa operabilia, quae sunt singularia et contingentia: non autem circa necessaria, sicut ratio speculativa. Et ideo leges humanae non possunt illam infallibilitatem habere quam habent conclusiones demonstrativae scientiarum."

Which scarcely keeps thee warm. But for true need—
You heavens, give me that patience, patience I need!
(II.iv.264–70)

According to R. S. White, sharing in Regan's implacable logic, Lear says this "in his unregenerate state, threatened with the disbanding of his personal followers." At his point, "he speaks without the experience of true need. He is rationalising 'superfluities.'"[38] Craig, however, calls it a "*pre*-philosophical view," but observes that it "is much closer to the truth than is the physiologist's view that he later espouses in the midst of liberating madness. One endlessly important respect in which human life differs from that of beasts is precisely in its being ruled neither by bare necessity nor by strict utility, and that *beauty*, in particular, is a natural human concern."[39]

As both St. Thomas (I-II, q. 91, a. 2) and Hooker (1:159–66) observe, there is a distinction between rational creatures or voluntary agents and "natural agents." Human nature transcends mere nature. Paradoxically, we truly *need* more than we *need* in strict material terms. Jonathan Dollimore gets it just backward in asserting, "Human values are not antecedent to these material realities but are, on the contrary, in-formed by them."[40] This is exactly Regan's line: "I pray you, father, being weak, seem so" (II.iv.201). As rational creatures capable of choice, men and women need to have their human dignity acknowledged. And this is not altered when someone, like Lear or like Gloucester, behaves badly. Although they both suffer in ways that seem poetically appropriate and significant—Gloucester is blinded in order to see; Lear loses his wits in order to understand—this does not mean that their children who subject them to this indignity and anguish are justified in doing so. Goneril's complaints against her father may have merit, and her sister's logic is impeccable: "How in one house / Should many people under

---

38. White, *Natural Law in English Renaissance Literature*, 202.
39. Craig, *Of Philosophers and Kings*, 183.
40. Dollimore, *Radical Tragedy*, 197.

two commands / Hold amity? 'Tis hard, almost impossible" (II.iv.240–42). But Lear's personal retinue is part of his identity, a crucial element in his sense of self-respect; to deny him his own men is to deprive him of his sense of self, to make him, in Oswald's surly phrase, nothing but "My lady's father" (I.iv.79). That Lear has, in large measure, brought his troubles on himself and has, strictly speaking, no right to act like a king anymore in no way excuses his ill usage.

Natural law teaching is, moreover, not revolutionary. Law should be changed, St. Thomas says, only for the gravest of reasons (*ST* I-II, q. 97, a. 2) The fact that Lear confronts need greater than his own in Edgar disguised as "Poor Tom," who stands in for the multitude of the dispossessed and destitute, does not make Lear's own need any less. His great speech of recognition and remorse on the heath is not a renunciation of his own requirements, but the realization of his responsibility to the needs of others whom he has neglected:

> Poor naked wretches, wheresoe'er you are,
> That bide the pelting of this pitiless storm,
> How shall your houseless heads and unfed sides,
> Your [loop'd] and window'd raggedness, defend you
> From seasons such as these? O, I have ta'en
> Too little care of this! Take physic, pomp,
> Expose thyself to feel what wretches feel,
> That thou mayst shake the superflux to them,
> And show the heavens more just. (III.iv.28–36)

Lear is not renouncing royalty; he is lamenting that he has not been a better king. He is not relinquishing the "superflux"; it is that which makes alms-giving possible.[41]

The trouble with the natural law is that it stipulates requirements for human nature that nature cannot fulfill, and it is in providing dramatic representation of this dilemma that *King Lear* becomes a profoundly Christian play. When Lear demands

---

41. See Kronenfeld, *King Lear and the Naked Truth*, 188–90.

love of his daughters, he is expressing a genuine need: men and women *need* to be loved. Even Edmund as he is dying takes perverse satisfaction in such love as he has elicited from Goneril and Regan: "Yet Edmund was belov'd! / The one the other poison'd for my sake, / And after slew herself" (V.iii.240–42). But as Edmund's comment shows, no one has a *right* to expect love from another individual simply because such a requirement cannot be enforced: Goneril failed to love her husband and killed for the illicit love of Edmund. Goneril and Regan also show that love can be feigned, that it can be expressed without being willed; but Cordelia's response, which so disappoints her father's expectation, shows all that one can actually *demand* of another, even if it is so much less than what one longs for:

> Good my lord,
> You have begot me, bred me, lov'd me: I
> Return those duties back as are right fit,
> Obey you, love you, and most honor you. (I.i.95–98)

Lear's frustrated response tells us what is missing: "But goes thy heart with this?" (I.i.104). It is just the *heart* that cannot be commanded.

Of course Cordelia is the ultimate embodiment of love in the play; it is she who, unlike her sisters, when her father is in despair, will *not* "reason the need"; that is, she offers the love that one need not—that one *could not* deserve. This factor alone would cast a Christian glow over the entire tragedy despite its pagan setting, but Shakespeare is at pains to associate Cordelia with Christian virtues and preoccupations by means of a number of explicit allusions. When she is cast off by her father, the King of France describes her in paradoxical terms reminiscent of the beatitudes in the Sermon on the Mount: "Fairest Cordelia, that art most rich being poor, / Most choice forsaken, and most lov'd despis'd" (I.i.250–51). When she returns to England at the head of a French army, she disclaims any ambition in words reminiscent of the twelve-year-old Jesus when his earthly parents find him in the Temple: "O dear father, / It is thy business that I go about" (IV.iv.23–24). The unnamed gentleman who seeks to bring Lear to his daughter says, "Thou hast [one] daughter / Who redeems nature from the general curse / Which twain have brought her to" (IV.vi.205–7). We are likely at first to think "twain" refers to Goneril and Regan, but it is Adam and Eve who caused the "general curse," and to "redeem" it is the work of the Savior. All of these lines, it should be noted, are in both the Quarto and Folio versions of the text.[42]

In the end, like Christ, Cordelia is "hanged on a tree" (Acts 5:30), and we last see her dead in the arms of her grieving father, a mirror image of the traditional *Pietà*.[43] The manner of Cordelia's death is also important because she *does not commit suicide*, as she does in the principal historical and literary sources such as Monmouth, Holinshed, *The Mirror for Magistrates*, and the second book of the *Faerie Queene*.[44] Suicide seems a highly significant issue for Shakespeare. Hamlet's fate seems more hopeful insofar as he draws back from the suicide he contemplates expressly because of Christian scruple (e.g., I.ii.131–32; III.i.55–81), while Othello seems to affirm his own sense of damnation in taking his own life (V.ii.277–80, 343–56). Even Puck, of all improbable spokesmen, condemns suicide in *A Midsummer Night's Dream* (III.382–87).

Most important is the scene when Lear awakens to find himself dressed in clean garments in the presence of his disinherited daughter, Cordelia. Filled with shame and guilt, he cannot believe that she will not spurn him:

> If you have poison for me, I will drink it.
> I know you do not love me, for your sisters
> Have (as I do remember) done me wrong:
> You have some cause, they have not.

---

42. See the parallel texts in *Norton Shakespeare*, which is based on the Oxford edition: Q 1.258–59 = F I.i.248–49; Q 18.24–25 = F IV.iii.23–24; Q 20.191–93 = F IV.v.195–97.

43. For these and numerous other scriptural references, see Milward, *Biblical Influences*, 156–204.

44. Bullough, *Narrative and Dramatic Sources of Shakespeare*, 7:315–16, 319, 331–34.

Cordelia's reply offers what is perhaps the most compelling vision of Christian charity and forgiveness in all of English literature: "No cause, no cause" (IV.vii.70–75). She does not *say*, "I forgive you," thus reminding him what he owes her. Instead, she wipes the slate clean as in the sacrament of penance or the divine forgiveness evoked in Psalm 32: "Blessed is he whose wickednes is forgiuen, & whose sinne is couered." The love that Lear sought to command in the play's opening scene is here bestowed freely upon him in the depths of his despair, "bound / Upon a wheel of fire" (IV.vii.45–46). This reconciliation scene is, then, a manifestation of hope for mortals who find that their own efforts to rectify the world by adhering to the law written in their hearts and exercising their own natural virtues are insufficient.

Cordelia returns to England to save her father's kingdom from her wicked sisters and to redeem him from despair. In so doing she dies. Any spectator or reader, in Shakespeare's day or ours, will almost inevitably be reminded of Christ's mission of redemption and his sacrificial death. Cordelia, however, is not Christ. She is a pagan woman who leads a French army into England, is defeated and captured, and brutally put to death by her captor. She will not rise from her grave in three days. In reminding us of the Christian Savior, she reminds us—and certainly Shakespeare's original audience—of what the world of *King Lear* did not have.[45]

This dénouement does not, however, validate Elton's conclusion that the "implicit direction of the tragedy [is] annihilation of faith in poetic justice and, within the confines of a grim pagan universe, annihilation of faith in divine justice" (334). What happens in *King Lear* is just what St. Paul might have predicted; it conforms perfectly with his admonition to the Ephesians concerning their life before they received grace and lived in a godless and hence hopeless world. Shakespeare looks at the pagan world

---

45. Hence Stanley Cavell's tortuous effort in *Disowning Knowledge*, 73, to show that Cordelia is not "a Christ figure" is simply beside the point.

of *King Lear* much as, according to J. R. R. Tolkien, the Christian *Beowulf* poet looked at the world of his hero: "One thing he knew clearly: those days were heathen—heathen, noble, and hopeless."[46] Elton's project to undermine "the optimistic Christian interpretation of *King Lear*" (335) was thus misconceived from the outset. Christianity is a religion of *hope* in a future life founded on grace, not *optimism*, and as St. Thomas Aquinas points out, "We should not seek other goods of God [besides salvation] except in the order of eternal blessedness. Hence hope also principally has regard for eternal blessedness; other things that are sought from God it holds in a secondary regard, and in the order of eternal blessedness" (*ST* II-II, q. 17, a. 2, ad 2).[47] Or as St. Paul puts it, "For we are saued by hope: but hope that is sene, is not hope: for how can a man hope for that which he seeth?" (Rom 8:24). Jesus Christ was tortured and brutally put to death, and his church was sustained and expanded by nearly three centuries of martyrdom. In Shakespeare's day Christians had been martyring one another for three generations: men and women endured terrible suffering and grisly death at the hands of those who were convinced that their hope was an illusion and without tangible evidence that "the purported benevolent, just, or special providence" was "operative" on their behalf.[48] Hooker's great exposition of natural law in the 1590s was precisely an effort—futile as it turned out—to moderate some of the sectarian passion that motivated this outburst of violence and cruelty. Shakespeare's starkly tragic revision of "the unconsciously comic and pietistic old *Leir*" need not be regarded as a rejection of Christian providence and divine justice, but rather a dramatic realization

---

46. J. R. R. Tolkien, "*Beowulf*: The Monsters and the Critics," in *An Anthology of Beowulf Criticism*, ed. Lewis E. Nicholson (Notre Dame, Ind.: University of Notre Dame Press, 1963), 71.
47. "Ad secundum dicendum quaecumque alia bona non debemus a Deo petere nisi in ordine beatitudinem aeternam; alia vero quae petuntur a Deo respicit secundario, in ordine ad beatitudinem aeternam."
48. Elton, *"King Lear" and the Gods*, 336.

that "poetic justice" and Christian hope are altogether different in kind and import.

Finally, Elton's relentless insistence on Lear's damnation—a literary critic's version of "Sinners in the Hands of an Angry God"—is as irrelevant to the meaning of the play as the question of "How Many Children Had Lady Macbeth?" "In every respect," Elton says, "Lear fulfills the criteria for pagan behavior in life and, according to Jewel's description, for pagan behavior regarding death; indeed, he even follows Jewel's heathen into total blasphemy at the moment of his irredeemable loss" (260). Elton might make a fitting addition to the company of Job's comforters: an old man who has endured insult, exposure, and mortification that have led him into madness; who has had his fondest hope briefly fulfilled and then dashed; who comes on the stage bearing in his arms the body of his beloved daughter whose death he knows to be the result of his own willful folly—this man is to have his dying words and actions scrutinized for doctrinal orthodoxy according to a doctrine that he never knew? It is highly unlikely that an audience of Jacobean Christians would be thinking along these lines; if their preachers admonished them about excessive grief, it was because they knew grief very intimately. The death of Cordelia and her father's anguished demise do not erase their scene of charity, forgiveness, and reconciliation: in the tragic, pagan world they inhabit, these Christian virtues furnish a reminder of the hope of grace and redemption without altering the dreadful consequences of sin and error in that world. The fact is, Shakespeare never allows the question of Lear's salvation (or anyone else's) to arise. If he did, it is probable that his view would be closer to Hooker's "Discourse on Justification" than to the fulminations of his more severe contemporaries, and it is Hooker who has the final word:

> Let me die, if ever it be proved, that simply an error doth exclude a pope or a cardinal, in such a case, utterly from hope of life. Surely, I must confess unto you, if it be an

error to think, that God may be merciful to save men even
when they err, my greatest comfort is my error; were it
not for the love I bear unto this error, I would neither wish
to speak nor to live.[49]

49. Richard Hooker's "A Learned Discourse of Justification" is included in the Everyman edition of Hooker, *Of the Laws of Ecclesiastical Polity*, 1:71.

8

The Tempest in the Academic Teapot

In the course of this study of Shakespearean drama there has been regular recourse to the opinions of various theorists of postmodern perspective, largely as a means of defining the playwright's relationship to Western civilization by way of contrast. Virtually all of the rhetorical devices and intellectual schemes of contemporary theory are polemical tactics in a long-term project to discredit altogether the culture of that civilization—artistic, moral, political, philosophical, and religious—along with the combination of reasonable discourse and revelation on which they rest.[1] As the premier literary representative of Western civilization, Shakespeare, as we have observed, has been subjected to pervasive and hostile suspicion. But none of his works have been the object of such relentless scrutiny as *The Tempest*, which is one of his finest plays and, to any healthy sensibility, most delightful.

One of Shakespeare's last plays, traditionally grouped with *Pericles*, *Cymbeline*, and *The Winter's Tale* among the romances, *The Tempest* offers a blend of comedy and lyrical enchantment shadowed by muted tragic overtones. Yet it has provoked virulent

---

1. See Linda C. Raeder, "Postmodernism, Multiculturalism, and the Death of Tolerance: The Transformation of American Society," *Humanitas* 30, nos. 1–2 (2017): 59–85, for a succinct but thorough account of the general cultural movement of which postmodern literary theory is a particular part.

rancor among contemporary academic critics. Although this academic "tempest in a teapot" about *The Tempest* could be regarded as a trivial matter in itself, it is important for what it tells us about the cultural crisis of our world. This concluding chapter will, therefore, examine a sample of critical responses to this play over the last few decades, including certain studies that affirm the dramatic integrity of the play in the face of the postmodern assault on our civilization and its principles.

Not too long ago, the highest praise for a critic's work was to say that it "sent you back to the text." Perhaps you did not altogether accept the critic's conclusions—perhaps you altogether rejected them—but he had raised important issues and made you see the text in a different perspective and think through your own views more rigorously. Literary criticism based on contemporary theory likewise sends the reader back to the primary text, but with a different motivation. The question is less likely to be "how did I miss that point?" or "will this passage bear that construal?" than "did this critic and I read the same work by the same author?" This is nowhere more apparent than in treatments of *The Tempest*.

As the preceding chapters have continually shown, the critical paradigms that currently dominate academic literary study—whether the rubric "new historicism," "cultural materialism," or "post-colonialism" is applied—all share a fundamentally materialist philosophical perspective. They begin with the assumption that every facet of reality can be reduced to and explained by physical processes. This assumption is not without moral and political consequences: the material conditions in which writers live and work and their situation among the power relations of society displace inspiration and vision as factors in the evaluation of literature. Most important are the metaphysical—or rather anti-metaphysical—consequences: the institution of literature, along with the particular literary work of art, ceases to exist.[2]

---

2. For the term "literary work of art," see René Wellek and Austin Warren, *Theory of Literature*, 3rd ed. (New York: Harcourt, Brace and World, 1962), 142–57. See also

"Literature" is a varying discursive formation constructed by the ideological energies and constraints of successive phases of social history, and any individual title, say, *The Tempest*, is likewise merely an empty signifier, the locus of diverse ideological constructs associated with an indeterminate number of ink and paper exemplars and the utterances and gestures of staged performances. It exists only in the sociopolitical uses to which it has been put by various interested parties in the course of the past four centuries.

The materialist literary critic, like the materialist psychologist, is a curiously ironic figure: both deny real existence to the putative object of their attention. A materialist critic ascribes the phenomenon of literature to the interaction of social forces even as his psychological counterpart treats the soul (or *psyche*) as the product of interactions between environmental factors and electrochemical reactions in the cerebral cortex. The question that arises about both researchers is, why are they here at all? Why not cut out the middleman and, in the case of the mentally troubled patient, go straight to the neurosurgeon and the pharmacist or, in the case of the play, to the political scientist or the sociologist? The substance of drama, as of all literature, lies, however, in the realm of intellect and imagination; and this is evinced by the persistence of rewarding scholarship on the play placing it in the context of classical literature and Christian scripture or investigating its poetic style and structure.

Criticism of the nineteenth and earlier twentieth centuries traditionally celebrated *The Tempest* as Shakespeare's triumphant, if somewhat nostalgic, farewell to the stage and the "magic" of his dramatic art. The dominant contemporary voices are engaged in the demystification of all Prospero's pretensions to nobility and integrity. Shakespeare's erstwhile heroic magician is now a figure of colonial oppression, and the play's real hero is Caliban, the embodiment of the indigenous victim. Upon the branches of this central trope, contemporary critics have hung,

---

Young, *At War with the Word*, esp. 16–22, for a further discussion of the implications of denying objective status to works of literature.

like ornaments on a Christmas tree, any number of the preoccupations of academic political correctness, from feminist sexual suspicion to racial conflict to psychoanalytic speculation. They have rifled the text for telltale hints of Prospero's perversion and ransacked history for instances of the play's complicity in racialist imperialism. The resulting account of *The Tempest* is unrecognizable to anyone who does not take for granted the ideological predilections of the contemporary academic establishment.

It is well to be clear from the outset that the entire dominant discussion of *The Tempest*, the terms of the discourse pervasive in the most prestigious journals and the greater part of the books issued by university presses, rests on a premise for which "absurd" would be a euphemism. There is no rational basis for identifying Prospero, either literally or figuratively, with colonialism. The victim of a palace coup d'état engineered by his own brother and the King of Naples, Prospero is set adrift in a small boat with his infant daughter. They wash up on a desert island somewhere in the Mediterranean—not with the design of founding a plantation, but by happenstance. Their life there is hardly more than subsistence, and as soon as the opportunity presents itself, they leave. There are terms for their status that create contemporary political resonance, but "colonialist" and "imperialist" are not among them. "Castaway," "exile," and—most suggestive—"refugee"—are far more appropriate. It is, in fact, passing strange that among academic literary scholars, who pride themselves on their political sensibilities at a time when the world is witness to the horrifying sufferings of millions of refugees from war and political oppression, no one seems to have noticed the connection.

Instead, Prospero is taken to task for failing to live up to the standards of contemporary bourgeois political correctness. An early example is Lorrie Jerrell Leininger's "The Miranda Trap: Sexism and Racism in Shakespeare's *Tempest*." This piece of "feminist criticism of Shakespeare" maintains that "Caliban is made to concur [presumably by Shakespeare?] in the accusation" of rape, because "Prospero needs Miranda as sexual bait, and then needs to protect her from the threat which is inescapable given his hierarchical world—slavery being the ultimate extension of the concept of hierarchy."[3] Since *The Tempest* was one of the plays presented as part of the festivities associated with the wedding of Frederick the Elector Palatine and Elizabeth, daughter of James I of England, Leininger speculates that it may have contributed to the poor Winter Queen's unrealistic expectations regarding the privileges of her position. "In our own century," the critic adds, "the play apparently continues to reflect ongoing societal confusions that may seduce women—and men—into complicity with those who appear to favor them while oppressing others."[4] Rather than banish *The Tempest* from the ideal republic, however, she prefers to rewrite it. She asks that we "invent a modern Miranda" who will denounce her father and "join forces with Caliban." To be sure, Caliban can be a rather scary character, so there is an alternative suggestion: "If either my father or I feel threatened by his real or imputed lust, we can build a pale around our side of the island, gather our own wood, cook our own food, and clean up after ourselves."[5] Of all the accusations leveled at Prospero, I think this is my favorite: that he neglects to develop a gated community on a desert island.

Such a rewriting is the antithesis of intelligent, critical reading: we learn nothing from this essay about *The Tempest*, only that this particular contemporary feminist would not like to be Prospero's daughter. If the *educational* purpose of literature is to *lead us out (educere)* of ourselves—of our preconceptions, our prejudices, our partisanship, and our interests—then "The Miranda Trap" fails to engage *The Tempest* as literature, much less on its own terms as a particular work of dramatic art. The essay is a signal example of what may be called temporal provincialism—

---

3. Lorrie Jerrell Leininger, "The Miranda Trap: Sexism and Racism in Shakespeare's *Tempest*," in *The Woman's Part: Feminist Criticism of Shakespeare*, ed. Carolyn Ruth Swift Lenz, Gayle Greene, and Carol Thomas Neely (Urbana, Chicago, and London: University of Illinois Press, 1980), 289.
4. Leininger, "Miranda Trap," 291.
5. Leininger, "Miranda Trap," 291–92.

namely, the heedless presumption that what my own generation takes for granted embodies eternal wisdom. As C. S. Lewis observes, sympathetic study of the past liberates us not only from "the present, from the idols of our own market-place," but also from "a fairly recent past."[6] Much current theoretical criticism seems to have been written under the assumption that the Victorian period extends back to the time of the Pharaohs.

Leininger represents a rather personal or individualistic version of feminism. *The Tempest* has more frequently been mutilated on the Procrustean bed of doctrinaire Marxism. Francis Barker and Peter Hulme, for example, maintain that *The Tempest* is "a play imbricated within the discourse of colonialism."[7] They deserve some credit for using the rather *recherché* term "imbricated" in a more or less plausible fashion. *Imbrication* is the overlapping pattern of scales on a fish, feathers on a bird, shingles on a roof, and so on; and for Barker and Hulme *The Tempest* or any other work of literature is merely one "scale" or "shingle" in an ideologically generated pattern of discourse. The concept of intertextuality, they aver, has begun to liberate literary study from such outmoded concepts as *genre* and *source*, "but has itself been unable to break out of the practice of connecting text with text, of assuming that single texts are the ultimate objects of study and the principal units of meaning. Discourse, on the other hand, refers to the *field* in and through which texts are produced."[8] While Leininger seems merely to have disliked Prospero so viscerally that she set about dismantling Shakespeare's particular play, Barker and Hulme have a theory that renders doubtful the identity and integrity of any work of literature. But the implications for literary interpretation are the same in each instance. Leininger says that "Caliban is made to concur in the accusation

---

6. C. S. Lewis, "De Descriptione Temporum," in *Selected Literary Essays*, ed. Walter Hooper (Cambridge: Cambridge University Press, 1969), 12.

7. Francis Barker and Peter Hulme, "Nymphs and Reapers Heavily Vanish: The Discursive Contexts of *The Tempest*," in *Alternative Shakespeares*, ed. John Drakakis (London and New York: Methuen, 1985), 204.

8. Barker and Hulme, "Nymphs and Reapers," 196–97.

[of rape],"suggesting that there is somehow an innocent Caliban who exists apart from Shakespeare's drama, in which he is forced to play such a humiliating role. Barker and Hulme spend several pages (198–203) distinguishing between "Prospero's play" and *The Tempest*, arguing that we cannot trust his account of the usurpation of the Duchy of Milan any more than we can trust his justification for usurping Caliban's place on the island. At first the idea seems to be that Prospero is analogous to the unreliable narrator of certain works of fiction, but they finally conclude "that *The Tempest* is ultimately complicit with Prospero's play in treating Caliban's conspiracy in a fully comic mode." Like Leininger, Barker and Hulme posit the existence of a "real" Caliban outside the play who has been cruelly betrayed by Shakespeare:

> Even before it begins, Caliban's attempt to put his political claims into practice is arrested by its implication in the "low-life" characters of Stephano and Trinculo, his conspiracy framed in a grotesquerie that ends with the dubiously amusing sight of the conspirators being hunted by dogs, a fate, incidentally, not unknown to natives of the New World. The shakiness of Prospero's position is indeed staged, but in the end his version of history remains *authoritative*, the larger play acceding as it were to the containment of the conspirators in the safely comic mode, Caliban allowed only his poignant and ultimately vain protests against the venality of his co-conspirators.[9]

Doubtless these gentlemen, like so many others, would have fascinating hypotheses to share about the girlhood of Shakespeare's heroines or the number of Lady Macbeth's children.[10]

---

9. Barker and Hulme, "Nymphs and Reapers," 203. The Leininger quotation is cited in n. 4.

10. I refer, of course, to the classic essay of L. C. Knights (first published in 1933), "How Many Children Had Lady Macbeth?," in *Explorations: Essays in Criticism Mainly on the Literature of the Seventeenth Century* (London: Chatto and Windus, 1951), 1–39. Knights, taking issue with A. C. Bradley's worrying over such matters as the effect of Macbeth's marriage upon his ambition, regards the title of the essay as a humorous parody of the tendency to treat the characters as if they had an existence apart from the play as a whole. But at least critics like Bradley and, more recently, Harold Bloom, in *Shakespeare: The Invention of the Human* (New York: Riverhead, 1998), are consistent with the individualism of their extreme romanticism. Materialist critics like Barker

The treatment of the characters of *The Tempest* as if they enjoyed an existence outside the confines of the play is pervasive in postmodern criticism. Eric Cheyfitz complains that although Prospero promises, "I'll drown my book" (V.i.57), it is "a promise he never carries out in the play proper." Crafty old Prospero! Are we to infer that he sneaks out of the play and recovers that naughty book? But it gets better: "The European's departure remains a promise, never fulfilled within the confines of the play."[11] Evidently the extra-theatrical Prospero is not only keeping his book of magic spells, but may well be joined by the members of King Alonso's party in deciding to forgo returning to his Kingdom even as Prospero gives up his Duchy in Milan, so that they can all lord it over Caliban and Ariel on a desert island in the Mediterranean, which Prospero has been trying to escape for twelve years.

Of course, according to Professor Cheyfitz, "while Shakespeare has literally (in the letters of the play) placed the island in the Mediterranean, somewhere between Tunis and Naples, the literal and the proper here are not identical. That is, the literal cannot escape its entanglement with the figurative in this case." In most of Professor Cheyfitz's argument, "proper" is identified with "literal" and opposed to "figurative"[12]—until it becomes convenient to do otherwise and relocate the island in *The Tempest* (literally? properly?) to the western Atlantic or the Caribbean. It is no wonder that this critic is sympathetic to Caliban: like him, he seems to have learned language only to be able to curse Western civilization.

Of course, it is a great relief to some commentators to find that Shakespeare is not altogether successful in his wickedness. Paul Brown, for example, agrees with Barker and Hulme about

---

and Hulme, when it is ideologically expedient, grant to dramatic characters an independence and substantiality that they ordinarily deny to actual human beings, who are reduced to socially constructed "subjects."

11. Cheyfitz, *Poetics of Imperialism*, 26, 74.
12. Cheyfitz, *Poetics of Imperialism*, 87. For the opposition between "proper" and "figurative," see 36.

the imperialist intentions of Shakespeare's drama, but doubts its effectiveness:

> *The Tempest* is not simply a reflection of colonialist practices but an intervention in an ambivalent and even contradictory discourse. This intervention takes the form of a powerful and pleasurable narrative which seeks at once to harmonise disjunction, to transcend irreconcilable contradictions and to mystify the political conditions which demand colonialist discourse. Yet the narrative ultimately fails to deliver that containment and may instead be seen to foreground precisely those problems which it works to efface or overcome.[13]

Poor Will. First, he loses his status as a great playwright, whose works are worth study for their own sake; now he is not even allowed to be a competent political hack. But then Brown is not much interested in Shakespeare in any case. Half his twenty-page essay is devoted to anecdotes and theorizing about the nascent Virginia colony and about the "plantation" in Ireland—a problem that the English have still not wholly resolved. A full three pages (49–51) take up John Rolfe's marriage to Pocahontas. Since Brown maintains that Rolfe's claim that he married the Indian woman in order to civilize her and save her soul was a rationalization of "potentially truant sexual desire," the incident is somehow supposed to be relevant to Prospero's "capacity to control not *his*, but his *subjects'* sexuality, particularly that of his slave and his daughter."[14] The connection is, however, altogether

---

13. Brown, "'This Thing of Darkness I Acknowledge Mine,'" 48.

14. Brown, "'This Thing of Darkness,'" 51. Of course Rolfe married Pocahontas in 1614, three years after the first production of *The Tempest*, and he only brought her back to England in 1616. John Chamberlain mentions the incident twice in letters to Dudley Carlton, once in passing (along with a list of the inadequate products brought back from Virginia) in a letter of June 22, 1616, and again ironically as "no fayre Lady and yet with her tricking up and high stile and titles you might thincke her and her worshipfull husband to be somebody, yf you do not know that the poore companie of Virginia out of theyre povertie are faine to allow her fowre pound a weeke for her maintenance." This is not a friendly observation, but it seems to be in keeping with Chamberlain's general view that the Virginia colony was a white elephant. Chamberlain plainly does not see the momentous implications in the Pocahontas affair that Brown wishes to read back into it. See John Chamberlain, *The Letters of John Chamberlain*, ed. Norman Egbert McClure (1939; repr. Westport, Conn.: Greenwood, 1979), 2:12, 57.

factitious. The importance of chastity, the tension between love and prudential marriage, and the threat of sexual violence were themes in Western literature long before Columbus sought an alternative route to the Indies.

In fact, the entire edifice by which *The Tempest* is assimilated to "the discourse of colonialism" rests on an exceedingly exiguous foundation. First, Gonzalo speaks about twenty lines describing the golden-age Utopian commonwealth he would establish on the island if he had "the plantation of this isle.... And were the king on't" (II.i.144, 146, 148–57, 160–65). The language of this passage is rife with echoes of the Florio translation of Montaigne's essay, "Of the Cannibals," which depicts the native inhabitants of "Antarctic France" leading a life of natural innocence and nobility that put to shame the greed, vanity, and treachery of Europeans. But Montaigne is a notoriously ironic and elusive author (even as Shakespeare is), and the material from the essay that turns up in the play is all absorbed into Gonzalo's comically inconsistent plan to be ruler over a community in which all rules are abolished. It is not certain that Montaigne is definitively anti-colonialist, and there is no evidence whatsoever that Shakespeare is doing anything more than appropriating useful material from a convenient source.

The second bit of evidence supposedly implicating the playwright in colonialism: Caliban gives the name of his father as "Setebos" (I.ii.373; V.i.261), which scholars have identified as a Patagonian god mentioned in accounts of the voyages of Magellan. There is no reason to suppose, however, that the use of an exotic name of obscure origin represents an investment by Shakespeare in colonialism. Again, it is a convenient appropriation of dramatically effective material. Third, Ariel makes reference to fetching dew from "the still-vex'd Bermoothes" (I.ii.229), but the point is that Bermuda is somewhere else a long way off. Finally, and the focus of most attention, it is widely accepted that the description of the storm in the first scene and the overall event of a ship that survives a terrible storm and runs aground on a providentially fertile and inviting island were inspired by William Strachey's account of the remarkable survival of the entire party of Sir Thomas Gates, whose ship ran aground on Bermuda in 1610. Strachey's narrative of the event was not published until 1625, so it is necessary to assume that Shakespeare read it in manuscript.

Even if the last assumption is granted, there is really not much here. Strachey makes the point that the Bermudas, which had been called the Devil's Islands and thought to be "given over to devils and wicked spirits," are in fact quite uninhabited but still "as habitable and commodious as most countries of the same climate and situation."[15] Shakespeare depicts an island rather more like what had been imagined by fearful mariners. It is certainly the abode of spirits and magic, although how wicked they are is a question posed by the play for its audience. If Shakespeare used Strachey's account of the Bermudas adventure of Sir Thomas Gates and his company, he did so with the same masterful insouciance with which he treated all his sources—appropriating what was useful to his own purposes and forging it anew in his imagination with no regard to the original author's intentions.

All the same, materialist critics make recourse to desperate shifts to persuade us that William Shakespeare was hand-in-glove with William Strachey, shareholder and secretary to the Virginia Company's Jamestown colony, and indeed with the entire British colonial enterprise. Stephen Greenblatt, the doyen of new historicism, furnishes a fair sample:

> I want to propose that the relation between the play and its alleged source is a relation between joint-stock companies. I do not mean that there was a direct, contractual connection.... In the case of Strachey and Shakespeare, there *are*, in point of fact, certain intriguing institutional affiliations: as Charles Mills Gayley observed many years ago, a remarkable number of social and professional connections link

---

15. I quote from excerpts reprinted in Stephen Orgel's edition of *The Tempest* (Oxford: Clarendon, 1987), 213.

Shakespeare and the stockholders and directors of the Virginia Company; moreover, Strachey in 1605 wrote a prefatory sonnet commending Jonson's *Sejanus* and in 1606 is listed as a shareholder in an acting company known as the Children of the Queen's Revels, the company that had taken over the Blackfriars Theater from Richard Burbage.[16]

Should Oliver Stone chance to read Stephen Greenblatt, we may surmise that the next Hollywood version of Shakespeare's life will not be *Shakespeare in Love* but *Shakespeare and the Colonialist Conspiracy*. And it will undoubtedly have just as much validity as the average conspiracy movie. If we remember that London was, by modern standards, little more than a big town with a very low literacy rate, it would be truly surprising if there were not multiple connections among the men involved in various enterprises requiring money and education (e.g., the Virginia Company and the theatre). Shakespeare dedicated *Venus and Adonis* (1593) and *The Rape of Lucrece* (1594) to Henry Wriothesley, Earl of Southampton, and Heminges and Condell dedicated the posthumous folio edition of Shakespeare's plays (1623) to William Herbert, Earl of Pembroke, and his brother Philip, Earl of Montgomery. Both Southampton and Pembroke have been advanced as candidates to be "Mr. W. H." to whom the *Sonnets* (1609) are dedicated, and both were directors of the Virginia Company. To infer from this information that *The Tempest* was therefore written to promote the Virginia colony is analogous to the inference that a man who wins a Ford Foundation grant to study art history must be somehow promoting the Ford Explorer and Expedition (names with definite colonialist overtones!).

But Greenblatt knows this. He backs away from the overt conspiracy theories and suggests a more subtle ideological connection:

Still, I should emphasize that these affiliations do not amount to a direct transfer of properties; we are dealing with a system of mimet-

---

16. Stephen Greenblatt, "Martial Law in the Land of Cockaigne," in *Shakespearean Negotiations*, 148–49.

ic rather than contractual exchange. The conjunction of Strachey's unpublished letter and Shakespeare's play signals an institutional circulation of culturally significant narratives. And as we shall see, this circulation has as its central concern the public management of anxiety.[17]

But once again this just won't do, and once again Greenblatt knows it:

> But the swerve away from these materials in *The Tempest* is as apparent as their presence: the island is not in America but in the Mediterranean; it is not uninhabited—Ariel and Caliban (and, for that matter, Sycorax) were present before the arrival of Prospero and Miranda; none of the figures are in any sense colonists; the departure is for home rather than a colony and entails not an unequivocal heightening of authority but a partial diminution, signaled in Prospero's abjuration of magic.[18]

But even though he concedes that "the direction of *The Tempest* is toward forgiveness," Greenblatt cannot refrain from reattaching it to repressive ideology. Having allowed that it raises "troubling questions about this authority," which is hardly news, he also maintains that "the play seems to act out a fantasy of mind control, to celebrate absolute patriarchal rule, to push to an extreme the dream of order, epic achievement, and ideological justification implicit in Strachey's text."[19] Greenblatt concludes his essay with one of his signature anecdotes. In this one H. M. Stanley burns his copy of Shakespeare, fooling the African natives into thinking it is his notebook containing his numerous "plans of falls, creeks, villages, sketches of localities, ethnological and philological details,"[20] which the natives thought an instrument of fatal magic. For Greenblatt, Stanley's notes on his observations in Africa are nothing but an instrument for the subju-

---

17. Greenblatt, "Martial Law," 149.
18. Greenblatt, "Martial Law," 154.
19. Greenblatt, "Martial Law," 156, 155.
20. Greenblatt, "Martial Law," 162.

gation of the continent and its peoples. The fact that a volume of Shakespeare's works is carried along on such an expedition and saves Stanley's notes means that Shakespeare is somehow implicated in the European conquest of Africa. But if we concede the point that Stanley's subterfuge represents the repressive deceit of European colonialism, nothing is thus proven about Shakespeare per se. *Any book* would have served Stanley's purpose, so it is literacy itself that must be regarded as the instrument of colonial oppression. Perhaps new historicist professors ought to stop writing books.

Greenblatt at least is willing to concede a certain ambiguity in the actual content of *The Tempest*, at least insofar as he grants it a definite content apart from its place in the historical unfolding of British ideology. Most materialist critics lack his finesse. Thomas Cartelli insists that because "the text of *The Tempest* continues to allow Prospero the privilege of the grand closing gesture; continues to privilege that gesture's ambiguity at the expense of Caliban's dispossession ... *The Tempest* is not only complicit in the history of its successive misreadings, but responsible in some measure for the development of the ways in which it is read."[21] Kim Hall combines a racial agenda with Lorrie Leininger's feminist preoccupations and concludes that Prospero's response to Caliban's attempt to rape his daughter has nothing to do with her safety and well-being: "It is in response to Caliban's claim of property rights that Prospero charges Caliban with rape, a rhetorical move that reinforces Valerie Smith's point that 'instances of interracial rape constitute sites of struggle between black and white men that allow privileged white men to exercise property rights over the bodies of white women.'"[22] Once again, while *The Tempest* itself is conceded no independent significance as a dramatic work, the character Caliban is assumed to exist apart from

---

21. Cartelli, "Prospero in Africa," 112. On this and the work cited in the following note, see Young, *At War with the Word*, 106–10.
22. Kim Hall, *Things of Darkness: Economies of Race and Gender in Early Modern England* (Ithaca, N.Y., and London: Cornell University Press, 1995), 150–51.

the play as an oppressed African or an African American victim of a lynch mob, led by that well-known Ku Klux Klansman, Prospero.

To be sure, although the race/class/gender perspective of new historicism and cultural materialism has been overwhelmingly dominant, there have been dissenting voices. Not all, however, are the basis for rejoicing. The psychoanalytic alternative, for example, is a cure that may only exacerbate the disease. Meredith Anne Skura carefully lists the shortcomings of the colonialist reading of *The Tempest*, pointing out that "we have no *external* evidence that seventeenth-century audiences thought the play referred to the New World," and remarking, "Caliban in fact is more like the devils Strachey expected to find on the Bermuda island (and didn't) than like the Indians whom adventurers did find in Virginia."[23] But Skura is careful to protect her political bona fides by inveighing against "New Critical 'blindness' to history and ideology" and "New Critics trying to isolate texts from contexts," although the only "New Critic" named is G. Wilson Knight, who, I suspect, would have been surprised to find himself in such company.[24] Skura's own reading, although dressed up in psychoanalytic argot, makes no real advance beyond traditional moral allegory (with which I have no necessary quarrel). Prospero's disproportionate rage with Caliban, she maintains, has more to do with the darker side of his own nature than with imperial dominion:

> At the moment of Prospero's eruption into anger, he has just bestowed Miranda on his enemy's son Ferdinand and is in the midst of presenting his pageant as a wedding gift, wrapped in a three-fold warning about chastity. If Prospero is to pass on his heritage to the next generation, he must at this moment repress his desire for power and for revenge at home, as well as any sexual desire he feels toward Miran-

---

23. Meredith Skura, "Discourse and the Individual: The Case of Colonialism in *The Tempest*," in *Critical Essays on Shakepeare's "The Tempest*," ed. Virginia Mason Vaughan and Alden T. Vaughan (New York: G. K. Hall, 1998), 64, 65.

24. Skura, "Discourse and the Individual," 63, 67–68.

da. Both desires are easily projected onto the fishily phallic Caliban, a walking version of Prospero's own "thing" of darkness. Not only has Caliban already tried to rape Miranda; he is now out to kill Prospero so that he can turn Miranda over to Stephano ... and Caliban does not even feel guilty. Caliban's function as a walking screen for projection may help explain why Caliban's sin does not consist in cannibalism, to which, one assumes, Prospero was never tempted, but rather in Prospero's own repressed fantasies of omnipotence and lust.[25]

Ruth Nevo is even more explicit and more suspicious. The banishment of Venus and Cupid from the masque of Ceres that Prospero stages for the betrothed couple strikes Nevo as peculiar (are an adulteress and a provoker of lust, one may ask, really necessary to bless a wedding?), and his disturbed breaking off of the masque when he recalls the conspiracy of Caliban, Stephano, and Trinculo clinches it: "How can we read this but as a stubborn return of the repressed, of the utterly tabooed, of his own unacknowledged desire, together with the terror that accompanies it and is then unleashed in rage upon Caliban?"[26]

How indeed can we read this? The idea that Caliban symbolically represents the dark, passionate side of human nature—against which Prospero, like every other mortal, must be vigilant—is hardly novel. Shakespeare takes pains to show his protagonist struggling against his (all too understandable) bitterness and anger—and succeeding:

> Though with their high wrongs I am strook to th'quick,
> Yet, with my nobler reason, 'gainst my fury
> Do I take part. The rarer action is
> In virtue than in vengeance. (V.i.25–28)

But there is no indication that he is struggling to overcome incestuous desire for his daughter, whether conscious or re-

---

25. Skura, "Discourse and the Individual," 73–74.
26. Ruth Nevo, *Shakespeare's Other Language* (New York and London: Methuen, 1987), 148. For a sensible explanation of why *Venus Cupiditas* is banished from the masque, see Maurice Hunt, *Shakespeare's Romance of the Word* (Lewisburg, London, and Toronto: Bucknell University Press and Associated University Presses, 1990), 135.

pressed. The only reason for adducing this notion is to explain what hardly requires explanation: that a man would feel fury at a scaly brute who tried to rape his daughter or behave with harsh caution toward even the most well-intentioned young suitor of that same daughter—a completely innocent yet very desirable girl experiencing the love of a young man for the first time. To demand an explanation is to assume that a father has no motive for protecting his daughter from rape or seduction except for his own wishes to exploit her sexually.

Efforts to expand the rather narrow new historicist focus from within by combining its basic outlook with old-fashioned philological or historical research have been undertaken, but with mixed results. *Shakespeare Quarterly*, which has been reliably materialist for many years, has nonetheless published essays that attempt to break the mold by applying careful scholarship rather than anecdotes of dubious relevance. Julia Reinhard Lupton, for example, invokes Caliban's status as a creature to open a new middle course:

> The political theology of the Creature avoids the traps presented by humanist/universalizing readings on the one hand and culturalist/particularizing readings of the play on the other. As part of Creation, Caliban shares the universe of Adam, thwarting attempts by both characters and readers to exclude him from the common lot of humanity. At the same time, his creaturely monstrosity foils any normative reading of this humanity which would raise Caliban into an exemplar of basic drives. The play includes him within the cosmos of Adam but only as its chaotic exception.[27]

Lupton is properly alarmed with "the impasses of culturalism, whose investment in identities conferred by national belonging uncannily links the progressive goals of liberal antiracism to the reactionary impulses of ethnic cleansing."[28]

While one may applaud her political idealism, the impulse to

---

27. Julia Reinhard Lupton, "Creature Caliban," *Shakespeare Quarterly* 51 (2000): 3.
28. Lupton, "Creature Caliban," 4.

bring world peace by redefining Caliban runs into trouble before it ever confronts a practical test. Lupton's thesis rests on the assumption that "creature" is in some measure or respect a pejorative term: "In modern usage *creature* borders on the monstrous and unnatural, increasingly applied to those created things that warp the proper canons of creation."[29] But the term "creature" is never applied to Caliban in *The Tempest*, a problem that Lupton tries to evade even as she acknowledges it: "Although in *The Tempest* the word *creature* appears nowhere in conjunction with Caliban himself, his character is everywhere hedged in and held up by the politico-theological category of the creaturely."[30] Despite a good deal of etymological speculation about a number of words, Lupton never actually supplies any primary evidence for the existence of this "politico-theological category" in which "creature" implies what is monstrous or unnatural. The evidence that springs readily to mind seems contradictory: Miranda famously exclaims upon first seeing all the survivors of the wreck, "O wonder! / How many goodly creatures are there here!" (V.i.181–82). To be sure, for her, "'Tis new," but the term "creature" can hardly be taken to indicate what is less than human. Or consider another contemporaneous example. In the *Book of Common Prayer*, in the course of the consecration in the service of Holy Communion, the minister prays, "Hear us, O merciful Father, we beseech thee; and grant that we receiving these thy *creatures* [emphasis added] of bread and wine, according to thy Son our Saviour Jesus Christ's holy institution, in remembrance of his death and passion, may be partakers of his most blessed Body and Blood."[31] *Creature* hardly suggests the "monstrous" in this familiar Elizabethan context. One suspects that Lupton has projected back into Shakespeare's time the overtones of the modern corruption "critter."

Finally, pursuit of her goal of reconciliation leads Lupton to

---

29. Lupton, "Creature Caliban," 1.
30. Lupton, "Creature Caliban," 2.
31. *Book of Common Prayer*, 263.

what can only be called a logical error. "If we want to find a new universalism in the play (as I believe, urgently, we must), we will do so not by simply reasserting that 'Caliban is human' but rather by saying that 'all humans are creatures,' that all humans constitute an exception to their own humanity, whether understood in general or particular terms."[32] This statement may be read thus: Caliban is a creature. All human beings are creatures. Therefore, all human beings are Caliban. This used to be known as the fallacy of the undistributed middle. Of course, Lupton may merely be saying that there is a Caliban lurking in all of us, but this view sounds suspiciously like original sin—a rather old-fashioned idea, which is even less amenable to current academic politics than unregenerate humanist universalism.

Barbara A. Mowat, unlike Lupton, suffers from no shortage of primary sources. Her essay "Prospero's Book" teems with fascinating material, much of it gleaned from the Folger Library collection, about the Renaissance *grimoire*, or manuscript manual of magical practice. Mowat begins by suggesting that among the books that Gonzalo has provided for Prospero there is such a book, and that it is this book to which he has recourse in saying, "I'll to my book" (III.i.94). But after more than twenty pages, it turns out that "Prospero's book is *not* a grimoire," or rather it "seems to be simultaneously a grimoire and a stage-prop (or romance-prop) grimoire." Finally, it turns out to be just a "book *per se*," which makes "possible Prospero's rule over his island kingdom"; that is, just colonialist technology.[33] In other words, we cannot be sure whether Prospero availed himself of a grimoire, but we know that he was an imperialist.

It is remarkable that, in the midst of such resolute (not to say, ruthless) subjugation of *The Tempest* to contemporary political

---

32. Lupton, "Creature Caliban," 21.
33. Barbara A. Mowat, "Prospero's Book," *Shakespeare Quarterly* 52 (2001): 1, 27, 29, 32. For Mowat's earlier take on Prospero as magician, see Mowat, "Prospero, Agrippa, and Hocus Pocus," in *Critical Essays on Shakespeare's "The Tempest,"* ed. Virginia Mason Vaughan and Alden T. Vaughan (New York: G. K. Hall, 1998), 193–213.

preoccupations, some critics have found new and interesting things to say about the play from more traditional perspectives. Russ McDonald, for instance, focuses on the poetic style and maintains that it eludes our reductive explanations: "In *The Tempest*, as in late Shakespeare generally, the effect of the poetry is to promote *un*certainty and to insist upon ambiguity, and attention to the verse makes one increasingly dubious about the bluntness of most political interpretation."[34] McDonald looks carefully at the rich and subtle patterning of poetic and rhetorical devices in the play and suggests that it is precisely in the seams of its ambiguities that significance emerges: "The verbal music is related to the oneiric and unreal atmosphere that attends and complicates the action of Shakespeare's late romantic forms; it promises much and delivers little, and I propose that it is just this dynamic that makes *The Tempest* uncommonly meaningful."[35] The *political* meaning of a play, McDonald contends, is just in the questioning of our ordinary political categories, of our proclivity for reducing reality to tidy ideological packages:

Poetic indeterminacy shows us how to evaluate the appropriation of the play by those who see it as a political act in the colonialist enterprise. It helps to complicate the ideology of *The Tempest*, indicating that the political ideas are more subtle and difficult than recent readings would suggest. Pleas for interpretative caution are often attacked as retrogressive politics, but the recognition that this is one of the most knowing, most self-conscious texts in the canon should warn us about pretensions to ideological certainty. On the very issues that have most deeply concerned materialist critics and their American cousins—power, social and political hierarchy, the theatre as a political instrument, freedom of action, education, and race—*The Tempest* is at its most elusive and complicated. The play valorizes ambiguity and irony, ironizing its own positions and insisting upon the inclusiveness of its

---

34. Russ McDonald, "Reading *The Tempest*," in Vaughan and Vaughan, *Critical Essays on Shakespeare's "The Tempest*," 216. The anthology put together by the Vaughans deserves high praise for the breadth—the genuine diversity—of the viewpoints it includes.

35. McDonald, "Reading *The Tempest*," 224.

own conclusions. The new orthodoxy, which exalts the colonized, is as narrow as the old, which idealizes and excuses the colonizer.[36]

This "new orthodoxy" is, apparently, so powerful and so unforgiving that McDonald immediately retreats from what he inaccurately calls a retreat: "This stylistic interpretation is not, however, merely another version of New Criticism, a retreat, that is, into the restful shadows of irony and ambiguity."[37] But irony and ambiguity, whatever else they may be, are never "restful"; and to find in the style of a sophisticated piece of literature or drama a complex unbalancing of the clichés by which we ordinarily muddle along—as McDonald does in *The Tempest*—is exactly the goal of the much-maligned "New Criticism." McDonald goes on to invoke Kenneth Burke in calling upon us to see how "*The Tempest* promotes in its audience a kind of moral and imaginative athleticism."[38] He might as justly have recalled Edmund Burke—or his twentieth-century disciple, Russell Kirk—on the moral imagination.

Another fine essay concerned with the style of *The Tempest*, although more concerned with larger, structural elements of the play, is Donna B. Hamilton's "Defiguring Virgil in *The Tempest*." She carefully lays out the various ways in which *The Tempest* is, in the best Renaissance sense of the term, an imitation of the *Aeneid*. In some instances, the imitation is direct and overt; in others it is oblique and hidden. Never simply a matter of copying the features of the model, imitation is rather a means of adapting another poet's techniques and strategies: "It involves the poet in the art, the workmanship, of the parent work, and it is the art that is often a primary object of imitation."[39] Hamilton explains how Virgil is more important than Virginia to an understanding of the political meaning of *The Tempest*. Shakespeare is typical of

---

36. McDonald, "Reading *The Tempest*," 228.
37. McDonald, "Reading *The Tempest*," 229.
38. McDonald, "Reading *The Tempest*."
39. Donna B. Hamilton, "Defiguring Virgil in *The Tempest*," in Vaughan and Vaughan, *Critical Essays on Shakespeare's "The Tempest,"* 20.

Renaissance thought in regarding political philosophy as dependent on ethics. Politics comes to life in *The Tempest* through the imitation of a poem that was routinely read as both an allegory of the soul and an exemplary account of political and military leadership:

> One way of explaining how Shakespeare responded to this tradition in his own imitation is to say that he invented a way to tell these two stories—the political story and the story of the soul's progress—as one. He structured the central political action of the play—Prospero's plot for regaining his dukedom in Italy—so that it incorporates a series of educational journeys.[40]

In this essay diligent philological scholarship combines with sophisticated analysis of a text to yield a happy critical result.[41]

Finally, attempts to interpret *The Tempest*, as well as the other romances, in Christian terms have recently appeared. Perhaps the most compelling and sophisticated of these treatments is by John D. Cox, who concedes a good deal of ground to the new historicists and cultural materialists in noting their displacement of the "idealist" or "formalist" readings that dominated the critical scene until the 1970s:

> Suspicion of Christian motives underlies the materialist critique, especially when Christian affirmation appears in the mouths of the powerful and the privileged, as it does in *The Tempest*, and especially when Christian aspects of the play are tied to Renaissance social assumptions, as they are in Kermode's edition. What I would like to suggest here is that a distinctive Christian account of the play can be offered apart from either of the dominant interpretive paradigms that developed in the second half of the twentieth century, and that that

---

40. Hamilton, "Defiguring Virgil," 34.
41. Also admirable is the treatment of the relation between Ovid and *The Tempest* in Jonathan Bate, *Shakespeare and Ovid* (Oxford: Clarendon, 1993), 239–63. An excerpt from this work is also reprinted in Vaughan and Vaughan, *Critical Essays on Shakespeare's "The Tempest,"* 39–59. John C. Briggs, "Catharsis in *The Tempest*," *Ben Jonson Journal* 5 (1998): 115–32, usefully applies Aristotle's classic concept of tragedy to consider Shakespeare's romance as a tragicomedy.

distinctiveness enables a recovery of Christian interpretation in the heyday of postmodernism.[42]

Cox provides a Christian alternative to the materialist reading, but only after maintaining, under the influence of Nicholas Lash, that Marxism and Christianity are "siblings" as well as "rivals" and "share a common concern for justice."[43]

In Cox's view, the materialists neglect the central thematic element of the play, Prospero's moral growth in his ability to forgive his enemies. Cox challenges Stephen Orgel's argument, for example, that Prospero's forgiveness is mere political maneuvering. While it is true that Prospero may be seen as embodying the absolute royal power for which James I longed, Shakespeare's character also embodies a moral lesson: "That Prospero actually possesses this kind of power and still recognizes the need for self-restraint and forgiveness of his enemies is perhaps the singly most remarkable feature of *The Tempest*."[44] On the other hand, Cox takes very seriously Caliban's status as a victim of colonialism rather than an allegorical figure for unruly passion and brutishness. "One reason that Shakespeare's Caliban cannot be reduced to an idealist allegory of bestiality," Cox maintains, "is that he is unmistakably human."[45] But here one may demur: Caliban's status is not really so self-evident: none of the other characters in the play seems willing to concede his humanity, and yet as a being capable of speech he is clearly rational, and his sexual interest in Miranda suggests human inclinations of another sort. It is precisely this ambiguity that leaves Caliban in an uncertain position, partly in the concrete world of the play, partly in a symbolic realm, without at all fitting into allegory in the mode of Spenser or Bunyan. And, of course, there is the further problem that Prospero is no colonist, and Caliban is merely another

---

42. John D. Cox, "Recovering Something Christian about *The Tempest*," *Christianity and Literature* 50 (2000): 31.
43. Cox, "Recovering Something Christian," 35.
44. Cox, "Recovering Something Christian," 37–38.
45. Cox, "Recovering Something Christian," 41.

castaway rather than the representative of an indigenous people (which could only be another allegorical role). Still, John Cox succeeds admirably in engaging the materialist critics on their own ground and demonstrating that Christianity provides a more satisfactory context for interpreting *The Tempest* even when a number of materialist assumptions have been granted.

There are additional recent interpretations of *The Tempest* in Christian terms, which also extend to the other late romances. Grace Tiffany, for example, observes that the later plays display the same preoccupations with human passions and mistakes as the tragedies themselves, but that "the dominant force in the romances is a providence that thwarts, overcomes, or undoes the crucial errors of the plays' would-be tragic heroes." What sets these plays apart is not an abandonment of tragic themes, but "the infusion of grace" that transforms them.[46] Although Tiffany is convincing in her suggestion that the romances manifest the workings of divine grace, the distinctive feature of her interpretation is that Shakespeare dramatizes "a grace conceived in Calvinist terms."[47]

The argument's shakiness is revealed when she turns to the sermons of Lancelot Andrewes for an example of Calvinist preaching.[48] Andrewes is hardly the first English cleric who comes to mind in this context, and, in fact, much of what Tiffany says about grace and all of the instances that she turns up in the romances are as compatible with Catholic as with Calvinist doctrine. Luther and Calvin maintained, for example, that the "repentance, which ... must precede our receipt of 'saving grace,' was itself prompted by an initiating grace"; but the teaching of St. Thomas Aquinas was essentially the same on this point. Likewise, when Belarius in *Cymbeline* (IV.ii.27) says, "Nature hath ... grace," he sounds more like St. Thomas than Calvin.[49]

---

46. Grace Tiffany, "Calvinist Grace in Shakespeare's Romances: Upending Tragedy," *Christianity and Literature* 49 (2000): 421.
47. Tiffany, "Calvinist Grace," 427.
48. Tiffany, "Calvinist Grace," 423–24.
49. Tiffany, "Calvinist Grace," 424, 427. See *ST* I-II, q. 112, a. 2 and I, q. 1., a. 8,

Maurice Hunt comes nearer the mark in *Shakespeare's Romance of the Word*. A dubious deployment of the Sapir/Whorf hypothesis in the introduction fortunately has minimal effect on the overall argument,[50] which concentrates on showing how the poetic words that Shakespeare gives his characters invoke the presence of the Word—that is, the influence of order and meaning and, very deftly, grace in the working out of the dramatic situations. Unsurprisingly, Hunt sees the convergence of the Word and grace culminating in *The Tempest*: "By forming a prayer, Prospero's epilogue fittingly concludes Shakespeare's romance of the word. The charity for which Prospero prays includes much more than the audience's good will, the plaudite."[51] Hunt thus offers an interpretation of *The Tempest*, as well as of the other romances in a very traditional mode: the resonance of words like "grace" and "word" itself implies a depth in the plays—a transcendence of their secular, mostly pagan plots—that again depends upon a combination of philological research and new critical sensitivity to paradox and the significant ambiguities of language.

It is reassuring to see that critics are still publishing readings of *The Tempest* based on sound scholarship and reasonable interpretive strategies, but somewhat disheartening to notice how most of these still hedge themselves about with disclaimers, insisting that they are not advocates of colonialism or patriarchy or—spare us the horror—New Critics. The crescendo of anti-colonialist and radical feminist hysteria directed at *The Tempest* is intimidating, especially for a young, untenured assistant professor who needs a livelihood and seeks a career. Still, the resistance must be made.

---

ad 2. For an account of the neglect of important convergences of Protestant and Catholic teaching on grace by the "Protestant Poetics" school of criticism, see R. V. Young, *Doctrine and Devotion in Seventeenth-Century Poetry: Studies in Donne, Herbert, Crashaw, and Vaughan* (Cambridge: D. S. Brewer, 2000), 5–80.

50. A shorthand phrase for the linguistic relativity principle, which maintains that the way a people perceives and thinks about reality is determined by the structure of its language. Edward Sapir (1884–1939) and his student, Benjamin Lee Whorf (1897–1941) are by no means the only proponents of this generally discredited theory, and they never actually collaborated on establishing the "hypothesis."

51. Hunt, *Shakespeare's Romance of the Word*, 140.

Efforts to accommodate this play as well as the rest of Shakespeare's works to the predilections and preoccupations of the current academic scene all have in common materialist presuppositions, and the common result is their failure as literary criticism. In the very strictest sense, all these approaches—whether called new historicism or cultural materialism or gender feminism—are anti-intellectual; that is, they deny the capacity of the human intellect to transcend its material circumstances. What is more, the import of this academic situation is not merely academic. The literary tradition of Western civilization is not just an important element of the civilization; it is also an analogue or metaphorical embodiment of that civilization. An attack on the literature of the West, especially in the work of one of its most important figures, is an attack upon the civilization itself. The plays that we have examined by Shakespeare in the course of this book provide lively, concrete images of the ideals of human endeavor and experience that have developed in the West, but they also show how they are corrupted and undermined by ideological preoccupations also of Western origin. Hence both the disease and its cure are present within our tradition. The prospect of restoration depends upon our wisdom and courage in resisting the destructive tendencies in our own way of life. It is up to us to determine whether the continued existence of a civilization of firm tradition continually renewed and reformed by a critical spirit is possible. Sound literary criticism will not save the world, but it can play a significant role in education, in leading young minds to an appreciation of the subtle wisdom of the idea of Western civilization as embodied in the drama of William Shakespeare.

Afterword

More than a quarter of a century ago, in *Appropriating Shakespeare*, Brian Vickers addressed many of the same postmodernist treatments of Shakespeare that are considered in this book. His account of postmodernist theory and its application is far more thorough—indeed, exhaustive—than what I have here attempted. He spends more than seventy pages documenting and explaining how the Parisian structuralists and deconstructionists distorted and exploited Ferdinand de Saussure's posthumously published *Cours de linguistic générale* (1916)—a problematic text in the first place—before discussing *Othello* as a "test case for language theory."[1] The concentration on expounding and criticizing various postmodernist theories, in fact, occupies all of part I, comprising more than 160 pages of the book.

In the remainder of his very substantial book, Vickers comprehensively shows the interpretative inadequacies of ideological criticism, including Deconstruction, New Historicism, Psychocriticism, Feminism, Marxism, and even Christianity, at least when it is deployed as an exclusive template for reading literature: "Shakespeare's plays, for so long the primary focus of the critic's and scholar's attention, are now secondary, subordinated to the imperialism and self-advancement of a particular group."[2] Vickers's painstaking critique of the applications of these various theories to Shakespearean drama is reinforced by his broad survey of numerous polemical studies by linguists,

---

1. Vickers, *Appropriating Shakespeare*, 74–91.
2. Vickers, *Appropriating Shakespeare*, xii.

philosophers, sociologists, anthropologists, and historians who effectively refute the original postmodernist theories on which the literary practice rests: "The cumulative impact of those iconoclastic theories has been damaging to literature, and I hope that my assemblage of a wide range of counter-criticism will have an appropriately deterrent, or liberating effect."[3] Combined with this "counter-criticism" from several disciplines, Vickers's attack on the postmodernist "appropriators" of Shakespeare is devastating. Or it ought to be.

But, alas, nothing much has changed over the intervening years since Vickers's book was published; it is business as usual at Academic Theory, Inc. To be sure, the luster of Deconstruction has certainly faded, but the damage—permanent damage—was already done. In a book published a year after the appearance of *Appropriating Shakespeare*, Stanley Fish, with his unerring eye for the shifting winds of academic politics, put it this way: "If there is now no vigorous discussion of deconstruction in the academy, it is because its lessons have been absorbed and its formulations—the irreducibility of difference, the priority of the signifier over the signified, the social construction of the self—have been canonized."[4] The implications of this "canonization" of deconstructive "formulations" had already been spelled out a year before Vickers's book by Henry Louis Gates, who said that, while it was fine to deconstruct "the Western male subject," the procedure was illicit when applied to "our attempts to reconstitute our subjectivity as women, as blacks, etc."[5]

Both Fish and Gates, at the time they delivered these comments, were professors in English departments; but both of their books have more to do with politics and the "culture wars" than literature, so it is not surprising that Vickers's scrupulous demonstrations of the vacuity of so many postmodernist inter-

---

3. Vickers, *Appropriating Shakespeare*, xvi.

4. Stanley Fish, *There's No Such Thing as Free Speech and It's a Good Thing, Too* (New York and Oxford: Oxford University Press, 1994), 57. See Young, *At War with the Word*, 31–33.

5. Henry Louis Gates Jr., *Loose Canons: Notes on the Culture Wars* (New York and Oxford: Oxford University Press, 1992), 35–36.

pretations of literature would be simply ignored. In what appears to be a moment of sheer exasperation with a reading of *Macbeth*, which equates "Macbeth and Lady Macbeth, regicides and murderers," with "innocent people murdered in their beds" as part of "official society," Vickers calls such an "'ideological analysis' ... not so much a critical theory as a new form of illiteracy."[6] But Terry Eagleton, the author of the truly absurd and offensive critique excoriated by Vickers, is not ignorant, certainly not illiterate. He simply does not care whether he is accurately explicating Shakespeare's text and making it accessible and enjoyable to students, his colleagues, or the public at large. Like so many of the Shakespeare critics whom both Vickers and I have cited and rebuked, his project is political, with the aim of revolutionary change of government and society. It is not just Shakespeare that has been appropriated; the humanities as a whole have been appropriated—I should say *expropriated*—to serve a political cause, which is the antithesis of the spirit of humanistic study.

When so distinguished a scholar as Brian Vickers has mounted so thorough and so powerful a rebuttal of the dominant currents in Shakespeare scholarship, with little discernible effect, it would be presumptuous, indeed, for me to suppose that this book will finally convince the contemporary academic establishment of the error of its ways and bring about a renewal of a more sensible, traditional approach to the study of our greatest poet and playwright. But such was never my principal aim. Although I should be gratified if *Shakespeare and the Idea of Western Civilization* should provoke lively debate in classrooms and faculty lounges across the United States, I do not expect this to occur to any great extent.

My hope is to provide a model of humanistic education, of teaching in the liberal arts, insofar as the study of Shakespeare is a part of that enterprise, especially in the English-speaking world. It is for this reason that my chief goal has been the exposition of Shakespeare's plays rather than the refutation of his post-

---

6. Vickers, *Appropriating Shakespeare*, 410.

Afterword

modernist critics. The latter have been frequently but not systematically invoked in order to clarify a particular idea illustrating a feature of Western civilization as it emerges from Shakespearean drama. The discussions of these ideas arising from the dramatic representation of men and women eventually converge to adumbrate the intellectual and imaginative arc of our civilization.

This book, then, seeks to engage individual scholars and teachers, individual students, and men and women in the general public who care about reading and thinking. To engage with a rich, challenging author such as Shakespeare is to embark on an investigation of the origins and nature of the culture in which we now live. To undertake this enterprise sincerely and resolutely ought to open the mind and heart and inform the intellect of the reader. With the aid of the insights available in Shakespearean drama, it should encourage a habit of reflection and patience in discerning what in our civilization is right and deserving of preservation and enhancement, and what is wrong requiring reform or even, in some instances, renunciation. The premise of liberal education, of which this book aspires to be a part, is that men and women who have read widely, thought deeply, and contemplated at length will be better suited to undertake such reform and reconstruction of society as may be needed than those who assume that, by tearing down the culture we have and substituting a utopian alternative, the individuals who constitute the society will be necessarily and spontaneously improved, even perfected.

Neither Brian Vickers nor I is going to alter very much the course of academic Shakespeare scholarship for the foreseeable future, but both of our very different books provide, for those who are or who may become disillusioned with the postmodernist Utopia, an image of a different approach to Shakespeare and to literary study as a whole and a reminder that things had been done differently in the not-too-distant past with no small measure of success. It is my hope that I have furnished some materials for the recovery of a more coherent and edifying literary culture in a not hopelessly distant future.

Bibliography

Alvis, John. "A Little Touch of the Night in Harry: The Career of Henry Monmouth." In *Shakespeare as a Political Thinker*, edited by John Alvis and Thomas G. West. Durham, N.C.: Carolina Academic Press, 1981.
Aquinas, St. Thomas. *Summa Theologiae*. Cura Fratrum Eiusdem Ordinis. 3rd ed. 5 Vols. Madrid: Biblioteca de Autores Cristianos, 1961–65.
———. *De Malo*. Edited by Brian Davies. Translated by Richard Regan. Oxford and New York: Oxford University Press, 2001.
Aristotle. *Poetics*. In *Aristotle, The Poetics; "Longinus," On the Sublime; Demetrius, On Style*. Edited and translated by W. Hamilton Fyfe and W. Rhys Roberts. Cambridge, Mass.: Harvard University Press, 1932.
———. *The Nichomachean Ethics*. Edited and translated by H. Rackham. Cambridge, Mass.: Harvard University Press, 1945.
Asquith, Clare. *Shadow Play: The Hidden Beliefs and Coded Politics of William Shakespeare*. New York: Public Affairs, 2005.
Bacon, Francis. *A Harmony of the Essays, etc., of Francis Bacon*. Edited by Edward Arber. 1871. Repr. New York: AMS, 1966.
Barker, Francis, and Peter Hulme. "Nymphs and Reapers Heavily Vanish: The Discursive Contexts of *The Tempest*. In *Alternative Shakespeares*, edited by John Drakakis. London and New York: Methuen, 1985.
Barthes, Roland. "The Death of the Author." In *Image, Music, Text*, edited and translated by Stephen Heath. New York: Farrar, Strauss and Giroux, 1977.
Barton, Anne. "Introduction" to *Much Ado About Nothing*. In *The Riverside Shakespeare*, edited by G. Blakemore Evans et al. 2nd ed. Boston and New York: Houghton Mifflin, 1997.
———. "Introduction" to *Troilus and Cressida*. In *The Riverside Shakespeare*, edited by G. Blakemore Evans et al. 2nd ed. Boston and New York: Houghton Mifflin, 1997.
Bate, Jonathan. *Shakespeare and Ovid*. Oxford: Clarendon, 1993.
Bell, Millicent. *Shakespeare's Tragic Skepticism*. New Haven, Conn., and London: Yale University Press, 2002.

Bibliography

Belsey, Catherine. *Shakespeare and the Loss of Eden: The Construction of Family Values in Early Modern Culture*. New Brunswick, N.J.: Rutgers University Press, 1999.

Berek, Peter. "The Jew as Renaissance Man." *Renaissance Quarterly* 51 (1998): 128–62.

Berger, Harry, Jr. "Text Against Performance in Shakespeare: The Example of *Macbeth*." *Genre* 15 (1982): 49–79.

Bernthal, Craig. *The Trial of Man: Christianity and the Judgment of the World in Shakespeare*. Wilmington, Del.: ISI, 2003.

Blitz, Jan H. *Deadly Thought: "Hamlet" and the Human Soul*. Lanham, Md.: Lexington, 2001.

Bloom, Allan. *Shakespeare on Love and Friendship*. London and Chicago: University of Chicago Press, 2000.

Bloom, Allan, with Harry Jaffa. *Shakespeare's Politics*. 1964. Repr. Chicago and London: University of Chicago Press, 1981.

Bloom, Harold. *Shakespeare and the Invention of the Human*. New York: Riverhead, 1998.

Bond, Ronald B., ed. *Certain Sermons or Homilies (1547) and a Homily Against Disobedience and Wilful Rebellion (1570)*. Toronto: University of Toronto Press, 1987.

The Book of Common Prayer: The Elizabethan Prayer Book. 1559. Edited by John E. Booty. Charlottesville: University Press of Virginia, 1976.

Born, Lester K. "Introduction." In Desiderius Erasmus, *The Education of a Christian Prince*. 1936. Repr. New York: W. W. Norton, 1968.

Bradley, A. C. *Shakespearean Tragedy*. 1904. Repr. New York: Fawcett World Library, 1968.

Brague, Rémi. *Eccentric Culture: A Theory of Western Civilization*. Translated by Samuel Lester. South Bend, Ind.: St. Augustine's Press, 2002.

Briggs, John C. "Catharsis in *The Tempest*." *Ben Jonson Journal* 5 (1998): 115–32.

Bristol, Michael. *Shakespeare's America: America's Shakespeare*. London and New York: Routledge, 1990.

Brown, Paul. "'This Thing of Darkness I Acknowledge Mine': *The Tempest* and the Discourse of Colonialism." In Dollimore and Sinfield, *Political Shakespeare*. 1985.

Bullough, Geoffrey, ed. *Narrative and Dramatic Sources of Shakespeare*. 8 vols. London and Henley: Routledge and Kegan Paul; New York: Columbia University Press, 1957–75.

Bibliography

Campbell, Oscar James. "The Salvation of Lear." *ELH* 15 (1948): 93–109.

Cartelli, Thomas. "Prospero in Africa: *The Tempest* as Colonialist Text and Pretext." In Howard and Connor, *Shakespeare Reproduced*. 1987.

Catullus. *C. Valerii Catulli Carmina*. Edited by R. A. B. Mynors. Oxford: Clarendon, 1958.

Cavell, Stanley. *Disowning Knowledge in Six Plays of Shakespeare*. Cambridge: Cambridge University Press, 1987.

Chamberlain, John. *The Letters of John Chamberlain*. Edited by Norman Egbert McClure. 2 vols. 1939. Repr. Westport, Conn.: Greenwood, 1979.

Chambers, R. W. *King Lear*. *Glasgow University Publications* 54 (1940): 20–52.

Champion, Larry S. *Perspectives in Shakespeare's English Histories*. Athens: University of Georgia Press, 1980.

Charney, Maurice. *Shakespeare on Love and Lust*. New York: Columbia University Press, 2000.

Cheyfitz, Eric. *The Poetics of Imperialism: Translation from "The Tempest" to "Tarzan."* Rev. ed. Philadelphia: University of Pennsylvania Press, 1997.

Cicero, Marcus Tullius. *De Amicita*. In *Complete Works of Cicero*. Hastings East Sussex: Delphi Classics, Kindle Edition, 2014.

Cohen, Walter. "Introduction" to *Troilus and Cressida*. In Greenblatt et al., *Norton Shakespeare*. 2016.

Coleridge, Samuel Taylor. *Coleridge's Writings on Shakespeare*. Edited by Terence Hawkes. Introduction by Alfred Harbage. New York: G. P. Putnam's Sons, 1959.

Copleston, Frederick, SJ. *A History of Philosophy*. 9 vols. New York: Doubleday, 1962–74.

Cox, John D. "Recovering Something Christian about *The Tempest*." *Christianity and Literature* 50 (2000): 31–51.

Craig, Leon Harold. *Of Philosophers and Kings: Political Philosophy in Shakespeare's "Macbeth" and "King Lear."* Toronto, Buffalo, and London: Toronto University Press, 2001.

Cressy, David. *Bonfires and Bells: National Memory and the Protestant Calendar in Elizabethan and Stuart England*. Berkeley and Los Angeles: University of California Press, 1989.

Danby, John F. *Shakespeare's Doctrine of Nature: A Study of "King Lear."* London: Faber and Faber, 1948.

Bibliography

Davidson, Basil. *The African Slave Trade: Precolonial History, 1450–1850*. Boston: Atlantic–Little-Brown, 1961.

Dawson, Christopher. *Religion and the Rise of Western Culture*. 1950. Reprint Garden City, N.Y.: Doubleday Image, 1958.

de Groot, John Henry. *The Shakespeares and "The Olde Faith."* 1946. Reprint Fraser, Mich.: Real-View, 1995.

de Sousa, Geraldo U. *Shakespeare's Cross-Cultural Encounters*. Houndmills, Basingstoke, Hampshire: Palgrave, 1999.

Dickens, A. G. *The English Reformation*. New York: Schocken, 1964.

Dollimore, Jonathan. "Foreword." In Dollimore and Sinfield, *Political Shakespeare*. 1985.

———. "Renaissance Antitheatricality and the Politics of Gender and Rank in *Much Ado About Nothing*. In Howard and O'Connor, *Shakespeare Reproduced*. 1987.

———. *Radical Tragedy: Religion, Ideology and Power in the Drama of Shakespeare and His Contemporaries*. 3rd ed. Durham, N.C.: Duke University Press, 2004.

Dollimore, Jonathan, and Alan Sinfield, eds. *Political Shakespeare: New Essays in Cultural Materialism*. Ithaca, N.Y., and London: Cornell University Press, 1985.

Donne, John. *The Sermons of John Donne*. Edited by George R. Potter and Evelyn Simpson. 10 vols. Berkeley, Los Angeles, and London: University of California Press, 1953–62.

———. *The Variorum Edition of the Poetry of John Donne*. Vol. 3, *The Satyres*, edited by Gary Stringer et al. Bloomington and Indianapolis: Indiana University Press, 2016.

Dryden, John. *An Essay of Dramatic Poesy and Other Essays*. Edited by George Watson. 2 vols. London: J. M. Dent, 1962.

Duffy, Eamon. *The Stripping of the Altars: Traditional Religion in England, 1400–1580*. New Haven, Conn., and London: Yale University Press, 1992.

Eccles, Mark. *Shakespeare in Warwickshire*. Madison: University of Wisconsin Press, 1961.

Eco, Umberto. *The Name of the Rose*. Translated by William Weaver. San Diego, New York, and London: Harcourt Brace Jovanovich, 1983.

Eire, Carlos M. N. *Reformations: The Early Modern World, 1450–1650*. London and New Haven, Conn.: Yale University Press, 2016.

Bibliography

Ellrodt, Robert. *Montaigne et Shakespeare: L'emergence de la conscience moderne.* Paris: José Corti, 2011.

———. *Montaigne and Shakespeare: The Emergence of Modern Self-Consciousness.* Manchester, UK: Manchester University Press, 2015.

Elton, W. R. *"King Lear" and the Gods.* San Marino, Calif.: Huntington Library, 1968.

Elyot, Sir Thomas. *The Book Named the Governor.* Edited by S. E. Lehmberg. 1907. Reprint New York: Dutton, 1962.

Empson, William. *The Structure of Complex Words.* 3rd ed. Totowa, N.J.: Rowman and Littlefield, 1979.

Erasmus, Desiderius. *Institutio Principis Christiani* (1516). Edited by O. Harding. In *Opera Omnia Desiderii Erasmi*, series IV, vol. 1. Amsterdam: North-Holland Publishing, 1974.

Erickson, Peter. "The Moment of Race in Renaissance Studies." *Shakespeare Studies* 26 (1998): 27–36.

Erikson, Erik. *Young Man Luther: A Study in Psychoanalysis and History.* New York: W. W. Norton, 1958.

Falco, Raphael. *Charismatic Authority in Early Modern English Tragedy.* Baltimore and London: Johns Hopkins University Press, 2000.

Fish, Stanley. *Is There a Text in This Class? The Authority of Interpretive Communities.* Cambridge, Mass.: Harvard University Press, 1980.

———. *There's No Such Thing as Free Speech and It's a Good Thing, Too.* New York and Oxford: Oxford University Press, 1994.

Flynn, Dennis. *John Donne and the Ancient Catholic Nobility.* Bloomington and Indianapolis: Indiana University Press, 1995.

Foucault, Michel. "What Is an Author?" In *The Foucault Reader*, edited by Paul Rabinowitz. New York: Random House, 1984.

French, Marilyn. "The Late Tragedies." In *Shakespearean Tragedy*, edited by John Drakakis. London and New York: Longman, 1992.

Fumaroli, Marc. "Rhetoric, Politics, and Society: From Italian Ciceronianism to French Classicism." In *Renaissance Eloquence: Studies in the Theory and Practice of Renaissance Rhetoric*, edited by James J. Murphy. Berkeley: University of California Press, 1983.

Gairdner, William. *The Book of Absolutes: A Critique of Relativism and a Defense of Universals.* Montreal, Kinston, London, and Ithaca, N.Y.: McGill-Queen's University Press, 2008.

Gates, Henry Louis Jr., *Loose Canons: Notes on the Culture Wars.* New York and Oxford: Oxford University Press, 1992.

Bibliography

Gray, Hannah. "Renaissance Humanism: The Pursuit of Eloquence." In *Renaissance Essays from the Journal of the History of Ideas*, edited by Paul Oskar Kristeller and P. P. Wiener. New York: Harper and Row, 1968.

Greenblatt, Stephen. *Renaissance Self-Fashioning from More to Shakespeare*. Chicago: University of Chicago Press, 1980.

———. *Shakespearean Negotiations: The Circulation of Social Energy in Renaissance England*. Berkeley and Los Angeles: University of California Press, 1988.

———. *Learning to Curse: Essays in Early Modern Culture*. New York and London: Routledge, 1990.

———. *Hamlet in Purgatory*. Princeton, N.J., and Oxford: Princeton University Press, 2001.

———. *Shakespeare's Freedom*. Chicago and London: University of Chicago Press, 2010.

Gregory, Brad. *The Unintended Reformation: How a Religious Revolution Secularized Society*. Cambridge, Mass., and London: Harvard University Press, 2012.

Gross, John. *Shylock: A Legend and Its Legacy*. New York: Simon and Schuster, 1992.

Hall, Kim. *Things of Darkness: Economies of Race and Gender in Early Modern England*. Ithaca, N.Y., and London: Cornell University Press, 1995.

Haller, William, and Malleville Haller. "The Puritan Art of Love." *Huntington Library Quarterly* 5 (1942): 235–72.

Hamilton, Donna B. "Defiguring Virgil in *The Tempest*." In Vaughan and Vaughan, *Critical Essays on Shakespeare's "The Tempest."* 1998.

Harrison, G. B., ed. *An Elizabethan Journal: Being a Record of Those Things Most Talked About During the Years 1591–1594*. New York: Cosmopolitan, 1929.

———. *Shakespeare's Tragedies*. London: Routledge and Kegan Paul, 1951.

Haydn, Hiram. *The Counter-Renaissance*. New York: Scribner's, 1950.

Hibbard, G. R., ed. *Hamlet*. Oxford and New York: Oxford University Press, 1987.

Hittinger, Russell. *First Grace: Rediscovering the Natural Law in a Post-Christian World*. Wilmington, Del.: ISI, 2003.

Hodgdon, Barbara, ed. *The First Part of Kind Henry IV: Texts and Contexts*. Boston: Bedford, 1997.

Honan, Park. *Shakespeare: A Life*. Oxford and New York: Oxford University Press, 1998.

Bibliography

Honigmann, E. A. J. *Shakespeare: The Lost Years*. Totowa, N.J.: Barnes and Noble, 1985.

———. "Introduction" to *Othello*. Walton on Thames, Surrey: Thomas Nelson & Sons, 1997.

Hooker, Richard. *Of the Laws of Ecclesiastical Polity*. Introduction by Christopher Morris. 2 vols. London: J. M. Dent, 1907.

Horace. *Q. Horati Flacci Opera*. Edited by E. C. Wickham. Revised by H. W. Garrod. 2nd ed. Oxford: Clarendon, 1912.

Howard, Jean. "Transgression and Surveillance in *Measure for Measure*. In Dollimore and Sinfield, *Political Shakespeare*. 1985.

———. "Introduction" to *As You Like It*. In Greenblatt et al., *Norton Shakespeare*. 2016.

Howard, Jean, and Marion F. O'Connor, eds. "Introduction." In *Shakespeare Reproduced: The Text in History and Ideology*. New York and London: Methuen, 1987.

Hughes, Philip. *The Reformation in England*. 3 vols. London: Hollis and Carter, 1950–54.

Hunt, Maurice. *Shakespeare's Romance of the Word*. Lewisburg, London, and Toronto: Bucknell University Press and Associated University Presses, 1990.

Hunter, Robert G. *Shakespeare and the Comedy of Forgiveness*. New York: Columbia University Press, 1965.

———. *Shakespeare and the Mystery of God's Judgments*. Athens: University of Georgia Press, 1976.

James, D. G. *A Dream of Learning: An Essay on "The Advancement of Learning," "Hamlet," and "King Lear."* Oxford: Clarendon, 1951.

Jardine, Lisa. "Introduction" to Erasmus, *The Education of a Christian Prince with a Panegyric for Archduke Philip of Austria*. Cambridge: Cambridge University Press, 1997.

Johnson, Samuel. "Preface" to *The Plays of William Shakespeare* (1765). In *Johnson on Shakespeare*, edited by W. K. Wimsatt Jr. New York: Hill and Wang, 1960.

Kerrigan, William. Review of *Hamlet in Purgatory*. *Ben Jonson Journal* 8 (2001): 385–90.

Knapp, Jeffrey. *Shakespeare Only*. Chicago and London: University of Chicago Press, 2009.

Knight, G. Wilson. *The Wheel of Fire: Interpretations of Shakespearean Tragedy*. 1930. Reprint London and New York: Routledge, 2001.

Bibliography

Knights, L. C. "How Many Children Had Lady Macbeth?" In *Explorations: Essays in Criticism Mainly on the Literature of the Seventeenth Century*. London: Chatto and Windus, 1951.

Kronenfeld, Judy. *King Lear and the Naked Truth: Rethinking the Language of Religion and Resistance*. Durham, N.C., and London: Duke University Press, 1998.

Lee, John. *Shakespeare's "Hamlet" and the Controversies of the Self*. Oxford: Clarendon, 2000.

Leininger, Lorrie Jerrell. "The Miranda Trap: Sexism and Racism in Shakespeare's *Tempest*." In *The Woman's Part: Feminist Criticism of Shakespeare*, edited by Carolyn Ruth Swift Lenz, Gayle Greene, and Carol Thomas Neely. Urbana, Chicago, and London: University of Illinois Press, 1980.

Leitch, Vincent B., ed. *The Norton Anthology of Theory and Criticism*. New York and London: W. W. Norton, 2001.

Lentricchia, Frank. *Criticism and Social Change*. Chicago: University of Chicago Press, 1988.

Levin, Harry. "Form and Formality in *Romeo and Juliet*." *Shakespeare Quarterly* 11 (1960): 3–11.

Lewalski, Barbara. "Biblical Allegory and Allusion in *The Merchant of Venice*." In *Twentieth Century Interpretations of "The Merchant of Venice*,*"* edited by Sylvan Barnet. Englewood Cliffs, N.J.: Prentice-Hall, 1970.

Lewis, C. S. *The Allegory of Love: A Study in Medieval Tradition*. London, Oxford, and New York: Oxford University Press, 1936.

———. *The Abolition of Man*. 1947. Reprint New York: Collier, 1962.

———. "De Descriptione Temporum." In *Selected Literary Essays*, edited by Walter Hooper. Cambridge: Cambridge University Press, 1969.

Lipsius, Justus. *Principles of Letter-Writing: A Bilingual Edition of Justi Lipsi Epistolica Institutio*. Edited and translated by R. V. Young and M. Thomas Hester. Carbondale and Edwardsville: Southern Illinois University Press, 1996.

———. *Justus Lipsius' Concerning Constancy*. Edited and translated by R. V. Young. Medieval and Renaissance Texts and Studies 389. Tempe, Ariz.: ACMRS, 2011.

Low, Anthony. "*Hamlet* and the Ghosts of Purgatory: Intimations of Killing the Father." *ELR* 29 (1999): 443–49.

———. *Aspects of Subjectivity: Society and Individuality from the Middle Ages to Shakespeare and Milton*. Pittsburgh: Duquesne University Press, 2001.

Bibliography

Lupton, Julia Reinhard. "Creature Caliban." *Shakespeare Quarterly* 51 (2000): 1–23.

Luther, Martin. *De Servo Arbitrio*. Nuremberg, 1526. Online at google.books.com.

Machiavelli, Niccolò. *Machiavelli's The Prince: A Bilingual Edition*. Edited and translated by Mark Musa. New York: St. Martin's Press, 1964.

Mack, Maynard. *King Lear in Our Time*. Berkeley and Los Angeles: University of California Press, 1965.

———. *Everybody's Shakespeare: Reflections Chiefly on the Tragedies*. Lincoln and London: University of Nebraska Press, 1993.

Marlowe, Christopher. *Complete Plays and Poems*. Edited by E. D. Pendry and J. C. Maxwell. London: J. M. Dent, 1976.

Martin, Thomas L., and Duke Pesta. *The Renaissance and Postmodernism: A Study of Comparative Critical Values*. New York and London: Routledge, 2016.

Maus, Katherine Eisaman. "Introduction" to *Julius Caesar*. In Greenblatt et al., *Norton Shakespeare*. 2016.

McDonald, Russ. "Reading *The Tempest*." In Vaughan and Vaughan, *Critical Essays on Shakespeare's "The Tempest."* 1998.

McLuskie, Katherine. "The Patriarchal Bard: Feminist Criticism and Shakespeare; *King Lear* and *Measure for Measure*." In Dollimore and Sinfield, *Political Shakespeare*. 1985.

Milward, Peter, SJ. *Biblical Influences in Shakespeare's Great Tragedies*. Bloomington and Indianapolis: Indiana University Press, 1987.

More, Thomas. *Utopia*. Edited by Edward J. Surtz, SJ, and J. H. Hexter. In vol. 4 of *Complete Works of Thomas More*, edited by Richard Sylvester et al. New Haven, Conn., and London: Yale University Press, 1965.

Mowat, Barbara A. "Prospero, Agrippa, and Hocus Pocus." In Vaughan and Vaughan, *Critical Essays on Shakespeare's "The Tempest."* 1998.

———. "Prospero's Book." *Shakespeare Quarterly* 52 (2001): 1–33.

Neville, Alexander. *Tragedy and God's Moral Judgments*. 1563. In *English Renaissance Literary Criticism*, edited by Brian Vickers. Oxford: Clarendon, 1999.

Nevo, Ruth. *Shakespeare's Other Language*. New York and London: Methuen, 1987.

Newman, John Henry. *The Idea of a University*. Edited by Martin J. Svaglic. Notre Dame, Ind.: Notre Dame University Press, 1982.

Bibliography

Newman, Karen. "'And Wash the Ethiop White': Femininity and the Monstrous in *Othello*. In Howard and O'Connor, *Shakespeare Reproduced*. 1987.

Nuttall, A. D. *A New Mimesis: Shakespeare and the Representation of Reality*. 2nd ed. New Haven, Conn., and London: Yale University Press, 2007.

Occam, William of. *Philosophical Writings*. Edited and translated by Philotheus Boehner, OFM. Revised by Stephen F. Brown. Indianapolis and Cambridge, Mass.: Hackett, 1990.

Orgel, Stephen, ed., *The Tempest*. Oxford: Clarendon, 1987.

———. "*Macbeth* and the Antic Round." In William Shakespeare, *Macbeth: A Norton Critical Edition*, edited by Robert Miola. New York and London: W. W. Norton, 2014.

Ornstein, Robert. *A Kingdom for a Stage: The Achievement of Shakespeare's History Plays*. Cambridge, Mass.: Harvard University Press, 1972.

———. *Shakespeare's Comedies: From Roman Farce to Romantic Mystery*. Newark: University of Delaware Press, 1986.

Pascal, Blaise. *Oeuvres Complètes*. Edited by Henri Gouhier and Louis Lafuma. Paris: Éditions du Seuil, 1963.

Pearce, Joseph. *The Quest for Shakespeare*. San Francisco: Ignatius Press, 2008.

Peter, John. *Complaint and Satire in Early English Literature*. Oxford: Clarendon, 1956.

Petrarcha, Francesco. *Opere*. Edited by Mario Martelli. 2 vols. Firenze: Sansone Editore, 1975.

Raeder, Linda C. "Postmodernism, Multiculturalism, and the Death of Tolerance: The Transformation of American Society." *Humanitas* 30: (2017) 59–85.

Reynolds, E. E. *The Field Is Won: The Life and Death of St. Thomas More*. Milwaukee: Bruce, 1968.

Riehl, Wolfgang. *Shakespeare, Plautus and the Humanist Tradition*. Cambridge: D. S. Brewer, 1990.

Rose, Mary Beth. *The Expense of Spirit: Love and Sexuality in English Renaissance Drama*. Ithaca, N.Y., and London: Cornell University Press, 1988.

Rosenberg, John. "King Lear and His Comforters." *Essays in Criticism* 16 (1966): 135–46.

Rymer, Thomas. *A Short View of Tragedy*. 1693. In *Critical Essays of the Seventeenth Century*, edited by J. E. Spingarn. 2 vols. Oxford: Clarendon, 1908.

Bibliography

Sams, Eric. *The Real Shakespeare: Retrieving the Early Years, 1564–1594.* New Haven, Conn., and London: Yale University Press, 1995.

Scarisbrick, J. J. *The Reformation and the English People.* Oxford: Basil Blackwell, 1984.

Schlegel, August Wilhelm von. *Lectures on Dramatic Art and Literature.* Excerpted in *The Globe Illustrated Shakespeare*, edited by Howard Staunton. 1979. Reprint New York: Greenwich House, 1983.

Schoenbaum, S. *Shakespeare: A Compact Documentary Life.* Oxford, London, and New York: Oxford University Press, 1977.

———. *Shakespeare's Lives.* Rev. ed. Oxford: Clarendon Press, 1991.

Scott, Sir Walter. *The Life of John Dryden.* In *The Delphi Complete Works of John Dryden.* Hastings, East Sussex: Delphi Classics (Kindle Edition), 2013.

Seneca, Lucius Annaeus. *Epistulae Morales.* Edited and translated by Richard M. Gummere. 3 vols. 1917. Cambridge, Mass.: Harvard University Press, 1989.

Sewall, Richard B. *The Vision of Tragedy.* New Haven, Conn., and London: Yale University Press, 1959.

Sewell, Arthur. *Character and Society in Shakespeare.* Oxford: Clarendon, 1951.

Shakespeare, William. *The Riverside Shakespeare.* Edited by G. Blakemore Evans et al. 2nd ed. Boston and New York: Houghton Mifflin, 1997.

———. *The Norton Shakespeare.* Edited by Stephen Greenblatt et al. 3rd ed. New York and London: W. W. Norton, 2016.

Shapiro, James. *Shakespeare and the Jews.* New York: Columbia University Press, 1996.

———. *Contested Will: Who Wrote Shakespeare?* New York: Simon and Schuster, 2010.

Sidney, Sir Philip. *An Apology for Poetry.* 1595. In *Elizabethan Critical Essays*, edited by G. Gregory Smith. 2 vols. London: Oxford University Press, 1904.

———. *Astrophil and Stella.* 1591. In *Sir Philip Sidney: The Oxford Authors.* Oxford and New York: Oxford University Press, 1989.

Sinfield, Alan. "Introduction: Reproductions, Inventions." In Dollimore and Sinfield, *Political Shakespeare.* 1985.

———. *Shakespeare, Authority, Sexuality: Unfinished Business in Cultural Materialism.* London and New York: Routledge, 2006.

Skura, Meredith. "Discourse and the Individual: The Case of Colonialism in *The Tempest*. In Vaughan and Vaughan, *Critical Essays on Shakespeare's "The Tempest."* 1989.

Speaight, Robert. *Nature in Shakespearean Tragedy*. 1955. Reprint New York: Collier, 1962.

Spencer, Theodore. *Shakespeare and the Nature of Man*. 2nd ed. New York: Macmillan, 1949.

Spenser, Edmund. *The Complete Poetical Works of Spenser*. Edited by R. E. Neil Dodge. Boston: Houghton Mifflin, 1908.

Spinrad, Phoebe. "'Too Much Liberty': *Measure for Measure* and Skelton's *Magnificence*." *MLQ* 60 (1999): 431–49.

Spitz, Lewis W. *The Protestant Reformation, 1517–1559*. New York: Harper and Row, 1985.

Stampfer, Judah. "The Catharsis of *King Lear*." *Shakespeare Survey* 13 (1960): 1–10.

Stewart, Stanley. *Shakespeare and Philosophy*. New York and London: Routledge, 2010.

Swinburne, Algernon Charles. *The Complete Works of Algernon Charles Swinburne*. Edited by Sir Edmund Gosse and Thomas James Wise, 1925–27. Reprint New York: Russell and Russell, 1968.

T. E. *The Law's Resolutions of Women's Rights: Or, the Law's Provision for Women*. 1632. In *Sexuality and Gender in the English Renaissance: An Annotated Edition of Contemporary Documents*, edited by Lloyd Davis. New York and London: Garland, 1998.

Taylor, Charles. *A Secular Age*. Cambridge, Mass., and London: Harvard University Press, 2007.

Taylor, Gary. *Reinventing Shakespeare: A Cultural History from the Restoration to the Present*. New York: Weidenfeld and Nicolson, 1989.

Thomas, Hugh. *The Slave Trade: The Story of the Atlantic Slave Trade, 1440–1870*. New York: Simon and Schuster, 1997.

Tiffany, Grace. "Calvinist Grace in Shakespeare's Romances: Upending Tragedy." *Christianity and Literature* 49 (2000): 421–45.

———. "Puritanism in Comic History: Exposing Royalty in the Henry Plays." *Shakespeare Studies* 26 (1998): 256–87.

Tillyard, E. M. W. *Shakespeare's History Plays*. 1944. Reprint Harmondsworth: Penguin, 1962.

Tilney, Edmund. *The Flower of Friendship: A Renaissance Dialogue Contesting Marriage*. 1568. Edited by Valerie Wayne. Ithaca, N.Y., and London: Cornell University Press, 1992.

Bibliography

Todorov, Tzvetan. *The Conquest of America*. Translated by Richard Howard. New York: Harper and Row, 1984.

Tolkien, J. R. R. "*Beowulf*: The Monsters and the Critics." In *An Anthology of Beowulf Criticism*, edited by Lewis E. Nicholson. Notre Dame, Ind.: Notre Dame University Press, 1963.

Trafton, Dain. "Shakespeare's Henry IV: A New Prince in a New Principality." In *Shakespeare as a Political Thinker*, edited by John Alvis and Thomas G. West. Durham, N.C.: Carolina Academic Press, 1981.

Traugott, John. "Creating a Rational Rinaldo: A Study of the Mixture of the Genres of Comedy and Romance in *Much Ado About Nothing*." *Genre* 15 (1982): 157–81.

Vaughan, Virginia Mason, and Alden T. Vaughan, eds. *Critical Essays on Shakespeare's "The Tempest."* New York: G. K. Hall, 1998.

Vickers, Brian. *Appropriating Shakespeare: Contemporary Critical Quarrels*. New Haven, Conn., and London: Yale University Press, 1993.

Weaver, Richard. *Ideas Have Consequences*. 1948. Reprint Chicago and London: University of Chicago Press, 1984.

Weber, Max. *The Protestant Ethic and the Spirit of Capitalism*. Translated by Talcott Parsons. 1934. Reprint New York: Charles Scribner and Sons, 1958.

Wellek, René, and Austin Warren. *Theory of Literature*. 3rd ed. New York: Harcourt, Brace and World, 1962.

Wells, Stanley. *Shakespeare: A Life in Drama*. New York: W. W. Norton, 1995.

White, R. S. *Natural Law in English Renaissance Literature*. Cambridge: Cambridge University Press, 1996.

Wilson, Richard. *Secret Shakespeare: Studies in Theatre, Religion and Resistance*. Manchester, UK, and New York: Manchester University Press, 2004.

Young, R. V. *At War with the Word: Literary Theory and Liberal Education*. Wilmington, Del.: ISI, 1999.

———. "Lipsius and Imitation as Educational Technique." In *Justus Lipsius Europae Lumen et Columen:* Supplementa *Humanisticae Lovaniensia* XV, edited by G. Tournoy, J. de Landsheer and J. Papy, 268–80. Leuven: Leuven University Press, 1999.

———. *Doctrine and Devotion in Seventeenth-Century Poetry: Studies in Donne, Herbert, Crashaw, and Vaughan*. Cambridge: D. S. Brewer, 2000.

———. "Academic Suicide." Review of *The Norton Anthology of Theory and Criticism*, ed. Vincent B. Leitch. *Modern Age* 44 (2002): 254–261.

Bibliography

———. "Constantia Nos Armat: Lipsius and the Trials of Constancy." In *Syntagmata: Essays on Neo-Latin Literature in Honour of Monique Mond-Dopchie and Gilbert Tournoy*, edited by Dirk Sacré and Jan Papy. Leuven: Leuven University Press, 2009.

———. "Stephen Greenblatt: The Critic as Anecdotalist." *Modern Age* 51 (2009): 262–71.

———. "'How Drie a Cinder This World Is': Dissociation of Sensibility Redux." *Ben Jonson Journal* 24 (2017): 163–86.

Index

Alvis, John, 127
Andrewes, Lancelot, 231
Aristotle: *Nicomachean Ethics*, 45, 192n33; *Poetics*, 20, 38, 96, 182, 193–94
Ascham, Roger, 120
Asquith, Clare, 104n1, 197n35
Augustine, Saint, 191n32

Bacon, Francis, 83, 183
Barker, Francis, 213–15
Barthes, Roland, 6n10
Barton, Anne, 38, 46n28, 68
Bate, Jonathan, vii, 229n41
Beaumont, Francis, 1
Bell, Millicent, 23–24, 164, 167, 180, 181
Belsey, Catherine, 26
Berek, Peter, 77–78, 81n8
Berlioz, Hector, 37–38
Bermuda, 217–20, 222
Bernthal, Craig, 88n15
Blitz, Jan, 148n22, 149
Bloom, Harold, 85–86, 96n20, 138–39, 143n14, 144, 145
Bloom, Harold, vii, 214n10
Book of Common Prayer, 35–36, 41, 225
Born, Lester k., 108n7
Bradley, A. C., 175, 214n10
Brague, Rémi, 13–14
Briggs, John C., 229n41
Bristol, Michael, 8
Brown, Paul, 4, 215–16
Bullough, Geoffrey, 67, 158n3, 203n43

Bunyan, John, 230
Burbage, Richard, 219
Burke, Edmund, 228
Burke, Kenneth, 228
Burroughs, Edgar Rice, 18

Calvin, John, 56, 187, 231
Campbell, Oscar James, 176n6
Carleton, Dudley, 216n14
Cartelli, Thomas, 221
Catholicism, 18, 40n19, 58, 81n8, 90, 101–12, 131–32, 147–51, 231
Catullus, Gaius Valerius, 45–46
censorship, 18
Cesena, Michael of, 60
Chamberlain, John, 216n14
Chambers, R. W., 176n6
Champion, Larry S., 129n28
Chapman, George, 67, 109
Charney, Maurice, 31–32
Chaucer, Geoffrey, 6
Cheyfitz, Eric, 9–10, 17–18, 215
Christendom, 23, 52, 57, 102, 106
Christianity: in Shakespeare's works, 25–32, 42, 46, 77–90, 99–102, 104–11, 120, 126, 132, 142, 154, 164, 168–69, 174–91, 201–6, 210, 229–32; in Western Civilization, 11–15, 21, 49, 68, 76, 99, 132
Cicero, Marcus Tullius, 140n11, 145
Cinthio, Giraldo, 96
Cohen, Walter, 68
Coleridge, Samuel Taylor, 95–96, 98, 141n12, 151, 153, 174–75

253

Index

Columbus, Christopher, 217
Condell, Henry, 219
Copernicus, Nicolaus, 109
Copleston, Frederick, S. J., 53n3
Cox, John D., 229–31
Cressy, David, 104n1
cultural materialism, 2, 4–5, 135, 146–47, 209–10, 222, 233

Danby, John F., 176n6, 183–87
Dante Alighieri, 37
Davenant, William, 10
Davidson, Basil, 97
Dawson, Christopher, 12–13, 15, 17
de Groot, John Henry, 104n1
de Souza, Gerald U., 35n15
Dickens, Charles, 179
diversity, cultural, 7–13, 227n34
Dollimore, Jonathan, 44, 135, 181, 191n32, 200
Donne, John, 101, 106, 109, 122
Dryden, John, *An Essay of Dramatic Poesy*, 1–3; and *The Tempest*, 10
Duffy, Eamon, 105n1, 151n27

Eagleton, Terry, 236
Eccles, Mark, 7
Eco, Umberto, 59–60
Edward I, King of England, 80
Eire, Carlos M. N., 57
Elizabeth, Princess (daughter of James I and VI), 212
Elizabeth I, Queen of England, 37, 77, 80, 98n26, 105, 134
Ellrodt, Robert, 23n39, 46n29, 164n8
Elton, W. R., 181–82, 185, 204–6
Elyot, Sir Thomas, 120, 128–29
Empson, William, 179–80
Erasmus of Rotterdam, Desiderius: 105n1, 106; *Education of a Christian Prince*, 106–32; *Praise of Folly*, 106, 107

Erickson, Peter, 18
Everett, Barbara, 181

Falco, Raphael, 120n18
feminism, 213, 234
Fiennes, Joseph, 6
Fish, Stanley, 235
Fletcher, John, 1, 33
Florio, John, 217
Flynn, Dennis, 106
Foucault, Michel, 6
French, Marilyn, 195n34, 198
Fumaroli, Marc, 133n2

Gairdner, William, 31n17
Gates, Henry Louis, 235
Gates, Sir Thomas, 218
Gayley, Charles Mills, 218
Geoffrey of Monmouth, 66n14, 203
Gianetto, Tale of, 79
Gower, John, 6
Gray, Hannah, 133
Greene, Robert, 7
Greenblatt, Stephen, 10–11, 48, 98–101, 105n1, 146–48, 157n2, 218–21
Gregory, Brad, 57
Gross, John, 79

Hall, Arthur, 67
Hall, Kim, 221
Haller, William and Malleville, 29n7
Hamilton, Donna, 228–29
Harrison, G. B., 80n8, 179n12
Haroun al Rashid, Caliph of Baghdad, 129n28
Hathaway, Anne, 106
Haydn, Hiram, 134n4
Heminges, John, 219
Herbert, Philip, Earl of Montgomery, 219

Index

Herbert, William, Earl of Pembroke, 219
Hibbard, G. R., 151n26
Hittinger, Russell, 185
Hobbes, Thomas, 183, 184, 186–87, 189, 191
Hodgdon, Barbara, 117n13
Holinshed, Raphael, 172, 203
Homer, 6, 11n20, 66–67
Homily Against Disobedience and Wilful Rebellion, 117
Honan, Park, 84n11
Honigman, E. J. A., 98n26, 104n1
Hooker, Richard, 183, 186–89, m190, 198–99, 200, 206–7
Horace (Quintus Horatius Flaccus), 6, 19
Howard, Jean, 44, 47–48, 135
Hulme, Peter, 213–15
Hunt, Maurice, 223n26, 232
Hunter, Robert G., 41, 178–79

ideology, 8, 22, 135–45, 159, 220–22, 227
Ignatius Loyola, Saint, 109
individualism, 58, 60–63, 113
Islam, 49, 102

James I VI, King of England and Scotland: 77, 157–65, 182 ; *Basilikon Doron*, 159
James, D. G., 179–80n12
Jardine, Lisa, 108
Jerome, Saint, 100–101
Jewel, John, 206
John XXII, Pope, 60
Johnson, Samuel, 1–2, 26, 27, 143–44, 153, 167, 173, 176
Jonson, Ben, 1, 7, 109, 219

Kermode, Frank, 119
Kerrigan, William, 147n21

Kirk, Russell, 228
Knapp, Jeffrey, 7n12
Knight, G. Wilson
Knights, L. C., 214n10
Kronenfeld, Judy, 187n25, 201n41

Lady Chatterley's Lover, 18
Lash, Nicholas, 230
law, natural, 160, 173, 174–205
Lee, John, 146
Leininger, Lorrie Jerrell, 211–12, 213–14
Lentricchia, Frank, 5
Lerner, Daniel, 11, 98
Levin, Harry, 59, 60
Lewalski, Barbara, 77–78
Lewis, C. S.: *The Abolition of Man*, 17n31; *The Allegory of Love*, 28, 29; "*De descriptione temporum*, 213
Lipsius, Justus: *Epistolica Institutio*, 133–34; *De Constantia*, 177–78
Lopez, Rodrigo, 80–81
Low, Anthony, 105n1, 148, 149–50
Lupton, Julia Reinhardt, 224–26
Luther, Martin, 55–58, 150, 231
Lydgate, John, 6

Machiavelli, Níccolo (Machiavellianism, 68, 80, 109–32, 168
Mack, Maynard. 102, 150, 172n13, 176–77, 178–79
Magellan, Ferdinand, 217
Marlowe, Christopher, 78–81, 84, 92
Marston, John, 109
Martin, Thomas, 10–11n20
Mary, Queen of Scots, 117
Maus, Katharine Eisaman, 142
Marxism, 213, 230, 234
McDonald, Russ, 227–28
McKluskie, Katherine, 4
Middleton, Thomas, 153
Milward, Peter, SJ, 176n6, 203n43

255

Index

Mirror for Magistrates, 203
Montaigne, Michel, 23, 164, 217
More, Saint Thomas: 105n1; *Utopia* 106, 107, 112n10, 126, 186
Mowat, Barbara, 226
multiculturalism, 7–134, 76, 208n1

nature, human, 15–22, 43, 48–51, 53–54, 72, 135, 164–67, 174, 181–201
Alexander, Neville, 177
Nevo, Ruth, 223
new criticism, 228, 232
new historicism, 2, 135, 146–48, 160n5, 209, 218, 233–34
Newman, Karen, 101
Newman, Saint John Henry, 42
nominalism, 51–58, 59–60, 63–65, 69, 113
Norton Anthology of Theory and Criticism, 5

Occam, William of, 51–55, 59–60
O'Connor, Flannery, 18
O'Connor, Marion F., 135
Olivier, Sir Laurence, 127
Orgel, Stephen, 157–63, 230
Ornstein, Robert, 78n3, 83, 87, 90n16, 130
Ovid (Publius Ovidius Naso), 6

Paracelsus, Philippus, 109
Pascal, Blaise, 178–79
Patriarchy, 6, 11, 58, 232
Paul, Saint, 36, 86–88, 190, 204–5
The Pawn Broker (film), 18
Pearce, Joseph, 104n1
Il Pecorone, 79
Pesta, Duke, 10–11n20
Peter, John, 180n12
Petrarch (Francesco Petrarcha), 30, 49, 145
Plato, 53

Plautus, Titus Maccius, 3
Pocahontas, 216
Protestantism, 29, 56, 105
Purgatory, 146–52
Puritanism, 90, 187, 199

race, ix, 2, 5n6, 76, 86, 91, 93, 97, 135, 222, 227
Raeder, Linda C., 208n1
Reagan, Ronald, 18
The Reformation, vii, 23, 40n19, 55–60, 104–10, 131, 134, 148–50, 178
The Restoration, Shakespeare's reputation in, 1, 10, 96
Reynolds, E. E., 112n10
Riehl, Wolfgang, 27
Rolfe, John, 216
Rose, Mary Beth, 43–44
Rosenberg, John, 180n12
Rousseau, Jean-Jacques, 186
Rymer, Thomas, 96–98

Salel, Hugues (translator of the *Iliad*), 67
Sams, Eric, 83n11, 100n1
Sapir, Edward, 232n50
Saussure, Ferdinand de, 234
Scaliger, Julius Caesar, 66
Scarisbrick, J. J., 104n1
Schlegel, August Wilhelm von, 13n26
Schoenbaum, Samuel, 16n29
Scott, Sir Walter, *Life of Dryden*, 10
secularization, 16–17, 57–58, 105, 109–10, 119, 152, 180–81
Seneca, Lucius Annaeus, 140n11, 177
Sewell, Arthur, 180n12
Sewell, Richard B., 187n25
Shakespeare, John, 7, 83
Shakespeare, William: as educational, 2, 20, 22–23, 49–50, 231, 236–37;

Index

first folio: 7, 219; plays: *All's Well That Ends Well*, 26, 70–72, 73; *Antony and Cleopatra*, 27; *As You Like It*, 20, 26, 46; *Cymbeline*, 26, 208, 231; *Hamlet*, 20, 26, 99, 134, 145–55, 156, 198n36, 203; *1Henry IV*, 64–65, 110, 120–23, 129–30; *2Henry IV*, 89, 110, 124; *Henry V*, 110, 120, 123–32; *1Henry VI*, 111; *2HenryVI*, 111; *3Henry VI*, 111–14; *Julius Caesar*, 134, 136–45, 154–55, 156; *King Lear*, 65, 99, 159–60, 173–207; *Macbeth*, 50, 156–72, 198n36; *Measure for Measure*, 70, 72–75; *The Merchant of Venice*, 31, 32, 33–37, 76–91, 102–3; *A Midsummer Night's Dream*, 203; *Much Ado About Nothing*, 31, 32, 33, 37–46, 69, 72; *Othello*, 18, 20, 26, 45, 76, 77, 90, 93–103, 198n36, 203, 234; *Pericles*, 208; *Richard II*, 110, 115–20; *Richard III*, 111, 115, 117, 131; *Romeo and Juliet*, 6, 27, 59–63, 65, 75; *The Taming of the Shrew*, 27; *The Tempest*, 4, 9–10, 18, 76, 208–33; *Titus Andronicus*, 27n4, 92–93, 153; *Troilus and Cressida*, 65–70; *Twelfth Night*, 33, 46, 69, 90; *Two Gentlemen of Verona*, 33; *Two Noble KInsmen*, 33; *A Winter's Tale*, 26, 208; Poems: *The Rape of Lucrece*, 218; *The Sonnets*, 16, 42, 44, 219; *Venus and Adonis* 219
Shakespeare in Love (film)
Shapiro, James, 16n29, 84–85
Sidney, Sir Philip: *Apology for Poetry*, 19, 21; *Astrophil and Stella*, 30
Sinfield, Alan, 4–5, 17
skepticism, 2, 23–24, 55–64, 164–67, 178–85
Skura Meredith Anne, 222–23
slavery, 11–12, 97, 108, 212
Smith, Valerie, 221

Speaight, Robert, 175–76
Spencer, Theodore, 176n6, 183
Spenser, Edmund: 6, 230; *Amoretti*, 29, 30; *Epithalamion*, 29, 30; *Faerie Queene*, 29
Spinrad, Phoebe, 105n1
Stampfer, Judah, 177
Stewart, Stanley, vii
Stone, Oliver, 219
Strachey, William, 218–20, 222
Swinburne, Algernon Charles, 175

T. E.: *The Law's Resolution of Women's Rights*, 40n19
Tarzan (character in Edgar Rice Burroughs novel), 18
Tasso, Torquato, 11n20
Tate, Nahum, 173–74, 176, 187
Taylor, Charles, 57, 58
Taylor, Gary, 3, 25–26
Thatcher, Margaret, 18
Thomas Aquinas, Saint, 40n19, 53, 186, 189–90, 191n32, 192, 199, 200, 201, 205, 231
Thomas, Hugh, 97n25
Tiffany, Grace, 122n21, 231
Tillyard, E. M. W., 123n23
Tilney: *The Flower of Friendship*, 33n14, 40n19
Todorov, Tzvetan, 9–10
Tolkien, J. R. R., 205
Trafton, Dain, 119

Vagina Monologues (stage presentation), 18
Vaughan, Virginia Mason and Alden T., 227n24
Velázquez, Diego: *Las meninas*, 157
Vickers, Brian, 234–37
Virgil (Publius Vergilius Maro), 6, 228–29

Index

Warren, Austin, 209n2
Watts, Cedric, 181
Weaver, Richard, 51, 55
Weber, Max, 56–57
Wellek, René, 209n2
Wells, Stanley, vii
White, R. S., 186–87, 189, 200
Whorf, Benjamin Lee, 232n50
Wilson, Richard, 104n1, 197n35
Wriothesley, Henry, Earl of Southampton, 219
Wyatt, Sir Thomas, 6

Xenophon, 107

Young, R. V.: "Academic Suicide," 5n9; *At War With the Word*, 17n31, 48n30; 160n5; 210n2, 221n21; "Constantia Nos Armat," 134n4; *Doctrine and Devotion in Seventeenth-Century Poetry*, 232n49; "How Drie a Cinder This World Is: Dissociation of Sensibility Redux," 57n9; "Lipsius and Imitation as Educational Technique," 134n4; "Stephen Greenblatt: the Critic as Anecdotalist," 11n21

Shakespeare and the Idea of Western Civilization
was designed in Verdigris and composed by Kachergis
Book Design of Pittsboro, North Carolina. It was
printed on 60-pound Natural Eggshell and bound by
McNaughton & Gunn of Saline, Michigan.

www.ingramcontent.com/pod-product-compliance
Lightning Source LLC
Chambersburg PA
CBHW070249010526
44107CB00056B/2401